PROPHETS OF REBELLION

STUDIES IN COMPARATIVE WORLD HISTORY
Under the General Editorship of
Philip D. Curtin, Bernard Cohn, and Edmund Burke III

PROPHETS OF REBELLION

Millenarian Protest Movements against the European Colonial Order

by Michael Adas

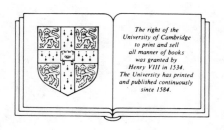

CAMBRIDGE UNIVERSITY PRESS

Cambridge
London   New York   New Rochelle
Melbourne   Sydney

Published by the Press Syndicate of the University of Cambridge
The Pitt Building, Trumpington Street, Cambridge CB2 1RP
32 East 57th Street, New York, NY 10022, USA
10 Stamford Road, Oakleigh, Melbourne 3166, Australia

First published 1979 by The University of North Carolina Press
First paperback edition 1987

Printed in the United States of America

Library of Congress Cataloging in Publication Data

Adas, Michael, 1943–

Prophets of rebellion.

Bibliography: p.
Includes index.

1. Colonies – Case studies.   2. Native races – Case
studies.   3. Government, Resistance to – Case studies.
4. Millennialism – Case studies.   I. Title.
JV305.A3   325′.34′09   78-26775
ISBN 0-521-33568-X paperback

TO MY MOTHER AND FATHER
AND HAM AND DOROTHY

Contents

Illustrations

Maps

Preface to the Paperback Edition

It has been suggested in both reviews and personal communications that I follow up the *Prophets of Rebellion* with a second study covering more recent movements with millenarian characteristics, such as the revolution in Iran. For a time I seriously considered this possibility. The Iranian revolt, with its striking parallels to the Mahdist rising in the Sudan in the late nineteenth century, was particularly tempting. Though the *ayatollah* Khomaini is revered as the *faghi* (the "trustee" who prepares the way for the prophet) and not the prophet himself, his personal history and style of leadership have much in common with the leaders who were pivotal to the rebellions dealt with in the present volume. The causes that gave rise to the Iranian revolution, the techniques of mobilization and protest employed, the theocratic nature of the postrevolutionary state that emerged, and the extensive use of talismans in the long border war with Iraq convinced me that comparisons between the Iranian upheaval and those that are the focus for *Prophets of Rebellion* would be extremely revealing. At the same time, the absence of a colonial regime as a target for the Khomaini revolution, its victory and its success in establishing a postrevolutionary state indicated important differences from the Saya San rebellion or the Java War that could be fruitfully explored in a second work. But the more I ruminated over the possibility of a sequel to the *Prophets* volume, the more clear it became to me that such an undertaking would run counter to the central purpose of comparative study. The Iranian revolution or other contemporary examples of millenarianism would simply provide additional cases to illustrate and perhaps modify the patterns that I have explored in depth in the present volume. Identifying these patterns was my main objective. My purpose was to explore the causation, nature and impact of a type of protest movement that I believe to be one of the most widespread and significant in both the era of European colonial dominance, from which the cases examined are drawn, and in the history of collective behavior more generally. Testing and expanding upon the patterns that I have identified is best left to other scholars—should they find them useful.

In tackling complex questions relating to causation, I was struck by usefulness of David Aberle's formulation of the relative deprivation approach for the analysis of this type of social protest. Though I was, and am, fully aware that relative deprivation is not at present in favor among social scientists, I found, and continue to find, it the most flexible and revealing way to tie together the diverse causes that gave rise to the movements under consideration. My current work on nineteenth-century intellectual history has reinforced my conviction that current approbation is no guarantee of long-term worth. More important, I have not found a more useful approach to causation for *this type of protest movement* in the years since the *Prophets of Rebellion* was first published. Aberle's formulation provides a temporal dimension and a framework that allows for serious attention to both material and ideological issues that I find essential in dealing with movements of this type. Though I did not intend it at first, one of my aims has become demonstrating the viability of the relative deprivation approach, shorn of its emphasis on predictability and the overly elaborate theoretical superstructure that understandably caused it to fall into disfavor.

Many scholars have shaped my thinking on protest in the years since the first edition of *Prophets,* but none as much as Theda Skocpol. At the very least I owe to her my determination to resist the inclusion of the term "peasant" (which others have argued would do much for sales) in the title of the paperback edition. As Skocpol has shown in her model of comparative study, *States and Social Revolutions,* elites and states are as fundamental to rebellions like those examined here as the peasants who have all but monopolized so many studies in recent years. I am also grateful to Jim Scott for his continuing and consistently insightful responses to my work, even though I still disagree with him about some of the central issues in this volume. Peter Carey and Paul Clark suggested corrections to the first edition. Unfortunately, it has proven prohibitively expensive to remedy in the Cambridge paperback edition the problem that Clark brought to my attention in a personal communication. The now accepted spelling for the Maori movement that forms one of the five main case studies is Pai Marire, meaning "good" and "peaceful". In one of the many retypings that went into the preparation of the first edition, the first "r" in Marire was dropped, and I did not catch the change until the manuscript was in press. The Maire variant was used in some nineteenth-century works and is in fact close to some of the English spellings for Maori words for "peaceful" listed by Bruce Biggs in a recent *English-Maori Dictionary* (Auckland, 1981), which includes "huumaarie" and "maarie" in addition to "aumaarire" and "huumaarire". Nonetheless, the reader should be aware that the preferred spelling for the movement is Marire. Finally, I wish to acknowledge the key roles played by Philip Curtin of The Johns Hopkins University and Frank Smith at the Cambridge University Press in making this paperback edition of the *Prophets of Rebellion* possible.

Rutgers University at New Brunswick   Michael Adas
June 1986

Foreword

Since the end of the Second World War, American universities
have passed through a whole sequence of revised attitudes toward
the societies beyond Europe and its offshoots overseas. In the postwar decade came the first realization that they had paid little attention to major countries like China, less still to ex-colonies like India
just emerging into independence, and even less to remaining colonial areas like Africa, which had been left to the attention of their
European overlords. The first response, and a somewhat slow response, was to make a place for non-Western studies in growing
postwar universities. The form of that response was to create area-
studies programs in the major universities, where a culture-area
like Latin America or South Asia could be brought under the collective scrutiny of specialists from the various social sciences and
human disciplines. At first, these centers were few, and no single
university tried to "cover" all of the major culture-areas in the
world. In time, however, the idea spread from large to small
universities. Several universities set out to establish area-studies
centers for most, if not all, of the world's important regions.

Historians participated in this spread of international studies,
and specialists in various fields of non-Western history, trained
initially in the area-studies centers, began to take their places in
departments of history, even in the smaller colleges and universities without formal area-studies programs. The traditional division of history departments into "Americanists" on one hand and
"Europeanists" on the other shifted to a tripartite division where
specialists in non-Western and Latin American history began to
function as a third group, often under the misnomer of "third-
world" history.

By the end of the 1950s, this tendency was clearly visible, and
it was to be more and more striking through the 1960s. While it
was clearly a net gain for American knowledge of the world overseas, it also posed some problems. Where historians had once
found it easy to have a passable knowledge of the discipline outside his own area of research, historical knowledge was now fragmented. The new range of course offerings now covered much of
the globe, but students had to choose from this wider range. They

were, in fact, confronted with a great variety of new courses and new programs in the university as a whole. The required courses in Western Civilization or American History became optional, and history enrollments began to decline. Students who specialized in history tended to know scattered bodies of historical information, rather than having a broad, if superficial, knowledge of the course of change in human societies.

By the 1960s the problem was obvious, but it was difficult to bring the explosion of knowledge under control. Some historians tried to reorient their teaching and writing so as to take in the whole of world history in a real sense, not the older "world history" that was actually the history of Europe with occasional mention of the peripheral regions. Another tendency was to reduce the number of time-place history courses in favor of more thematic approaches like "Twentieth-Century Revolutions" or "Industrialization." All history is comparative in some sense, but the pursuit of a theme across national or cultural boundaries was more self-consciously comparative than most historical study had been in the past. From that point, it was only one step further to make comparisons explicit and to use this approach to discover principles that can be taken to be broadly true of human experience.

Studies in Comparative World History, of which this book is the first volume, grew out of this general ferment of the 1960s and 1970s. Most of the authors of projected volumes were connected in one way or another with the Program in Comparative World History at the University of Wisconsin, as Michael Adas and I both were. The program itself was founded in 1959 as a way of helping Ph.D. candidates in various fields of non-Western history to avoid the problem of fragmented historical knowledge. In addition to the interdisciplinary training of the typical area-studies program, it insisted on cross-area training within the discipline of history as a counter-weight to excessive area specialization. A large proportion of the hundred or so doctoral candidates who emerged from the program in the 1960s and early 1970s went on to teach at least one course that crossed the cultural divisions of world history.

The project of a series of books in comparative world history arose from the opportunity to make this teaching experience available in a more permanent and accessible form. The Wisconsin Program in Comparative World History sponsored a summer seminar in 1975, financed by a grant from the Carnegie Corporation of New York. Michael Adas and a half dozen or so prospective authors brought manuscripts-in-progress for a summer of mutual discussion that ranged from the kinds of comparative history that might be attempted, through the techniques for presenting comparative data and conclusions, down to the specific and detailed criticisms that could come from specialists with a home base in a variety of different culture-areas. The result should therefore be something more of a joint enterprise than are most historical series, in which intellectual interchange rarely moves beyond a dialogue between the series editor and the individual authors.

As general editor, I find it especially gratifying to introduce Michael Adas's work. It represents the kind of cross-area breadth so often missing in the new non-Western history of recent decades. It should serve to remind us that history is and should be the study of how and why human societies change through time. It underlines the fact that societies quite different from our own can tell us a great deal about the human condition—even more, that history, or any other social science, needs a wide range of data from differing cultures to separate general patterns of the human past from the special cases that occur in particular cultures.

The Johns Hopkins University   Philip D. Curtin

Acknowledgments

A comparative study of this kind must draw on the work of many specialists, and I have acknowledged their indispensable contributions in footnote references. In addition, I have received assistance, valuable critiques, and suggestions from many sources. Funds for research and writing were provided at various stages by the Fulbright, Danforth, and Carnegie Foundations—the latter through a grant from the Comparative World History Program at the University of Wisconsin. I have also received financial support from the Rutgers University Research Council. My research could not have been done without the assistance of the staffs of the India Office Library and Records, the British Library, the library of the School of Oriental and African Studies of the University of London, the New York City Public Library, and the libraries of the universities of Wisconsin, Rutgers, Cornell, Yale, and Princeton.

James C. Scott provided useful critiques of both the early drafts and the completed version of this study. The members of the Comparative World History Workshop at the University of Wisconsin —Philip Curtin, Joseph Miller, John Richards, Leo Spitzer, Allen Isaacman, and Dick Eaton—made detailed suggestions for revising the original draft of the manuscript. Joseph Brennig, David Henige, and Bruce Cruickshank also made helpful suggestions for revision at this stage, and Steve Feierman directed me to a number of productive source materials. At several points, the incisive critiques of the members of the Social History Group at Rutgers University forced me to reconsider or rework materials. For this, I owe a special debt to my colleagues Rudy Bell, Traian Stoianovich, Donald Weinstein, and Allen Howard. I am also grateful to Herb Rowen for his detailed suggestions concerning my writing style and manner of presentation. In England, I received valuable assistance from a number of scholars, especially Patricia Herbert of the British Library and Merle Ricklefs and the members of the Southeast Asia seminar at SOAS. I am most indebted to Peter Carey of Magdalen College, Oxford University, for generously providing supplemental source materials, fine insights, and extensive and cogent critiques. My wife, Jane, and my children, Joel and Claire, patiently endured my attempts to work out problems involving angry prophets over meals and during walks in nearby parks and provided wonderful diversions from research and writing.

London   Michael Adas

Introduction

Near the town of Dedaye in Lower Burma in January 1931, a well-armed party of colonial police was confronted by an irregular mass of nearly seven hundred Burman peasants. Despite warnings from the British officer in command that they would be fired upon, the peasants, armed only with knives, spears, and a few antique firearms, advanced fearlessly across open ground toward the ready guns of the Indian and Burmese mercenaries who made up the bulk of the colonial military forces. As they marched, the leaders of the rebel throng chanted cabalistic incantations to stupefy the enemy troops and rang sacred gongs to render their adversaries' rifles and machine guns useless. The rank-and-file clutched protective talismans, which had been distributed before battle, and displayed magic symbols tattooed on their chests and arms, which were intended to confer invulnerability. The peasants did not hesitate, for their victory seemed certain. All signs indicated that the forces of the cosmos were on their side. Many believed that Saya San, the prophet who had exhorted them to rebellion, was the Coming (*Metaya*) Buddha or the Buddha's messenger. He had promised an end to the infidel's rule and restoration of the Burman monarchy and the Buddhist religion. Through their prophet leader, the peasants sought to usher in a golden age of harmony and prosperity. They thought themselves invincible. No threats, no show of force could turn them back. As the closely packed ranks of the rebel band drew near to an embankment where the colonial forces had taken cover, the police opened fire. Nearly two hours later the bewildered remnants of the rebel force withdrew leaving hundreds of their comrades dead or wounded on the field of battle.

Since the early nineteenth century, this scene has been played out hundreds of times. The actors, settings, and cultural idioms have been different; the tragic endings have been similar. The Saya San rebellion in Lower Burma represents one type of a class of social movements for which Anthony Wallace's term "revitalization" is the most inclusive and useful label. Wallace defined revitalization intentionally in broad terms as "a deliberate, organized, conscious effort by members of a society to construct a more satisfying culture." This process presupposed that the participants in such movements felt that major aspects of their existing culture were no longer viable. Revitalization involved changes that affected "not merely discrete items," but would lead to the creation of "a new cultural system."[1] Wallace's concept of revitalization covers a wide range of social movements, including those which have been called "nativistic," "millennial," "messianic," "nostalgic," "sectarian," and "revivalist," to cite just the most prominent labels employed.[2]

These movements have erupted in radically different societies and diverse locales in almost all areas of the globe. They represent one of the oldest forms of collective behavior known to man. They have varied widely in scale, ranging from localized and spontaneous outbursts to well-organized rebellions that have engulfed whole societies. The form and content of revitalization movements have also differed greatly. Some have involved violence and organized resistance; others have stressed peaceful reform or passive withdrawal. Many have focused on the formation of new religious sects or separatist churches, and often these organizations have become involved in political agitation. In certain movements the participants have consciously sought to revive "traditional" customs and beliefs and to purge their culture of alien elements. On the other hand, adherents of movements like the Cargo Cults of Melanesia have been obsessed with acquiring foreign material goods and imitating alien forms of organization and behavior.

The concerns expressed little more than a decade ago that revitalization movements would be treated as mere ethnographical curiosities or as bizarre episodes on the fringes of more fundamental historical events[3] have proven unfounded. In recent years there has been a great outpouring of detailed monographs and a number of theoretical and comparative studies dealing with these movements over a wide range of geographic areas.[4] These works have clearly demonstrated both the historical importance of this form of collective expression and the great potential for theoretical analysis which revitalization phenomena offer to those working in a number of disciplines, particularly anthropology, sociology and history. Revitalization movements and the situations that gave rise to them provide superb materials for the study of the dislocations and deprivations, as well as the impetus for innovation, that result from culture contact and the process of acculturation. They provide excellent opportunities to examine the stresses produced by accelerated change and some of the potential responses to it.[5] With regard to societies in colonial or post-colonial Africa, Asia, and Oceania, which have been the focus of many recent studies, revitalization movements have been seen as key examples of social protest against the conditions resulting from European colonial rule. They have been viewed as attempts to create viable new ideologies, institutions, and social bonds in situations where long-standing world views and customary relationships were eroded by the transformations that resulted from European conquest. A number of writers have also seen in revitalization movements the beginnings of mass political mobilization and expressions of embryonic nationalist sentiments among colonized peoples.[6] Increasing stress has been placed on the ways in which the symbols and demands of these movements were eventually recognized and put to use by Western-educated African and Asian elite groups in their struggles to create independent nation-states.[7]

Although I will refer to examples drawn from the broader class of revitalization movements, in this study I am primarily concerned with a particular form of this type of collective behavior. I will focus on revitalization movements which took the form of *prophet-inspired rebellions* among *non-Western peoples* against *European-dominated colonial regimes*. Since each of these characteristics played a key role in my selection of case examples for comparison, it is important that I explain at some length my use of these terms in the present study.

My central purpose is to explore the relationships between the rise of prophetic leaders and violent protest. The participants in the movements under consideration sought to transform sociocultural systems which they perceived to be unacceptable by extralegal means rather than constitutional agitation, by force rather than reform, withdrawal, or passive resistance. Each of the groups studied here mounted rebellions aimed at overthrowing not only existing political regimes but also the sociocultural order as it then existed. In this sense, their aims were revolutionary, even though their visions of alternative orders were vastly different from those that social scientists have come to associate with "true" revolutions. One of my main concerns will be to analyze the causes of discontent and frustration that were so intensely felt that people were willing to kill and in turn risk their own lives in order to alleviate them. In addition to what it tells us about the specific type of movement under study, this analysis should provide insights into the effects of the diffusion of aspects of the commercial-industrial revolutions in western Europe to diverse societies in Africa, Asia, and Oceania. This process of diffusion-transformation, which is central to modern global history, offers a common framework for comparing the movements selected and for attempting to identify general patterns.

Each of the cases considered here involved not only violent protest but violent protest that was intimately linked to the rise of a prophetic leader. As I use the term in this study,[8] a prophet is a person who believes and is able to convince others that he or she has special contacts with supernatural forces by means of dreams, visions, and special revelations. The prophet's followers are convinced that he or she possesses superhuman powers, which are frequently displayed in predictive or healing abilities.[9] In some cases the prophet may claim to be or may be regarded by the faithful as an incarnation of the divine. More important for the origins of social movements, the prophetic figure serves as a channel for divine revelations that provide a plan of action for oppressed groups and present fundamental challenges to existing beliefs and institutions. The prophet promises his followers salvation, expressed through millenarian visions, which vary according to the cultural idiom in which he works. Although I will qualify somewhat Norman Cohn's typology[10] of the basic components of these millenarian visions, his definition provides a useful starting point for the analysis of the millenarian themes in the movements under study. Each of these movements exhibited salvationist beliefs that involved radical transformations within the terrestrial realm. Supernatural forces were expected to play some part in these transformations that would usher in a perfect world order which would be enjoyed by the faithful as a group.

Given current expectations regarding the terminology employed in discussions of the appeal of leaders of this type, it is necessary that I state at the outset my reasons for deliberately avoiding the use of the term "charisma" in this study. Though there is much of value in Max Weber's discussion of the "charismatic leader," which he sets forth as one of three ideal types of authority figures, the term itself, as he defines it and subsequent authors have employed it, raises many problems. Weber's original definition of the term is at best ambiguous.[11] A brief quotation from a key introductory passage demonstrates the problems inherent from its inception. Weber states that the concept should be applied to a leader who possesses ". . . *a certain quality* . . . by virtue of which he is set apart from ordinary men and treated as endowed with supernatural, superhuman, *or at least specifically exceptional* powers or qualities" (italics mine).[12] The opportunities for imprecision and misunderstanding provided by this passage are multiplied as Weber's equivocation continues in his treatment of such key issues as whether a charismatic leader's authority comes from his divine calling,[13] his followers' perception,[14] his consistent success, or a combination of all of the above.

Despite a number of serious attempts in recent years to tighten up Weber's definition and develop criteria that might be empirically tested,[15] the meaning of "charisma" has, if anything, become more ambiguous. Popularizers have reduced it to a catch-all label for leaders who excite mass adulation. The term has been applied to persons as disparate as Jesus, Adolf Hitler, and Leonard Bernstein. The vagueness of Weber's and subsequent formulations of the meaning of charisma contribute to a second major deficiency, the concept is fundamentally circular. A leader is charismatic because he is perceived by his followers to have charismatic qualities.[16] Since a reformulation of the term clearly lies beyond the scope of this study, I will forego the use of the concept and employ instead the term prophet, as defined above.

Although a great deal of recent scholarly attention has been devoted to violent protest movements and the meaning of prophetic and millennial expression, few writers have attempted to study the links between the two and the ways in which they reinforce each other.[17] This study focuses on the relationships between these two forms of collective behavior and an analysis of the key factors which have caused them to fuse in prophetic rebellions. To explore these connections, I shall investigate the causal grievances that tend to direct rebellion into millennial channels and examine in detail the cultural settings, available options, and other circumstances that determine which mode of expression is adopted by dissident groups. I shall pay special attention to the complex relationships between rebellion and millenarianism as they affect patterns of leadership, mobilization, and organization, and as they influence the outcome and impact of particular protest movements. Although an exploration of the roles of myths, religious beliefs, and forms of ritual expression is an integral part of this analysis, these elements are not examined for their own sake or for what they may contribute to the study of religion or comparative theology. I am interested in these aspects of prophetic movements primarily for what they reveal about the genesis, expression, and outcome of violent social protest.

All of the movements examined displayed in varying degrees nativistic tendencies. Each movement represented "conscious" and "organized" attempts on the part of its participants "to revive or perpetuate selected aspects of [their] culture."[18] These movements also involved efforts to destroy or expel the agents, ideas, and artifacts of alien, but dominant, cultures. At the very least, their participants hoped to destroy the European colonial regime and expel white settlers and Christian missionaries, as well as alien non-European officials, mercenary troops, and mercantile groups. In each of the movements considered, however, there was some ambivalence toward foreign imports and the degree to which they should be purged. Each movement reflected widely varying degrees of acculturation in ideology, behavior, and organizational patterns. Rather than pure nativism or total assimilation, these movements exhibited a blend of the two. In this respect, they can best be compared when plotted on a continuum ranging between two "ideal types," with nativism at one pole and assimilation at the other. This continuum provides the basis for a general typology of these movements which takes into account important variations in causation, leadership patterns, rank-and-file composition, mobilization, and modes of organization and expression.

Because my interest is primarily in the general patterns exhibited by prophetic rebellions, I have chosen to study these movements through a comparison of a number of examples rather than devote a monograph to the details of a single rising. To avoid emphasis on straight chronology and description, I have concentrated my analysis on five main examples. These are (in chronological order): the revolt led by Prince Dipanagara in the Netherlands East Indies (1825–1830); the Pai Maire or Hau Hau movement of the Maoris of New Zealand (1864–c.1867); the Birsa disturbances among the Mundas of Chota Nagpur in east-central India (1895–1900); the Maji Maji rebellions in German East Africa (1905–1906); and the Saya San risings in Burma (1930–1932). Limiting the number of cases allows me to examine in some depth both the sociocultural contexts of these rebellions and the patterns displayed by each movement.

In addition to these five core cases, I will draw on a large and growing literature on different types of revitalization movements, particularly those works dealing with various forms of prophetic social protest. My intent in comparing these cases is not to construct a rigid model that systematically defines all aspects of prophetic rebellions, for I have found that contexts and movements vary so greatly that a more flexible frame of analysis is desirable. Therefore, within each category of analysis (causation, modes of expression, etc.) I have attempted to identify variations on basic patterns. I have intentionally selected examples that differ widely in terms of geographical location, sociocultural context, the nature and timing of European colonial penetration, and the patterns displayed by the movements themselves. Although these differences mean that the case evidence does not always fit neatly into my general typologies, they provide important qualifications for and variations on common themes. They indicate the importance of an often overlooked principle of comparative analysis—that differences within the type can be as meaningful as similarities. In attempting to come to terms with the problems for comparative analysis raised by these differences, I hope to minimize some of the perils involved in the comparison of revitalization phenomena that have been noted by numerous students of these movements.[19]

As in all research, my selection of case examples has been strongly influenced by the quality and quantity of source materials available. For only one of the five cases, the Saya San rebellion, have I conducted extensive research in archival materials. For the other four movements, secondary works and published government reports and documents have been my main sources of evidence. In both primary and secondary sources, I have encountered a major problem that has come to be associated with the study of social protest, excepting the relatively well-documented "Great Revolutions" of Europe and China. With rare exceptions of documents like the diary kept by Saya San and the post-rebellion histories written by Prince Dipanagara and other Javanese nobles, most of the contemporary materials on the movements under study were compiled by hostile observers. Very often information comes from military commanders or judicial officials charged with the task of suppressing the disturbances and meting out punishment to their participants. In addition, the administrators who gathered the great bulk of materials on these movements were foreigners—either Europeans or immigrant Asian or African functionaries attached to the European colonial bureaucracy. Although these events might not have been recorded at all had it not been for the European penchant for investigations and written reports, there are nonetheless a number of special problems involved in selecting and interpreting such source materials. Normally neither the officials who wrote at the time of the outbreaks nor the authors who published accounts shortly afterwards had any special anthropological or ethnological training, though there were sometimes administrators present who were somewhat knowledgeable about the peoples and cultures involved. Not only did these early observers ask questions different from ones that trained social scientists might have posed, they were also less concerned than social scientists to "render intelligible . . . symbolic system[s] and mode[s] of understanding" that they did not share.[20] In addition, non-European, immigrant or indigenous informers, translators, and subordinate officials very often supplied most of the information about a particular rising. These agents frequently screened or distorted information to protect or advance their own position, or to harm their rivals.[21]

The nature of the colonial sources compels the social scientist to develop new ways of approaching and analyzing the limited materials available about revitalization movements. He must glean evidence of rebel expression and activities from government reports and published accounts dominated by narratives of official disputes and military engagements. This information must be cross-checked for consistency and accuracy and combined with available statistical and textual materials on social and economic conditions. Additional evidence can also be drawn from accounts of the lives of the agitators who led these movements, the grievances proclaimed in the rebels' recruiting speeches and polemical tracts, and, most especially, in the testimony of participants and observers during the trials and special inquiries that frequently resulted from these outbursts of protest.

Social scientists must also correct for the deep-seated prejudices that permeate the colonial sources. These biases are reflected in sweeping judgements on rebel motives and modes of expression, indiscriminately applied labels like "bandit" or "witch doctor," and condescending remarks about the childlike mentality or superstitious nature of the peoples involved. Recent research on the movements under consideration and the societies which produced them are essential aids in this process of revaluation and reconstruction. Even these recent studies, however, must be used with caution. They have been produced in a scholarly climate strongly influenced by what has been termed an "apologetic reaction"[22] associated with the era of decolonization. This is particularly true of the more fervently anti-imperialist studies where prophetic leaders tend to be transformed into nationalist heroes marching in the vanguard of struggles for independence, which appear inevitable only in retrospect.

Although European colonial situations provide a common context for the movements under consideration, there are significant variations in colonial regimes and the societies they dominated, as well as in the nature of the changes that resulted from the interaction of the two. Three different European imperialist powers—Great Britain, the Netherlands, and Germany—are represented in situations that range from the in-depth, direct control achieved by the British in Lower Burma to the indirect rule exercised by the Dutch in the princely states of central Java. One of the cases, the Maori Pai Maire movement, involved European settlers. In all of the others, non-European migrant groups played key roles as administrators, merchants, and moneylenders, and, in some instances, as landlords and laborers. Thus, two basic variants of what have come to be known as "plural societies" are examined. Christian missionary influence played an important role in the Pai Maire and Birsa movements, a peripheral role in the Maji Maji rising, and virtually no part in the rebellions in Burma and Java.

Perhaps the most important reason for differences in European colonial regimes and their impact was the timing of the European advance in each area. The cases considered are spread fairly evenly over the century that saw European global expansion peak and then begin to recede. The degree of European penetration and the extent of the changes effected (or contemplated) were largely determined by the degree to which the metropolis of each of the colonial areas had undergone the process of industrialization in the different time periods considered. The length of the period of colonial rule before an outbreak also had an important bearing on a movement's nature and impact, as contrasts between the Saya San and Maji Maji rebellions will clearly reveal.

I have selected my case examples from societies in Africa, India, Southeast Asia, and Oceania. All of the societies selected were primarily agrarian and, before the coming of European control, oriented to family or community-based production that was only marginally linked to market networks. When I first conceived this study, I intended to focus specifically on peasant[23] protest, but as I gathered evidence it became clear that elite groups played key roles in the genesis and development of these movements. Therefore, although the scope of my enquiry remains confined to rebellions concentrated in rural areas and supported mainly by agriculturists, I have given special attention to indigenous leadership groups, in addition to their peasant subjects or kinsmen. I do not intend that my concentration on rural-based movements limit the applicability of my general findings; in fact, I hope that some of these will be useful for the analysis of prophetic protest among other kinds of groups, such as the urban poor, vagabonds, and déclassé townsmen.

The sociocultural milieus of the core cases range from those representative of the "Great Traditions" of Islam and Buddhism to the isolated and predominantly animistic Maori people of the North Island in New Zealand. Two of the societies studied (those in Burma and Java) had developed fairly centralized political systems before the European conquest; the remaining three were decentralized and acephalous socities with political institutions based on blends of kinship and local influence. The historical geography of the five cases includes examples of frontier regions, marginal hill retreats of former plains-dwelling groups, and densely populated core areas. The scale of the rebellions varies from the Java War, which involved hundreds of thousands of combatants and affected millions of persons, to the Birsa rising, which was a small and relatively localized outbreak.

Although this is a study of a particular kind of response to European overseas expansion, I have deliberately not used an analytical framework based on the tradition-modernity dichotomy that has dominated recent research on former colonial societies. Even a cursory review of the vast literature on "modernization" reveals how difficult it is to determine with any degree of precision or consensus the content of tradition and modernity as ideal types. In addition, as the studies of Lloyd and Susanne Rudolph, Milton Singer, and others[24] have clearly demonstrated, the dichotomy between tradition and modernity is in many ways a false one. Customary or traditional ideas and institutions often persist through the process of modernization and contribute significantly to both group and individual adjustment to change. Equally important, the tradition-modernity dichotomy implies that all peoples are "developing" (or *should* develop) on the pattern of western European or North American industrialized societies, an inference that is clearly challenged by the experience of the non-Western nations in the postcolonial era.

Despite these reservations regarding the tradition-modernity dichotomy, change and its accompanying dislocations are central to the movements under consideration. The societies that produced them were far from stagnant in the centuries before the arrival of agents of European industrial civilization and that contact greatly accelerated their rates of change. In some cases European activities mainly intensified patterns that had already been set in motion by indigenous forces. In other cases they introduced new forces of innovation and disruption. In none of these movements was the response to change merely a blind retreat into an idealized pre-European past, although there was always some appeal to customary ways. Rather, they represented creative efforts to repair the fabric of societies rent by forces over which the indigenous peoples had little or no control. These prophet-inspired rebellions involved restoration and reformulation of customary ideas and institutions as well as the introduction of foreign elements and a millenarian vision of a new society. Their adherents were not faced with a choice between a traditional and a modern order, but with the problems of coping with accelerated change and intense culture contact. In bits and pieces, rather than by some grand design, they rejected or adapted, revived and reworked ideas, artifacts, and patterns of behavior in an effort to create a more viable social order.

Prophets of Rebellion

ONE

Contexts for Five Rebellions

Although European expansion and contacts between cultures provide a common basis for comparing the rebellions considered here,
these movements arose in contexts that were very different in
ecology and geography and in sociocultural and historical development. Understanding these differences is obviously necessary to
analyze the patterns of protest displayed by each movement, but
they must also be kept in mind in developing a body of case evidence from which comparisons can be made and general themes
identified. Differences in social systems or historical circumstances
often caused important variations in the broader patterns that
are the focus of this study. In this chapter I will underscore the
most important contextual differences and introduce the areas,
peoples, cultures, and movements from which most of my empirical evidence is drawn. In succeeding chapters I will move from
this general discussion to a consideration of specific patterns of
causation, organization, and rebellion. Implicit in my approach is
the conviction that specific historical causes have little meaning in
and of themselves. They are significant only when related to other
causal factors in a sequential framework that the historian must
reconstruct.[1]

Dutch Advance and the Slow Death of Mataram: The Java War of 1825–1830

The extension of Dutch control over the island of Java was almost
totally the product of the early, preindustrial phase of European
expansion into Asia. Javanese responses to this advance were similar to those of the peoples of India, Ceylon, and "Indianized"
Southeast Asia.[2] The foothold established by the Dutch at Batavia
on the northwest coast of Java in 1619–1620 was not intended as a
base from which to conquer the island. The Dutch viewed the port
as the central point in a maritime trading empire that they were
struggling to build throughout Asia. Dutch control was established
on the wreckage of the Portuguese system that preceded it and in
defiance of British as well as Southeast Asian and Arab rivals. Sea
power, based on superior ship design and the deployment of artil-

lery in sailing vessels, was the most decisive European advantage over all but the Chinese in the early centuries of Western involvement in Asia. Sea power permitted the Dutch to defend their trading posts on Java and elsewhere from the attacks of Asian princes, to gain partial control over the lucrative East Indies spice trade, and to expand their share of the increasingly important Asian interport commerce. Dutch power was confined largely to the sea lanes, the tiny spice islands, and sections of the coastal regions of India, Ceylon, and the Indonesian archipelago. Until the end of the seventeenth century, the Dutch at Batavia faced the sea and avoided as far as possible costly entanglements in the complex inter- and intra-state struggles that periodically erupted in the Javanese hinterland. For over half a century after the founding of Batavia, the Dutch continued to maintain the fiction that they were the vassals of the Sultan of Mataram, whose kingdom dominated all but the western extremities of the island. The Dutch showed only limited interest in either the ruler or his kingdom and the ancient and sophisticated civilization they represented. Even in the eighteenth century, when the Dutch became deeply involved in the complex political struggles in the interior, they did so at first largely without premeditation. Although their maritime empire was becoming increasingly obsolete, they were very reluctant to convert it into a land-based colonial system of the sort that would be associated with European imperialism in the late nineteenth century.

As did the British in India, the Dutch advanced on Java mainly by exploiting the rivalries, internal weaknesses, and persistent errors that undermined the indigenous kingdoms. The rulers of Mataram, who began the seventeenth century as overlords of most of the island and who represented by far the most formidable defense against outside domination, misjudged Dutch capacities and intentions and underestimated the dangers posed by these alien invaders. In these failings they shared much with the princes of India, the rulers of west and central Africa, and the emperors of the Amerindian civilizations of the New World. After Sultan Agung's failure to dislodge the Dutch from their fortified seaport at Batavia in 1628 and 1629, the monarchs of Mataram came to tolerate the Dutch as vassals who paid their tribute punctually while harboring suspicions of them as potential allies for rebellious princes or rival states like Banten. The location of Batavia and other areas of early Dutch penetration on the north coast and in the west, outside the heartland areas in central and east Java, contributed significantly to the tendency of the rulers of Mataram to play down the importance of the growing Dutch presence on the island. After nearly a century of strong leaders and sustained growth, the kingdom of Mataram began to disintegrate in the 1670s because of forces that have clear counterparts in the cycle of dynastic rise and decline characteristic of precolonial states in India and "Indianized" Southeast Asia. Mataram itself had risen from the ruins of preceding states that had shown similar weaknesses. In the late seventeenth century, however, it was an alien power and not a neighboring rival that would begin to forge a territorial empire on the ruins of the once-mighty Javanese kingdom.

Succession disputes, the loose—often nominal—control exerted by the court center over the geographically divided regions that made up the kingdom, and an aristocratic bureaucracy whose loyalty was personal rather than systemic and whose support was derived from the localities were the key causes of the slow death of Mataram. Javanese dynastic disputes were rarely resolved through compromises aimed at maintaining unified strength in the face of external enemies. Princely claimants and rebellious nobles not only openly battled for dominance but repeatedly called on the Dutch for assistance. Military intervention gave the Dutch an ever greater role in the internal affairs of the island and, perhaps most significantly, upset the pattern of consensual support on which the power of Javanese rulers had previously depended. As Dutch backing became increasingly vital to the maintenance of the Sultan's position, the allegiance of Javanese nobles and local officials declined in importance. Foreign support also resulted in a loss of legitimacy, which gave rise to further dynastic disputes and bloody intramural strife. In 1674, a major rebellion by the Prince of Madura against Sultan Agung's son and successor (Amangkurat I) began a succession of civil wars and regional revolts that reduced Mataram to puppet impotence within a century and made the Dutch the paramount lords on the island. The Javanese vision of a hierarchic realm with the Sultan's *kraton* or palace-city at the center, extending through the core regions of central Java to the peripheral northern coastal areas and island extremities, was reversed as Batavia and its hinterland rose to become the new focal points of Javanese history. This process culminated in 1755–1757 in the division, supervised by the Dutch, of the remnants of the kingdom of Mataram in central Java and along the southern coast (see Map 1). Four princely states were formed, of which Yogyakarta and Surakarta were by far the largest and most important. In less than a century,

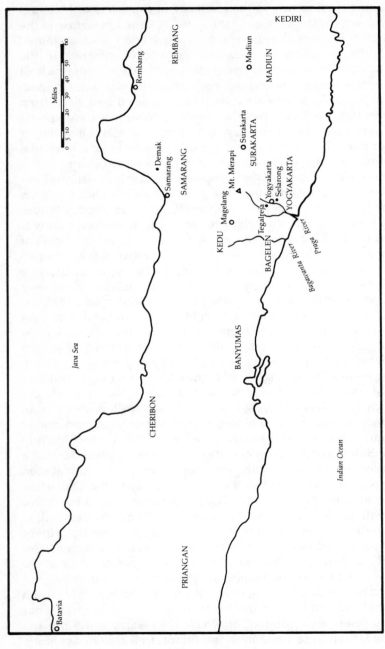

1. Central Java in the Nineteenth Century. Source: H. A. van Coenan Torchiana, *Tropical Holland* (Chicago, 1921).

through piecemeal concessions by Javanese princes in desperate straits, the Dutch had obtained direct rule over all save these lingering vestiges of Javanese sovereignty. In the "Vorstenlanden" the Dutch exercised increasingly effective control through European residents and their assistants, through regulation of appointments, and through manipulation of the chief ministers of the princely realms.

The political decline of Mataram was accompanied by severe social and economic dislocations. The monarchs of Mataram themselves contributed to the downfall of the commercial centers of the north coast of Java by their repeated military campaigns. The loss of these once thriving areas to the Dutch meant that the inland court centers had fewer trading outlets to the sea and thus they were deprived of important sources of revenue. The remaining local and inland trade was sizable but it gradually fell into the hands of the Chinese, who served both the Javanese and Dutch as middlemen, tax farmers, and landlords.[3] The Dutch annexed one outer province after another, and eventually took over even those provinces that bordered on the central core areas. These annexations deprived the indigenous princes and administrative nobility of land and, more important, of manpower that supplied the produce and labor services on which the monarchy and bureaucracy rested. Thus, the political collapse of Mataram was intimately related to the worsening position of the indigenous elites and in turn to general social and economic breakdown. All these factors were to prove conducive to rebellion in the 1820s.

Despite these important repercussions of Dutch-Javanese interaction, the degree of direct control exerted by the Dutch over Javanese society and the extent of the transformations effected up to the time of Dipanagara's rebellion in the late 1820s were considerably less profound than those in most of the other areas considered in this study. As I have noted, this difference can be explained by the timing of the Dutch advance and the nature of the European metropolis that stood behind it. Dutch overseas expansion was a product of the great commercial transformations in western Europe whose roots extended far back into the Medieval period, rather than of the industrial revolution that would shape the nature and effects of European involvement in the other areas examined in this study. Beyond trade, which was centered in areas outside of Java, Dutch activities in the Indonesian archipelago until the mid-nineteenth century were mainly political and military. Even in these spheres, Dutch influence on Java itself was limited.

Although new European bureaucratic ideas and institutions had begun to be introduced into Dutch-controlled areas in the last decades of the eighteenth century, the administrative structure of both the areas directly ruled by the Dutch (beyond Batavia and its environs) and those remaining under the indigenous princes was still predominantly Javanese in personnel, structure, and ideology in the prerebellion period. The persistence of indigenous forms was perhaps best exemplified by the continuing importance of Javanese officials or regents in regional and local administration, and the fact that the Dutch exploited the land and labor resources of the interior primarily through tribute systems, which closely resembled pre-European revenue arrangements and administrative precedents.[4] Like Javanese lords, Dutch officials traveled about under umbrellas decorated according to their rank, while the Javanese nobility clung to their ancient dress, protocol, and modes of behavior. Before the mid-nineteenth century, the Javanese adopted few of the new military and political forms which the Dutch brought to the island. In the sociocultural spheres, the disinclination of the Javanese to imitate or borrow from those whom they viewed as uncouth foreigners was even more pronounced. As a result, the changes in court organization and even lifestyles that the Dutch and the British (during the interregnum period 1811–1816) attempted to introduce in the first decades of the nineteenth century were all the more disruptive and disturbing. They would prove to be among the major irritants that eventually prodded Prince Dipanagara and his numerous adherents into open revolt.

Although there was considerable disagreement among Dutch observers about the underlying causes of Dipanagara's rebellion or the Java War of 1825–1830, most saw it as the last in a long succession of dynastic squabbles in the princely states.[5] Dutch officials argued that Dipanagara's widespread personal popularity and the chronic state of instability and unrest in Yogyakarta transformed what should have been a petty palace quarrel into the greatest rebellion against the Dutch in Indonesia before the 1945–1949 revolution. In the contemporary Dutch view, the conflict arose primarily from Prince Dipanagara's disappointment at being denied the throne of Yogyakarta and his resentment of the disrespect shown to him by his Javanese rivals and Dutch officials. Dipanagara's refusal to obey the Dutch Resident Smissaert's summons to the court at Yogyakarta in July of 1825 precipitated nearly five years of hostilities. The prince's escape from the Dutch and Javanese troops sent to his residence at Tegalreja to bring him forcibly to court was the signal for numerous local outbreaks of violence led by regional lords, Muslim religious leaders, and bandit chiefs. Dipanagara himself built up a substantial following among the local notables and villagers from his estate and nearby areas and among those court officials, royal relatives, and palace troops who rallied to his standard. In the opening days of the rebellion, the struggle was concentrated in the region around the court center at Yogyakarta. Rebel forces attacked and burned neighboring villages and market centers, as well as houses and official residences in the capital itself. Dipanagara's rivals at court fled to the Dutch fort for protection. In the following weeks the revolt spread into the districts fringing the Yogyakarta core area, like Kedu and Bagelen. Within months there were outbreaks in areas as distant as Demak in Samarang on the north coast and Madiun to the east.

The sudden escalation of palace squabbles into open rebellion caught the Dutch completely off guard. Most of the European troops stationed in the Netherlands East Indies at the time were involved in expeditions in the Celebes and elsewhere in the "outer islands," and had to be quickly recalled to Java. Dutch officials who survived the early risings could do little more than retreat to the nearest fortifications and attempt to withstand rebel sieges until relief columns arrived. In late July, Hendrik Merkus de Kock was named commander-in-chief of the Dutch and indigenous forces opposed to the rebellion. He began at once to send the limited forces at his disposal to relieve embattled garrisons in the disturbed districts. De Kock also personally went into the field. His timely arrival at the court of Surakarta and his forceful dealings with the Sunan and other nobles there averted the potential defection of the second of the Javanese princely houses and turned it into a captive but important ally. The loss of Surakarta to the Dutch cause would have been a severe blow to their attempts to reassert their control over central Java. With the arrival of the Dutch expeditionary force from the Celebes in late August, De Kock led his army and their allies over to the offensive. The rebel siege of Yogyakarta was lifted and Sultan Menol reinstalled in the palace. In the same period rebel forces in the Samarang region were routed. In October Dutch columns drove Prince Dipanagara and his closest supporters from their base at Selarong. The Dutch pursued the rebels from village to village south of Yogyakarta, but Dipanagara managed to evade capture and established a new center of operations across the Praga river.

Successive operations mounted by the Dutch and their allies

in the Yogyakarta area and surrounding districts appeared to have brought the revolt under control by June 1826. Rebel actions at this time were largely confined to the area north of Yogyakarta, where government columns were still in hot pursuit of Dipanagara and his main forces. A series of stunning rebel victories completely reversed the Dutch momentum, however, and led to renewed resistance in Bagelen, Kedu, and other areas. In these engagements Sentot Prawiradirja emerged as the most brilliant of Dipanagara's generals and was soon elevated to supreme commander of the rebels' armies. The slaying or capture of a number of Dutch officers and allied Javanese nobles in these clashes greatly enhanced Dipanagara's prestige among the general populace and brought new supporters flocking to the rebel standards. In mid-October the Dutch and their allies managed to stem the rising rebel tide somewhat through victories in two major engagements. In the first at Gowok, Dipanagara himself was wounded; in the second, the rebel threat to the vital Solo river valley region was removed.

By 1827, De Kock had finally gathered enough European and indigenous troops and amassed the necessary guns and supplies to begin a systematic campaign to end the rebellion. Employing a strategy based on the use of small forts called *bentengs* linked by mobile columns, the Dutch sought to reduce steadily the area of rebel operations and to deny the enemy their village-based sources of supplies and new recruits. After a series of defeats dealt to Dipanagara's supporters in July and August, the rebels attempted to negotiate a settlement and there was a brief cessation of hostilities. The unwillingness of either side to compromise led to renewed struggle, which was rekindled by a major rising in the Rembang Residency on the northeast coast. Although the revolt would continue for over two years more, the Dutch had clearly gained the advantage by the end of 1827. The final years of the rebellion were characterized by small skirmishes rather than large pitched battles. The Dutch made increasingly effective use of their mobile forces. Through the *benteng* system the Dutch were able to hold areas from which they had driven rebel forces and, by late 1828, serious resistance had been confined to a stretch of heavily wooded, hilly, and riverine country between the Praga and Bagawanta rivers west of Yogyakarta.

Sentot managed a number of small victories as late as August 1829, but the Dutch gained an ever-increasing preponderance of manpower, firearms, communications control, and logistical support. Gradually Dipanagara's major commanders and advisors surrendered or defected. Some were killed in the endless skirmishes that continued right up to Dipanagara's surrender. Although the prince indicated his willingness to treat with the Dutch commander, De Kock, in February 1830, he refused to concede that his cause had been unjust or to give up his demand to be the supreme arbiter of religion on Java. His stubborness and continuing popularity among the Javanese, despite his many reverses, forced De Kock's hand. Feigning negotiations, De Kock lured Dipanagara to Mage-lang, where the prince was arrested on 28 March 1830. His capture and exile to Menado in the Celebes marked the end of the last major attempt of a Javanese prince to use force to halt the advance of Dutch colonial rule.

In area affected and lives lost, the scale of the rebellion led by Prince Dipanagara was comparable to the largest of the Mahdist movements, which was led by Muhammad Achmed in the Sudan in the late 1880s. As many as 200,000 Javanese were killed during the struggle; the Dutch and their indigenous allies lost over 15,000 men. Much of the heavily populated core region of central Java was ravaged by the long years of warfare, which directly affected the lives of over two million people.[6]

The End of Maori Isolation and the Pai Maire Movement in New Zealand, 1864–c. 1867

Like the Amerindian peoples of the New World, the Maoris of New Zealand lived in isolation for centuries before the arrival of European whaling and merchant ships at the end of the eighteenth century.[7] Although the period of Maori isolation was far briefer than that of the peoples of the Americas, the impact of European technology, plants, animals, and diseases was as sudden and their effects were as far-reaching in New Zealand as in the New World. The sustained European influx that began in the last decades of the eighteenth century eventually resulted in the destruction of much of the Maori world order and brought about profound transformations in the Maori way of life.

The predominantly Polynesian people whom the Europeans would call Maoris migrated to New Zealand in intermittent waves from the tenth to the mid-fourteenth century, probably from home-lands in the Society Islands.[8] In the comparatively harsh envi-ronment of their New Zealand landfalls, they developed a tribal culture that was common to virtually all of the peoples of the islands before the arrival of the Europeans. Maori identity was rooted in these tribal units, whose members traced their descent from common ancestors and whose names were derived from the fleet canoes of the semimythical adventurers who settled the islands at least three hundred years before. The Maoris had no designation for themselves as a whole people; they identified so completely with their tribal units that they often spoke of tribal accomplishments as "the war I won," or "the village I established."[9] Relations between tribes were dominated by blood feuds and intermittent warfare, although temporary alliances were occasionally formed. Law and authority existed only within tribal boundaries. Intertribal relations were a nebulous middle ground where hostility and force overwhelmed apparently feeble efforts to forge larger political units or establish permanent channels for peaceful intercourse.

The *hapu* or subtribe, which was normally composed of kinship-linked families living in the same village, was the focus of the Maori's everyday life. The *hapu* was in turn subdivided into extended families normally spanning three generations. The heads of each household represented family interests in the village council, which regulated all aspects of Maori life from the allotment of land to the adjudication of civil disputes or criminal offenses. Chiefs, who were chosen on the basis of a combination of descent and ability, were found at both *hapu* and tribal levels, but they were far from absolute sovereigns. Their decisions depended heavily on the advice and opinions expressed in the tribal councils. The Maori, like many nonliterate peoples, developed a high level of oratorical skill. Council meetings and debates over tribal issues, together with warfare, provided the high points in the life of the Maori male. Military prowess was an essential attribute of a Maori chief. Wars were frequent but, compared with those of the Euro-Asian mainland civilizations, were not costly in property or human lives. The Maori genius for building military fortifications was particularly noted by early European observers, and European armies suffered heavy casualties in the wars of the nineteenth century while trying to take a number of brilliantly constructed Maori *pas* or stockades.

Despite their tightly knit social units and military achievements, the Maoris lacked a number of key technological and organizational elements in their culture that left them both receptive to European penetration, at least initially, and vulnerable to European designs for dominating and colonizing their island home. Their tools and weapons were of wood and stone. Their staple crops were limited in variety and nutritive value, consisting mainly of sweet potatoes and taros, which were cultivated near their settlements, and fern roots, which were gathered in the forests. Since New Zealand lacked large mammals, the Maoris emphasized fishing and bird-snaring. The Maori economy was oriented to self-sufficiency. The chiefs and freemen of each tribe alloted land to *hapu* and family groups for agricultural production, and each group was given its own areas for hunting and fishing. The group acquired only the right to use the designated lands. They did not own them and could not transfer their land rights to other groups without the consent of the whole tribe. Labor was provided largely through mutual assistance within the *hapu* or by slaves, who were usually prisoners-of-war. There was little trade in the usual sense, but tribal exchanges were often effected through gift giving. One tribe or *hapu* would present special foods, precious stones, or handicraft goods to another with the understanding that the recipients were obligated to reciprocate at some future date.

Their first extended contacts with Europeans, which began in the 1790s, were largely detrimental to the Maoris.[10] Merchants seeking *kauri* timber and whalers in search of rest and amusement established small quasi-settlements that led to contacts with tribal groups dwelling near the coast. These initial contacts resulted mainly in the spread of prostitution, liquor and drunkenness, syphilis, and a number of respiratory diseases, as well as the introduction of firearms among the Maoris. The European guns, for which the Maoris eagerly traded wood, food, flax, or whatever else the whites desired, radically altered long-standing patterns of Maori warfare. Precontact tribal balances were upset, and under innovative military chiefs like Hongo, war became far more devastating. Historians have emphasized the role of firearms in the ensuing population decline, but probably a greater toll was taken by epidemic diseases. Because the Maoris' long isolation had left them with few immunities, diseases ranging from smallpox and tuberculosis to the common cold spread rapidly through the islands with devastating effect. Disease and war between them took the lives of tens of thousands of Maoris in the sorrow-filled decades which began the European influx into New Zealand. In 1769 there were an estimated 125 to 135 thousand Maoris in the islands. By the 1840s there were between 80 and 90 thousand.[11] Substantial areas were depopulated and major shifts in Maori distribution occurred. Of special importance was the southwest corner of the North Island, which was to become the major battleground for land control between the Maoris and European settlers (see Map 2).

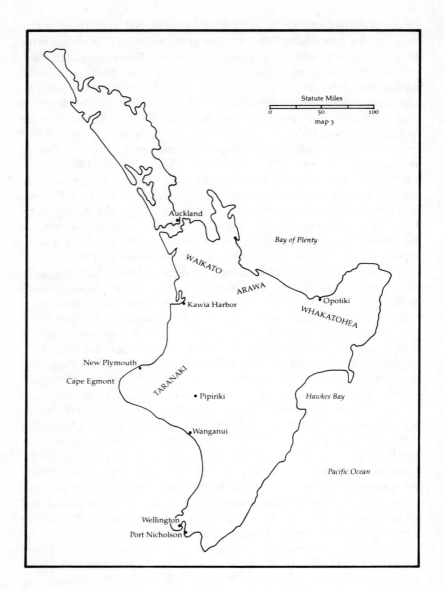

Statute Miles

map 3

Auckland

Bay of Plenty

WAIKATO

ARAWA

Kawia Harbor

Opotiki

WHAKATOHEA

New Plymouth

Cape Egmont

TARANAKI

Pipiriki

Hawkes Bay

Wanganui

Pacific Ocean

Wellington

Port Nicholson

2. The North Island of New Zealand during the Maori Wars.
Source: Arthur P. Douglas, *The Dominion of New Zealand* (London,
1909).

Despite these early catastrophes in which coastal tribes were affected much sooner than those of the interior, the Maoris continued to take great interest in the Europeans and their material culture. This interest soon extended far beyond guns and brightly colored blankets and began to yield substantial returns for those Maoris who survived the years of bitter inter-tribal warfare, which began to taper off in the North Island by the mid-1830s. The survivors quickly accepted foods and animals that their native environment lacked and the Europeans' clearly superior technology. Such rapid adaptation can be attributed to both basic elements in the precontact Maori sociocultural order and the nature of their early interaction with the European invaders. The Maoris' struggle for survival in the harsh New Zealand environment had made the *hapu* unit flexible and adaptable. In addition, *hapu* and tribal divisions resulted in intense competition between different Maori groups. If one chief or *hapu* head acquired firearms or new tools, the leaders of neighboring groups also had to obtain them or lose prestige and risk defeat by better-armed rivals. The Maoris highly revered physical power, material achievement, and military prowess, and the Europeans were well endowed in all of these areas. The Maoris integrated European technology and new organizational patterns on a collective basis into *hapu* and tribal units, which remained largely intact and in control of their own affairs. Change was filtered and distributed in such a way that some stability was preserved. Once the initial shocks—inflicted mainly by firearms and disease—had been absorbed, *hapu* units that survived and adapted extensively were able to improve their life styles and material standards considerably.[12]

New crops, animals, and tools were adopted, and many Maori *hapus* entered with remarkable skill into the international market network that suddenly extended to their once-isolated homeland. They cultivated foodstuffs on a mutual-assistance basis, and sold them to European missionaries and settlers or export merchants. They cut timber, grew flax on demand, built windmills to process their grains, and purchased small European-built vessels to carry their goods to market and European wares home again. In the early 1840s, European travelers contrasted the prosperity of Maori settlements near Port Nicholson, with their fat cattle, horses, plows, and windmills, to the squalor and plowless poverty of the early European settlements on the North Island.[13] A high price had been paid in lives lost to disease, war, and European pleasure seekers, but for a brief period in the 1830s and early 1840s, many

Maori *hapu* units appeared to have adjusted reasonably well to the sudden influx of influences from overseas.

In addition to the acceptance of European material culture and involvement in a market economy, the Maoris began to respond with considerable enthusiasm to the conversion efforts of Christian missionaries.[14] After decades of fruitless toil following the establishment of the first mission station in 1814, considerable numbers of Maoris, whom many Europeans argued were weary of bloody wars and fearful of new diseases, began to adopt Christian beliefs and rituals in the 1830s. Although critical European observers questioned the depth of the Maoris' understanding and the firmness of their convictions, well over half of the Maori population was attending Christian services by the mid–1840s. The missionaries, who were staunch "humanitarians" and advocates of a theocratically oriented "native" preserve in New Zealand, called upon reluctant British ministers to formally annex the islands to the global empire. Successive governments rebuffed these suggestions, not because they held to a concept of a "Little England", which has been shown to be a fiction,[15] but because control of the islands' warlike population threatened to require costly expeditions that its nonstrategic location and apparent lack of resources could not justify. Eventually, however, the threat of rival European penetration into the area forced a preemptive British annexation. This move was bolstered by the Treaty of Waitangi which was signed by many Maori chieftains in 1840.

In the same year, a new and very different phase of Maori-European relations began—one that would reverse many of the Maoris' gains and again plunge them into misery and despair. As part of the grand designs of Edward Gibbon Wakefield to siphon off surplus laborers from squalid English industrial towns and establish them productively in fertile, but sparsely populated, colonies, the first band of permanent European settlers arrived in New Zealand. They immediately began to lay claim to the lands that made up the ancient Maori home. Although Wakefield's schemes proved abortive, his settlers spread the word about the potential in New Zealand for grazing sheep and cultivating grain and tapping mineral wealth. Soon, from a handful of refugees on the coastal fringe, the European population grew until in the late 1850s it surpassed that of the Maoris, whose numbers once again began to decline.[16] After laying claim to the South Island, which the Maoris had never populated heavily, the Europeans began to settle extensively in the North Island heartland of the Maori people.

Settler political pressure quickly rendered most British colonial officials amenable to their designs. Even government agencies created to protect Maori interests fed the settlers' seemingly insatiable hunger for Maori land. In 1852, the Colonial Office hesitantly granted representative government to the people of New Zealand, which effectively meant the European settlers. It became increasingly obvious to the Maoris that they must organize and resist further encroachments or perish. They first tried constitutional organization and agitation through the King Movement and then made futile attempts to expel the Europeans by force. The resulting frustrations and dislocations gave rise to the Pai Maire movement in the mid-1860s. In desperation many Maori *hapus* flocked to the messengers of a prophet who promised salvation and a paradise without Europeans. At the time there seemed to be few other options.

To the contemporary English observer, the Pai Maire movement was a half-crazed reversion by certain Maori tribes to the savage beliefs and practices that decades of contact with the Europeans had supposedly eradicated. At first, European settlers and missionaries saw the prophet, Te Ua Haumene, and his visionary teachings as something of a sad joke—the rantings of a psychopath, which his defeated and embittered people seized upon as their last hope for deliverance. One Englishman accurately captured the general European attitude in the following summary of the movement's main features: he wrote that it consisted of "A large infusion of Judaism, some leading features of Mormonism, a little mesmerism, a touch of spiritualism, occasional ventriloquism, and a large amount of cannibalism."[17]

When the prophet's disciples began to use his teachings to arouse the Maoris to make war on the Europeans, however, the attitude of settler and government official alike quickly changed. Even European observers who had been sympathetic to the Maori struggle for survival roundly condemned the followers of the prophet as barbarous savages wallowing in ignorance and superstition. The Pai Maire rebels' decapitation of slain enemies and revival of ancient Maori customs, such as cannibalism, outraged the European community and led to strident demands that the movement be ruthlessly and quickly suppressed.

Once full-scale warfare was underway, victories for the followers of Te Ua were few.[18] After success in an initial ambush of a small party of British soldiers near New Plymouth in the Taranaki in April 1864, the rebels assaulted a British redoubt on Sentry Hill at the end of the same month and were severely defeated. In the middle of May came a second major setback, when loyalist tribesman of the lower Wanganui region routed a large band of Pai Maire warriors in a pitched battle on the island of Moutoa east of Taranaki. In both of these engagements and in equally unsuccessful attempts to storm British fortifications at Pipiriki in mid-July, the Pai Maire warriors employed special ritual gestures and war chants that they believed would cause the European and loyalist Maori bullets to miss their mark. The rebels fearlessly charged enemy positions over open ground, but their charms failed miserably and many of the Pai Maire faithful were left dead or wounded on the field of battle.

Despite early defeats, the new religion of renewal and resistance continued to spread along the west coast and was carried by Te Ua's chief disciples across the interior of the North Island to the Bay of Plenty and down the eastern coast to Hawke's Bay (see Map 2). European travelers reported that the flagstaff-like *niu* pole, the most prominent symbol of the resistance cult, could be seen in Maori villages over large stretches of the island. European settlers anxiously watched neighboring Maori villages for signs of the Pai Maire rituals, but there were few encounters between adherents of the movement and government troops between late July 1864 and the first months of 1865 when the government launched a number of military campaigns aimed at crushing the rebellion. Because of the growing European obsession with the movement, however, all Maori resistance came to be attributed, often incorrectly, to the "Hau Haus"—as the Europeans scornfully referred to the followers of the Pai Maire.

The campaigns against the tribes on the west coast appeared to have broken the movement, but an incident at Opotiki on the other side of the island brought it new notoriety. At the instigation of Pai Maire agitators, members of the Whakatohea tribe murdered a German missionary named Carl Volkner. The leader of the rebel band rendered the killing even more horrific by plucking out the victim's eyes and eating them, then passing around a chalice of the murdered man's blood to be drunk by all who had joined in the killing. The murder of Volkner and several other incidents renewed the determination of the Europeans and the tribes allied to them to wipe out the movement completely. A new series of government campaigns, involving seemingly endless sieges of Pai Maire fortresses and villages in the last half of 1865, led to costly defeats for the rebels on both the east and west coasts. Although Maori assaults on European settlements were attributed to the "Hau Haus" as late as the 1870s, the movement was effectively dead after the defeats of 1865 and the capture of Te Ua in March 1866. Leadership of the Maori resistance then fell to new prophets and other movements, like Te Kooti and his Ringtau sect. The violence inspired by the Pai Maire faith cannot be distinguished from that resulting from the Maori–settler wars generally, but the movement contributed substantially to the thousands of lives lost in the decade of confrontation that determined who would be the master of New Zealand.

The Mundas and the Birsa Rising in Chota Nagpur (East-Central India), 1899–1900

> Then was the Satyug[19]—now the Iron Age.
> Gone is the Golden Age of Old!
> Then reigned the Satyug,—now the reign of Kal,[20]
> On Earth has come with woes untold.
> Men in that blessed ancient Age of Gold,
> Had nothing to do but drink their ale.
> Now that the accursed Kali reigns supreme
> Horrible death from hunger prevails.
> Oh! for the days when men knew no cares,
> But drank their fill of home-brewed ale.
> Woe to this age when men on earth below
> Do daily die of famine.[21]

This folk song, sung by the Munda people of east-central India as late as the early 1900s, embodies a number of key elements of their long history and expresses the deep yearning for a lost golden age that would give rise to the prophet Birsa in the late 1890s.[22] The Mundas were the losers in a contest which provides one of the central themes in the history of the peoples of a vast and diverse Asian expanse running from north-central India across mainland Southeast Asia and into south China: the struggle for control of fertile river valleys. The Mundas were among the dark-skinned, plains-dwelling peoples that the nomadic Aryan invaders from Central Asia drove before them as they advanced into northwest India in the third and second millennia B.C.[23] Although the available sources are too sketchy and myth-laden to provide a precise chronology, the Mundas appear to have retreated for centuries before the relentless pressure of the invaders, whose advantage grew as Brahmanic civilization developed. The Mundas grew weaker in numbers and their cultural level declined. Many former skills were lost because of the defeats and prolonged wanderings that eventually brought them to the plateau highlands of Chota Nagpur in east-central India (see Map 3). Like many other vanquished peoples, the Mundas retreated to inaccessible forests and hills where they established a new society that was based on kinship-linked, communally oriented villages.

Until the first centuries A.D. the Mundas recognized no authority beyond that of their village headmen, councils of elders, and *mankis*, or the elected chiefs of loose intervillage confederations. Links between villages were maintained mainly by marriages, which led to extravillage contacts because the *killis* or kin-settlement units were exogamous and Munda society patrilocal. Except for the *mankis*, who functioned primarily in times of war, political ties between settlements were weak and trade peripheral. Land rights were vested in the descendants of those who had originally cleared forest and waste areas and were passed on to their descendants. Full members of the "village-family" controlled the available land collectively and regulated the usufruct to the fields on which the Mundas raised their dry rice and maize staples.

Because the region's soil was poor and the Mundas were unwilling or unable to construct irrigation systems, crop output was scanty and food shortages endemic. In this early period, however, a low population meant that in all but periods of prolonged drought the Mundas could maintain a reasonable standard of living. Although small voluntary contributions were given to village heads and the *mankis*, no taxes, rents, or labor services were paid by the landholders of the settlements. In addition to the sedentary cultivation of lands near the villages, shifting agriculture was practiced in the hills surrounding Munda settlements. Vast virgin forests also provided plant and animal food supplements, building materials, and wood and metals for tools.

Like all else in their culture, Munda religion was village oriented. Although the Mundas had a supreme creator-deity called Sing-Bonga, their worship focused on village gods and ancestral and nature spirits. They also propitiated malevolent demons, who they believed were the arbiters of good or ill fortune in their everyday lives.

Although even less centralized and hierarchic, early Munda society bore strong resemblances to that developed by the Maoris of New Zealand. Munda history, however, followed a far different

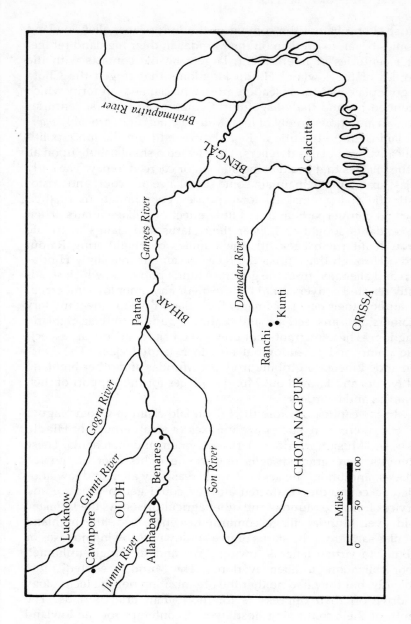

3. East-Central India in the Nineteenth Century.

course. Long before the coming of the Europeans, alien lowland peoples began to press in on the Mundas in their highland refuge. After centuries of intermittent, largely hostile contacts with the peoples of the lowland Hindu kingdoms that ringed the Chota Nagpur plateau, Munda leaders arose who claimed authority which extended beyond the village unit. Sometime in the first centuries A.D., an ambitious family of local Munda chieftains (probably *mankis*) laid claim to the title of Raja, borrowed from the more politically advanced plains dwellers. They levied a small tribute upon all of the villages that could be persuaded or coerced to pay. The early Rajas, struggling to maintain some semblance of a court and aristocratic life style, remained for centuries poor imitations of their lowland counterparts and had little effect on village affairs. Their descendants sought to bolster their status and claims to tribute through intermarriage with the families of neighboring Rajput lords. Through these links the Rajas became increasingly Hinduized and alienated from the general Munda populace, which steadfastly resisted conversion to Hinduism or any other lowland creed. To support their new self-image, the Rajas strove to attract military retainers, artisans, scribes, and Brahman pundits to their highland kingdom. These migrants not only gave rise to a court of respectable pomp and splendor but also to a landed class. The Rajas demanded increased tribute from the Mundas and other highland cultivators and farmed out Munda villages for the support of their retainers and courtiers.

In the centuries before the British laid claim to Chota Nagpur in 1765, there were successive influxes of small groups of Hindu, Sikh, and Muslim warriors, clerks, holymen, and merchants. These migrants were granted *jagirs* or revenue rights over designated villages, and under the aegis of an increasingly alien and lowland-oriented court, they extracted all they could get in produce and services from the Mundas and other agriculturists. As the *jagirdars'* hold over Munda village communities increased, the highland peoples sank from the status of free landowners, owing no taxes or tribute, to virtual tenants, owing rents and seemingly unlimited labor obligations to alien overlords. The Mundas resisted, often violently, but they had neither the organization nor the technology to drive off their oppressors for more than brief periods. The depth of their continuing hostility and contempt for the lowland infiltrators was captured in folksongs, which declared with scorn:

> Men of mean blood are found in high places
> Owls[24] pose as lords, the owls of low birth.

The vain peacock struts in glory of plumage,
Owls pass for lords, the owls of low birth.

and lamented:

Mundas of hamlets now tremble with fear.
Terror supreme now reigns everywhere,
Mundas of hamlets have lost their old cheer.[25]

The basic conditions that would lead to the Munda revolt under Birsa in the 1890s were established long before European influence became an important factor in the region. During the period of British control, which began formally in the last decades of the eighteenth century, landlord exactions merely increased and the position of the Mundas and other hill peoples worsened as long-standing methods of exploitation were intensified. Because of their ignorance of the area and their lack of trained manpower to devote to effective control, the new overlords left the Raja and his often truculent retainers in charge of administration and revenue collection. Until late in the nineteenth century, there were few checks on their arbitrary and self-serving rule. Corrupt and often distant police officials and courts, ineffective government regulations designed to provide relief for hard-pressed cultivators, and Christian missionaries' promises that could not be fulfilled added to old Munda grievances and distrust. The British represented, after all, a lowland-based empire. Consequently, the "Pax Britannica" in nineteenth-century Chota Nagpur was periodically shattered by riots and rebellions by the Mundas and other hill-dwelling groups. These protest movements culminated in the prophetic rebellion led by Birsa Munda, who promised supernatural solutions for problems that human efforts had not been able to resolve.

Contemporary British officials and Christian missionaries believed that the prophet Birsa was a clever imposter who had managed to gain a substantial following among his people through bogus claims of healing powers and promises to deliver them from their oppressors. Many other observers argued that Birsa was the dupe, or at least the figurehead, for long-established Munda agitators collectively known as the Sardars. These malcontents, they held, used Birsa's popularity and bizarre teachings to mobilize mass support for their campaign to drive out lowland invaders by force. The Sardars gradually transformed Birsa's amorphous and unrealistic eschatological preachings into an ideology of rebellion. In Birsa's name, these more politically oriented Munda leaders organized secret night meetings in remote forest clearings. Amid "frenzied" dancing about great bonfires, they recruited followers and planned the coming revolt. The rising—the briefest and least destructive of life among all the movements considered in this study—began on Christmas Eve 1899.[26] Rebel bands attacked mission stations in central and eastern Chota Nagpur. They burned buildings and shot arrows at missionaries and Munda converts. These assaults were apparently intended to frighten Christian Mundas into apostatizing and joining the Birsite efforts to liberate the highlands. In these first assaults, several Mundas were killed and two European missionaries wounded.

In the last days of December, police stations and government officials became the targets of rebel attacks. There were also a number of abortive attempts to sack landlord estate houses. A group of rebels led by one of the most determined Birsite disciples, Gaya Munda, killed a small contingent of constables sent to arrest them on 5 January 1900. A larger party of rebels armed with bows and arrows and spears mobbed the Khunti police station during this same period. The five policemen on duty fired on the crowd as it approached the police station, but in their haste and panic they completely missed their targets. The crowd, mistaking the constables' bad aim for proof of the prophet's promise that his followers would be invulnerable to bullets, rushed and sacked the police station. Four of the five policemen fled in the confusion, but a fifth officer was caught and beaten to death by the enraged crowd.

These early successes of the Birsite rebels spread panic among the lowland migrant population, which was concentrated in major towns, like Khunti, and in the district capital, Ranchi. For a time it appeared that other hill peoples would join the Mundas and the rising would spread over much of the central highland area. Finally admitting the seriousness of the threat, the British moved to suppress the rebellion. They strengthened the police forces in the threatened areas and sent in reinforcements from the lowlands. The latter formed military parties to seek out and, if necessary, destroy rebel bands.

A successful assault on 9 January by government troops on a large party of Birsites entrenched on a hill near the town of Dombari brought the rising to an abrupt end. Although rebel casualties were apparently not heavy (the estimates range from two to four hundred), the British were able to arrest most of the leaders of the movement. During the clash the prophet Birsa ignominiously abandoned his followers and fled into the nearby forest. The rest of January was dominated by government "beat and search" operations in the forest zone. These finally led to the arrest of Birsa on 3 February. He was imprisoned and died of cholera on 9 June while awaiting trial. The prophet's capture ended the last and most serious Munda attempt to forcibly expel the invaders of their highland home.

A Century of Upheavals and the Maji Maji Rebellion in German East Africa (Tanzania), 1905–1906

The Maji Maji rebellion, which broke out in German East Africa in 1905, was not a single movement but a combination of often uncoordinated risings. These outbreaks were spread over an area of more than 100,000 square miles and involved over twenty different, and previously disunited, ethnic groups.[27] In this study I will focus on the core areas of the rebellion, particularly the heartlands of the Matumbi and Ngindo peoples in the Kilwa hinterland (see Map 4). The grievances of these peoples sparked the initial risings. They supplied the earliest and staunchest adherents to the prophet, Kinjikitile Ngwale, and the Maji Maji cult beliefs which were essential to the spread of the protest movement to distant and often hostile peoples. The Matumbi also proved to be the most formidable adversaries of the Germans and their African allies during the period of open rebellion from mid-1905 through 1906.[28]

For the peoples of German East Africa as a whole, the nineteenth century was a period of upheaval and substantial change.[29] Historians have traditionally viewed these transformations as predominantly or wholly disruptive. Recent research has shown, however, that in the midst of the destruction and suffering that were so graphically recorded by European explorers and missionaries, there was also significant innovation and growth. Depopulation, increased warfare, and the brutalization of life did indeed follow the Arab slave traders as they advanced inland from the Swahili coast, but so did new caravan routes and new patterns of exchange that provided the impetus and revenue base for the rise of larger political units.

While some decentralized peoples were cruelly ravaged, others, like the Nyamwezi and the Yao, responded by forging alliances which eventually led to consolidated kingdoms. These larger political units were better able to defend themselves and even to join in the lucrative business of slave and ivory hunting. The incursions of the warlike Ngoni, who had originally fled from Shaka's legendary military machine in southern Africa, caused great hard-

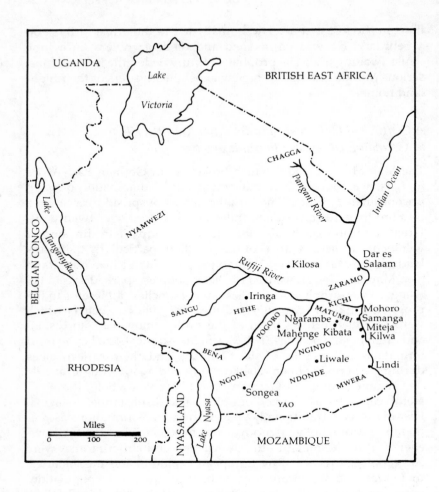

4. German East Africa in 1912. Source: John Iliffe, *Tanganyika under German Rule, 1905–1912* (Cambridge, 1969). By permission of the Cambridge University Press.

ship for some decentralized societies, like the Ngindo. For other peoples, these invaders provided military and political models from which new kingdoms would emerge in the interior. The regimental organization, short stabbing spears, and large oval shields, which were the hallmarks of Zulu and Ngoni military prowess, were adopted by peoples like the Sangu, Hehe, and Bena. These innovations, which were in some cases supplemented by firearms, led to the growth of formidable standing armies. Slave raiding, trade, and cattle raising supplied the resource base for these military forces and the beginnings of professional bureaucracies and centralized states. The latter arose from the consolidation of village units, or more commonly the *ntemi* or localized chieftainships that had been established in preceding centuries. Thus, change set in motion largely by external forces resulted for some peoples in a shift from religious to military based authority and increases in the scale and complexity of organization and degree of specialization. These innovations and the general turbulence of the period also led to the introduction or internal gestation of new beliefs and cult movements which may have played important roles in the shaping of the ideas and organization of the Maji Maji rebellion.

Although these transformations had important effects on the Ngindo and Matumbi who first rallied to Kinjikitile's call, these people did not develop centralized states or large-scale military systems, nor did they participate extensively in the new patterns of trade. The peoples of the hill and plateau complex where the Maji Maji movement originated held to their customary clan-based units, which were organized into loose localized chieftainships. Clan leaders and village headmen were chosen largely according to their personal merit, and their authority was limited to small clusters of kinship-linked settlements. Clan heads acted as the mediums between their followers and the ancestral spirits, as the mediators of family and intra-clan disputes, and as war leaders. They were also responsible for allotment of clan lands for the use of individual families. Although they levied no formal tribute, clan heads were periodically offered gifts or services by their kinsmen in return for the time they devoted to community affairs. As among the Maori, clan and village councils exercised great influence and advised elected leaders, who represented local interests rather than those of some higher authority. In addition to clan and village heads, decision making was shared by extremely influential *mgangas* (in Matumbi) who were experts in religio-magical affairs. These "medicine men" (as they are commonly labelled in European

sources) performed a wide range of vital functions, from propiti-
ating ancestral and nature spirits and presiding over ritual observances to finding and expelling witches and interpreting omens.

In the decades before the German conquest, the decentralized
societies of the Matumbi and the Ngindo were developing different
kinds of organization. In both cases, the external challenges had
important effects on these processes of change. Colonial observers
argued that the Matumbi people was made up of originally disparate groups that had fled from their former homes to the rugged
forest zone that came to be known as the Matumbi hills. Making
the fullest use of the terrain that they had adopted as their homeland, the Matumbi developed an elaborate intersettlement warning
system and defended their villages with fierce, guerilla-style assaults on outside invaders. The success of their tactics and their
reputation as bold and stubborn fighters discouraged depredations
by slave traders from the Swahili coast or by neighboring peoples.
As a result, the population of the hill region increased, and cooperation in defense gave impetus to more centralized sociopolitical
organizations. Before the Germans came in the 1890s, clans had
begun to coalesce into larger units. Supra-clan leaders, called
jumbes, appear to have gained positions of some influence, particularly in times of war.

Unlike the Matumbi, Ngindo society became even more fragmented in the nineteenth century than in earlier periods. The
Ngindo and the closely related Ndonde people were concentrated
in the more exposed plateau country west of the Matumbi hills.
Their clan-oriented settlements proved tempting targets for Swahili
slave traders moving in from the coast and Yao warriors from the
south, who also came in search of slaves. In the middle decades of
the nineteenth century, Ngoni armies descended on Ngindo country from the west and south, destroying settlements and killing or
dispersing their populations. Some Ngindo survivors fled to small
clearings in the dense forests that covered portions of their plateau
homeland; others migrated west and north to less accessible areas.
Under the pressure of external assaults, Ngindo clan organization
was considerably weakened. Some clan groups disappeared completely. Others broke into smaller units that consisted essentially of
several loosely allied households or an extended family. Although
a number of writers have argued that the central areas of Ngindo
settlement around Liwale were densely populated on the eve of
the Maji Maji rebellion in 1905,[30] their assertions are not supported
by oral evidence collected in the decades after the rising, by con-

temporary German maps, which indicate sparse population, or by British censuses taken in the years after the First World War.[31]

Both the Matumbi and Ngindo peoples practiced a mixture of shifting and sedentary agriculture, supplemented by cattle herding. In both societies land was controlled by the clan, which as a group granted rights of occupation and use to individual family heads. Fruits, green vegetables, sweet potatoes, and other crops were grown in small gardens near the family household or in family plots located in fertile and well-watered valley bottoms. Possession of these plots was a central attribute of Matumbi clan membership. Through shifting cultivation on a mutual-assistance basis in the fields surrounding the clan settlements, the Matumbi and Ngindo raised the grain staples, like sorghum and maize, that were central to their diet. Each household received a share of the common produce of the outlying fields. Like leadership succession, inheritance of land use rights was patrilineal. Although the Matumbi and Ngindo traded to some extent with neighboring peoples and bartered crops and cattle for the guns and cloth offered by the traders of the Swahili coast, their societies were largely self-sufficient. Neither the Matumbi nor the Ngindo played an important role in the development of the great nineteenth-century caravan routes inland to the rift lakes.

In the east African interior as in Chota Nagpur, the penetration of the Europeans was not the starting point for far-reaching change but an additional element in an ongoing process of transformation.[32] Despite the attention they receive in Western accounts of this period, the early inroads of European explorers and missionaries made little lasting impact on the peoples who inhabited the area that became German East Africa. Until the mid-1880s, European activity was largely commercial and concentrated on the island of Zanzibar and the port centers adjacent on the Swahili coast.

Major European involvement in the affairs of the mainland peoples can be traced mainly to the schemes and initiatives of the self-styled Napoleon and archchauvinist, Carl Peters, who arrived at Zanzibar in November 1884 disguised as a ship's mechanic. Peters, with a number of his expansionist-minded countrymen, had founded the Society for German Colonization in the same year. The society was established expressly to obtain support for and to lend a sense of legitimacy to Peters' designs for the creation of a "Deutsches Indien in Afrika," which he envisioned as some day stretching from the Zambezi to the Nile.[33] His reasons for seeking a colonial empire—market outlets for Germany's manufacturers, raw materials for its factories, and land for its settlers—were also the central motives for Germany's belated overseas expansion. Bismarck, perched precariously atop an anachronistic social and political order that was threatened by depression and revolution, had long taken an antiimperial stance, but he reversed himself in the 1880s in an effort to provide ideological props and economic ballast for the young and unstable German nation. Through Peters, Bismarck's grudging pursuit of overseas empire overtook the peoples of east Africa.[34]

By early 1885, the bogus treaties of "protection," which Peters and three of his countrymen had foisted on a number of mainland notables of widely varying importance, had been approved by the German government and accorded international recognition. In the next decades, the control established by the Germans as they advanced inland to establish their premier colony was extremely uneven and largely indirect. Although a number of the peoples who took part in the Maji Maji disturbances were involved in the primary resistance to imposition of German rule,[35] the most serious opposition came from more centralized peoples like the Hehe, Nyamwezi, Yao, Chagga, and the Arabs of the Swahili coast. Even the martial Ngoni, who would join in the Maji Maji revolt, had not seriously tested German military capabilities in major battles during the period of conquest. Equally notable, in the years of consolidation after the German government assumed direct control of the colony from the German East African Society in 1891, the northwest, not the area of the rebellion in the southeast, became the focus of German settlement and plantation development.[36] The extension of administrative and communications systems, commercialization, and resource exploitation had little effect on the areas associated with Maji Maji risings until the first years of the twentieth century. As Wilhelm Methner, the German official in charge of much of the territory in rebellion, admitted some years later, right up to the eve of the disturbances the southeast portions of the colony remained largely a "terra incognita."[37]

Despite their ignorance, however, the Germans had begun to demand labor services from the general populace and increased loyalty from indigenous leaders in the southeastern portions of the colony in the years just before the 1905 outbreaks. These new demands, coupled with longstanding abuses by Swahili government agents or *akidas* and nonindigenous African mercenary troops, were critically important in the spread of Kinjikitile's influence and the revolt that, he prophesied, would drive the Germans from east Africa. In seeming contradiction to the generally accepted theory that revitalization movements have been reactions to extensive changes, the core areas of the Maji Maji movement had remained on the periphery of the great transformations, both colonial and precolonial, that dominated the nineteenth-century history of east Africa. Germany, one of the most advanced and industrialized of the European colonial powers, had achieved less control over the peoples who rebelled against its rule than had any of the imperial powers considered thus far. But the changes that came, came abruptly and, because of German ignorance of the peoples involved, were badly mismanaged. The Matumbi and Ngindo had fought for decades to safeguard their communities and customary ways from the threats posed by alien invaders, and they were determined not to let the Germans destroy their heritage through decrees issued by distant officials on the Swahili coast.

Over two weeks before the outbreak of the initial Maji Maji risings in late July 1905, the Arab *akida* at Kibata reported that the local population was increasingly resistant to his orders. He also wrote of secret meetings and other unusual activities that indicated that a widespread conspiracy was afoot. His warnings passed through the hands of several colonial bureaucrats, but no action was taken until *after* the first rebel assaults of a massive revolt that at its peak would engulf most of the southern districts of German East Africa.[38] German officials, like the Count von Götzen and Captain Moritz Merker, thought that the rebellion had been plotted by disgruntled African leaders who had been replaced or demoted for incompetence or drunkeness. According to this interpretation, these leaders had conspired with local "witchdoctors" and the seers from a number of oracles in the Matumbi hill region to organize a resistance movement that was based primarily on their manipulation of the childlike superstition, ignorance, and credulity of the colonized peoples. The single element that linked the diverse and previously disunited peoples who supported the movement was a water-based medicine, which the Africans believed to have magical powers. The agitators who distributed the water (in Swahili, *maji*) medicine claimed that the potion was magic and would render their followers impervious to European bullets. Emboldened by these assurances, many villages and whole peoples rose up to assault the scattered government outposts, mission stations, and merchant houses which gave evidence of the European colonial presence in the interior.

The rebels struck first in late July and early August at the towns of Samanga and Miteja north of Kilwa near the coast and at several points in the Matumbi and Kichi hills. War parties, reported to be as large as 2,000 to 2,500 men, burned buildings, cut telegraph lines, and killed government officials and missionaries or sent them in flight to the coastal towns. These early successes seemed to confirm the claims made regarding the magical power of the *maji* medicine and encouraged the rapid spread of the revolt. In early August disturbances took place north of the Matumbi hills near the capital at Dar es Salaam. At the same time the revolt spread up the Rufiji river complex and into the rugged plateau region around the town of Mahenge. Rebel bands threatened the important town of Kilwa on the coast, and a series of risings occurred among the Ngindo, Mwera, and Ndonde peoples in the interior around Liwale. With the fall of the town of Liwale to the rebel forces and the murder of the Roman Catholic Bishop Spiess and a small party of missionaries in mid-August, the revolt took on new fervor. Despite scattered victories by German-led mercenary forces in the last weeks of August, the revolt continued to spread to the northwest and especially to the southwest where the *maji* medicine was accepted by the Pogoro and, most ominously, by the martial Ngoni and Bena.

Like the Dutch in Java, the Germans were caught completely unprepared for the rebellion. There were very few German administrators and colonial troops in the affected area, and for weeks the revolt spread unchecked from one people to the next. During the early days of the revolt the Germans could do little more than call for reinforcements from abroad and recruit volunteer defense corps from the settler and merchant communities in the colony. They were unable to undertake major military operations for over a month after the initial outbreaks. The outcome was not to be determined entirely by German actions, however. By the middle of August, a number of decisions had been made by different groups of colonized peoples that would gravely affect the course of the rebellion. Most of the coastal peoples, many of whom were Muslim and Arab in culture, refused to support the revolt. A number of key groups in the interior, most notably the Hehe, also refused to join the movement. The Hehe decision, which was strongly influenced by their earlier defeats by the Germans and the decisive actions of a bold German captain named Nigmann, was critical because it checked the spread of the revolt to the north and west of the colony. Equally important, it was clear by late August that the African mercenaries recruited into the colonial armed forces could and would fight the rebels, despite their initial uneasiness over the powers attributed to the *maji* medicine.

The slaughter of large numbers of rebel warriors at Mahenge on 30 August, in what was perhaps the largest assault during the revolt, was a severe blow to the Maji Maji movement. Rebel spears and massed assaults were no match for German machine guns; German-led African mercenaries fought bravely; and one of the key military stations in the interior held firm. In early September rebel forces suffered severe reverses in the Ngoni areas and further north, where a major assault on the town of Kilosa was repulsed —again with very heavy rebel casualties. When additional reinforcements arrived in mid-September, the Germans went on the offensive. In this period there was also a major shift in rebel tactics in many areas, from sieges and frontal assaults to increasingly localized guerilla resistance. The Germans divided the areas in revolt into identifiable zones and systematically deployed the limited available colonial forces first to contain and isolate and then to seek out and kill or capture rebels operating in these areas. As conventional warfare gave way to loosely organized guerilla resistance, the Germans employed scorched earth tactics and other measures that were aimed at reducing the capacity of the civilian population to support the rebels.

A series of German victories in the last months of 1905 and a crushing defeat which they inflicted on the Ngoni at Upangwa on 12 April 1906 made the hopelessness of the rebel cause all too apparent. By early March 1906 the rebellion had been completely suppressed in the Matumbi hills and in the areas near the coast. In May and June, the major centers of continuing resistance around Mahenge and Ifalara and in the Ngindo region around Liwale were brought under control. By mid-1906, government operations had reduced rebel activities to the grim struggle of scattered bands to avoid capture. By the early weeks of 1907, most of the important rebel leaders had been captured or killed, and German officials could confidently report that the rebellion was over.

The Maji Maji movement ranks as one of the greatest efforts by sub-Saharan African peoples to resist European colonial dominance by violent means. Minimal German estimates placed the number of African lives lost at seventy-five thousand. Later British writers and African historians have argued that, if one includes casualties due to the widespread famines that resulted from German scorched earth tactics, the deaths caused by the revolt numbered in the hundreds of thousands.[39]

Laissez-faire Colonialism in British Burma and the Saya San Rebellion of 1930–1932

In contrast to German East Africa, the changes resulting from the imposition of British colonial rule over Lower Burma, or the Irrawaddy Delta region (see Map 5), were as dramatic and profound as those which occurred in any area which came under European imperialist control.[40] Since the fall of the commercially oriented Mon kingdoms of the coastal Delta in the late sixteenth century, Lower Burma had been reduced to a sparsely inhabited backwater that periodically served as a battleground for the seemingly interminable wars between the Buddhist kingdoms of mainland Southeast Asia. Following an audacious but feebly-based Mon attempt to conquer the Burman[41] Dry Zone heartland in the 1750s, the Burmans under Alaungpaya, the founder of their last and most powerful dynasty, annexed the Irrawaddy Delta area to the ascendent Konbaung empire. Under the Konbaungs the region remained a frontier, its fertile and well-watered plains sparsely settled and little cultivated. Restrictions on the export of rice and other commodities, rigidly-enforced sumptuary laws, and the heavy tolls and expensive gifts demanded by Konbaung officials from the few traders who ventured to shabby Delta ports discouraged commercial development on any scale. Hostile inhabitants, endemic malaria, dysentery, insect pests, wild animals, and the considerable labor and low returns involved in clearing the Delta lands for cultivation limited migration from the drought-prone and relatively heavily populated Dry Zone to a small trickle in the Konbaung era.

Before the British conquest in 1852, Burman cultivator-settlers were largely confined to the upper Delta provinces. Burman administrators, monks, and soldiers clustered in the larger towns, which were circled by wooden fortifications to ward off attacks by rebellious Mons or Karens. The latter groups made up the majority of the population in the wild and, to the Burman rulers, uncivilized districts of the lower Delta. The population of the Delta region was predominantly engaged in either irrigated wet-rice or shifting dry-rice agriculture. Most cultivators settled along the banks of the many rivers and small creeks that branched from the mighty

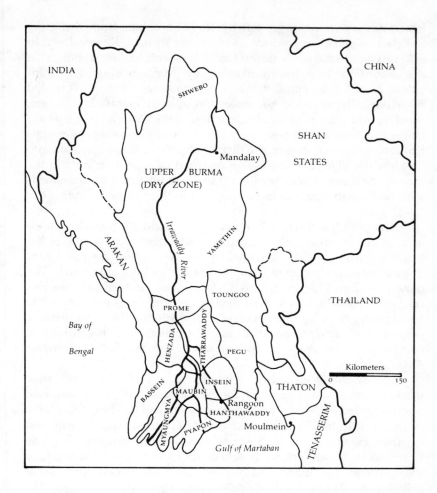

5. British Burma, Showing Delta District Divisions. Source: Michael
Adas, *The Burma Delta: Economic Development and Social Change on an
Asian Rice Frontier, 1852–1941* (Madison, 1974). By permission of
The University of Wisconsin Press.

Irrawaddy or in clearings cut by their ancestors from the great forests that once covered much of Lower Burma. Karens lived in self-sufficient villages patterned after their original tribal homes in the mountainous Salween river valley. Burman and Mon cultivators huddled in small hamlets, which were often surrounded by makeshift palisades for protection against marauding troops, bandits, and wild animals. The portion of the Delta's sparse population that was effectively controlled by the Konbaung monarchs from their court centers in the distant Dry Zone was organized into "regiments." These groups were required to provide tribute in the form of produce, labor, or military services for those Burman lords who had the misfortune to be assigned to the frontier provinces of the Delta.

Except in the towns, there were few Buddhist pagodas, monasteries, or monks. The hazardous and rather dreary life of the frontier settler was little relieved by the cycle of festivals and rites of passage that were an integral part of village life in the north. The once proud and highly civilized Mons, who centuries before had transmitted Buddhism to their Burman neighbors, were reduced to constant flight or dismal servitude. In response they increasingly emphasized their pre-Buddhist animist beliefs, which continue to coexist with Theravada Buddhism over all of mainland Southeast Asia.[42]

The British long had been interested in Burma as a potential market outlet and source of foodstuffs and raw materials but, operating from their growing empire in India, they were able to make little headway against the determined isolationism and (as they viewed it) xenophobia of the Konbaung monarchs. The Burmans stubbornly resisted British attempts to place them under the informal diplomatic and commercial controls characteristic of British colonial policy in the mid-Victorian period.[43]

Misunderstandings, mutual recriminations, a good deal of arrogance on both sides, and border disputes in the Assam-Manipur frontier zone between the Indian and Konbaung empires eventually led to the first Anglo-Burman war of 1824–1826. Despite the considerable ability of their commanders and the courage of their troops, the Burmans were decisively defeated and forced to cede the coastal provinces of Arakan and Tenasserim. Though the Konbaung monarchs became uncomfortably familiar with British advantages in technology, organization, and manpower, the Burmans continued to resist British demands that they "open" their kingdom to trade and diplomatic intercourse along Western lines.

In conjunction with continued advances in India proper, Burma was again drawn into war with the British in 1852. This conflict ended in a second defeat for the Burmans and Lower Burma was annexed to the Indian Empire in the same year. Despite heroic efforts by the Konbaung ruler, Mindon Min, to save the rump Burman state through reforms and innovations based on Western models, the remaining portions of the once mighty Burman empire were absorbed after a third war and Burman defeat in 1886.

British colonial control in Burma resulted in a reversal of the Dry Zone's centuries-old dominance of the Delta and other neighboring areas. The British focused on the development of the plains of Lower Burma, an area that was not only vast and fertile but lightly settled and poorly cultivated. British administrators rightly perceived that they could effect the greatest innovations in this frontier region, where the hold of custom and pre-British institutions was less restrictive than in the Dry Zone or other less accessible areas. They used the Delta, albeit only semi-intentionally, as a giant test tube, and for nearly fifty years the experiment seemed a resounding success for all of the major participants. British merchants and administrators, Indian and Chinese moneylenders and laborers, and Burmese rice brokers, merchants, and above all cultivators combined to transform a subsistence-oriented frontier wilderness into one of the richest provinces of the British Empire and the world's largest exporter of rice. This transformation resulted in soaring production and trade totals and greatly increased revenue receipts. It also provided real income gains and higher living standards for indigenous cultivators and hundreds of thousands of permanent settlers and seasonal laborers who migrated to Lower Burma from the Dry Zone and other areas within Burma.

Burma became a major destination for millions of Indian migrants who flocked from the overpopulated and poverty-stricken coastal districts of eastern India in search of jobs and, in times of famine, mere subsistence. The British intended to create a market-oriented economy based on the surplus production of small-holding peasants, and until the 1890s their goal appeared to have been realized. A new society with a high degree of both vertical and horizontal mobility and dominated by peasant proprietors evolved on the basis of Burmese responses, British policy decisions, and the administrative and communications grid which was established after 1852. At least until the first decades of the twentieth century, no one noticed the price that had been paid in terms of the neglect and impoverishment of Burman culture and village cohesiveness.

The Burma rice industry grew up in the chronically unstable ideological and institutional context of nineteenth-century liberalism and laissez-faire capitalism. The British administrators who plotted the course of its development provided few safeguards to protect the inexperienced peasant or to check the avarice of land speculators and moneylenders. There were virtually no buffers against severe market fluctuations or disruption of international communications. A combination of global economic shifts and the closing of the land frontier within Lower Burma itself in the early 1890s were key elements in a complex of factors that began to undermine the position of the small landholder and the aspiring tenant or laborer. As the population came to greatly exceed available outlets for productive employment, heightened competition, agrarian indebtedness, land alienation, rack-rented tenants, and unemployed or underemployed laborers came to be the dominant features of a once prosperous Delta economy.

When the new socioeconomic order in which they had participated so eagerly and apparently so ably began to crumble, the cultivating and laboring classes of Lower Burma became increasingly aware of what they had lost due to the decline of their customary social and cultural systems. This awareness coincided with the emergence of a Western-educated, Burmese nationalist elite and both fed a growing hostility toward the political domination exercised by alien European overlords and their numerous Indian subordinates. The result was a revival of proto- or pre-European[44] Burman nationalist sentiment that was reinforced by deep resentment by the Burmese of the prominent positions of Indian and Chinese merchants and moneylenders and the competition of Indian laborers. Saya San, who was a Burman rather than a Burmese prophet, effectively focused mounting dissatisfaction with a foundering colonial order. He aroused deep yearnings in both peasants and Buddhist monks for the return of an idealized world of the past. Out of economic depression and sociocultural disintegration, he forged a rebellion that at one point in 1931 threatened to engulf most of Burma and to put a sudden and unexpected end to British colonial rule.

Three main types of disturbances made up the Saya San rebellion of 1930–1932: (1) organized insurrections aimed at towns, villages, and government positions or military columns; (2) outbursts of communal violence between Burmese and Indians; and (3) depredations by bandit gangs, whose motives ranged from anticolonial feelings to a desire for booty pure and simple.[45] British colonial officials in seeking the sources of the disturbances tended to play down the significance of socioeconomic dislocations, although some admitted that the adverse effects of the Great Depression on Lower Burma's export-oriented economy might have contributed to the spread of the rebellion and sparked communal clashes. Most British observers stressed the role of disgruntled Burmese monks and necromancers (Saya San was an ex-*pongyi*) in fomenting the disburbances. As in the other movements considered, colonial officials attributed the agitators' widespread support among the peasant masses to superstition and gullibility.

The organized insurrections, which posed the most serious threat to the British colonial regime, generally followed the pattern of the initial risings in the Tharrawaddy and Insein districts north of the capital at Rangoon. In late December 1930, the rebels raided Burmese villages to obtain the firearms possessed by the headmen and followed with attacks on railway lines and stations. The rebels also cut telegraph lines and smashed telegraphic equipment in several places. In the next days several isolated Europeans were killed and the rebels began frontal assaults on police stations and government military columns. In the last days of December, the forces under Saya San increased to over fifteen hundred rebels, and for several days much of the upper Delta region lay open to their forays. A well-executed raid by government forces against rebel headquarters on 31 December broke the momentum of the rebellion. Saya San panicked and fled to the north. Those under his command who had escaped death or capture scattered or went into hiding, and British officials assumed that the disturbances had peaked and would soon die out.

Official optimism was dispelled by a third insurrection, organized by agitators from Lower Burma, that broke out on the plains of Yamethin on the southern fringe of the Dry Zone on 7 January 1931. This action was feeble and short-lived, but it was soon followed by a large-scale rising in the Pyapon District far to the south in the Delta coastal region. In the following months, there were major outbreaks in several districts in both the lower and upper Delta, and Saya San reemerged to lead a rising in the Shan States to the east of the Dry Zone. Although Saya San was captured in late August and subsequently executed, one last major rising occurred in the Pegu District northeast of Rangoon in late September 1931. To put down the rebel assaults, the British called for reinforcements from India and reorganized the provincial police and military forces, which were recruited heavily from indigenous minority peoples like the Karens and Kachins. Machine guns and eventually airplanes were used against rebel forces, whose firm belief in protective amulets led to repeated frontal assaults on well-armed government columns.

In many areas major rebel insurrections gave rise to the other forms of violence associated with the Saya San rebellion. Bandit gangs took advantage of temporary lapses of government authority to operate with impunity. In addition, these gangs found ready recruits, and new bandit groups were formed from the remnants of defeated rebel bands in many districts. In several instances government troops drove bandit gangs into neighboring districts, where there had been no major risings but where the terrain was more suited to their activities. Many gangs were well organized, and in a number of cases they were voluntarily supported by the local villagers. Their guerilla-style tactics proved much more difficult for the British to counter than were the frontal assaults of the major insurrections, and the "dacoit" (robber) phase of the rebellion continued until late 1932.

Major rebel uprisings also touched off widespread Burman rioting aimed at Indian moneylenders, landlords, and poverty-stricken laborers. Communal disturbances were most severe in the lower Delta, where unknown numbers of Indians perished and Indian shops, homes, and crops were burned. Tens of thousands of Indians fled to the relative safety of Rangoon and other Delta towns. Many booked passage back to their original homes in east and south India.

By the end of 1932, at least seventeen hundred persons had lost their lives in violence related to the rebellion, which was by far the largest during the period of British colonial rule in Burma.[46] For the British, who had long viewed Burma as one of the model provinces of their empire, the revolt was a stunning blow. Shaken by the depth of popular hostility to the colonizers which it revealed and the great numbers of peasants who fell in unequal combat, British observers generally concluded that the Saya San rebellion was a "sordid and miserable affair."[47]

Variations and Common Themes

European colonial expansion and its concomitant intercultural exchanges provide something of a common ground for the movements of prophetic protest under study, but these movements differed profoundly in terms of the situations and events which gave rise to them. Historical and cultural milieus into which the Europeans advanced differed widely, as did the nature and intensity of cultural contacts and the pace of change which these confrontations accelerated. In New Zealand and Lower Burma, change began abruptly, and primarily as the result of contacts with the agents of European capitalist-industrial civilization. Previous Maori isolation and the Delta's former position as a frontier outlier gave them a potential for radical transformations, which when they came were effected in very different ways. In both cases, but for varying lengths of time, the indigenous peoples adjusted to the original forces of change unleashed by the European influx. They proved unable, however, to cope with the new systems that resulted, particularly as these continued to evolve in response to internal and external influences.

In the princely states of central Java, the pace of change resulting from contacts with the slowly expanding Dutch empire was far more gradual and its effects, at least until after 1810, were less disruptive than in New Zealand or Lower Burma. Yet, as I shall attempt to show, the Javanese commitment to "homeostasis"—a harmonious, highly stable sociocultural order—was much more pronounced than that of either the Maoris or the Burmans. Therefore, even gradual and comparatively peripheral alterations were acutely felt by both the Javanese nobility and their peasant subjects.

The societies in which the Maji Maji and Birsite rebellions arose had experienced profound transformations long before the advent of European control. Nonetheless, in the case of the Maji Maji rebellion, attempts by the new German overlords to intervene in local affairs and alter indigenous political and economic patterns represented for the Matumbi and Ngindo instigators a departure from earlier experiences. Arab slavers and Ngoni warriors had caused severe disruption among the Ngindo and neighboring peoples, but these invaders had made no attempt to impose ongoing political control or to enforce regular economic demands. Outside forces had had even less effect on the Matumbi. Their basic beliefs, institutions, and way of life changed only gradually, and then as a result of their own initiative rather than at the commands of alien conquerors. Thus, the Matumbi and Ngindo viewed the initial changes brought by the Germans and their Swahili subordinates as very different and much more radical than earlier transformations. These changes were judged to contain the seeds of destruction for the indigenous order.

In contrast to German East Africa, little was left of the pre-Raja order in Chota Nagpur when the first British officials reached the highland settlements of the Mundas in the late eighteenth century. Over a period of centuries, agents of preindustrial lowland civilizations had introduced new political arrangements and economic demands that had gradually reduced the Mundas to servitude. In one sense, the British conquest merely froze an institutional framework in which Munda decline could continue. From another viewpoint, it resulted in the introduction of new forces—law courts, government regulations, and Christian missionaries—which revived Munda hopes for liberation from their oppressors. When these hopes were frustrated, the Mundas turned to violence and supernatural agents to gain deliverance.

Despite important variations in timing and intensity, there were common elements in the processes of culture contact and change discussed above. All of the peoples considered came to be dominated by the agents of an alien civilization that possessed a marked superiority in technology and organizational techniques. Although the European powers were at varying stages of socioeconomic development, each of them carried aspects of the commercial-industrial revolutions of Western Europe to the diverse non-Western peoples they sought to rule. In every case the colonizers shaped their policies, institutions, and activities to conform to the demands of a common capitalist order and the global commercial network that it had spawned. With colonization came new groups (both European and non-European), new institutions, modes of organization, and patterns of exchange. European dominance introduced new standards by which to gauge status and achievement, shape aspirations, and judge morality and worth. Imported agents and influences displaced or demoted indigenous leaders and undermined patterns of thinking, evaluation, and behavior that had been forged by centuries of experience.[48] These changes led to disorientation, a sense of *anomie*,[49] among the colonized peoples. The norms that had once governed social intercourse and human behavior were no longer fully adhered to. There was a growing lack of consensus on goals and a decrease of meaning in everyday life. Bewilderment and insecurity compounded the colonized peoples' deep sense of social and economic decline and led them to idealize the precolonial past as a golden age.

TWO

Causes for Revolt:
Colonial Transformations
and Relative Deprivation

The views of the Europeans who .witnessed the prophetic rebellions under study and fought to repress them can tell us a good deal about these movements beyond administrative responses and mere chronology. Contemporary European accounts often capture the participants' fanatical belief in their cause and the underlying desperation of their resistance. European observers also rightly perceived that these movements were destined to fail because their adherents simply did not have the means to reverse the changes that had resulted from cultural contact and colonization. The colonizers never doubted that prophetic visions would prove illusory, that magical charms would not prevent European guns from firing, and that the groups in rebellion would suffer or die fighting for a hopeless cause.

Despite the important information contained in contemporary European accounts of the course and outcome of these movements, most European observers missed much of the meaning that these expressions of violent protest held for their participants. The prophets who inspired these revolts and the groups that supported them acted in response to grievances and in accordance with belief systems that the Europeans did not understand or refused to accept. The adherents of these movements believed their causes to be righteous, their means potent, and their prophets' solutions effective. Their perceptions of the events that gave rise to their protest and the factors that determined their mode of expression provide very different explanations of these prophetic rebellions than those offered by the European colonizers.

To understand the causes of these movements from the participants' perspective, we must move from the general contexts of rebellion, outlined in Chapter 1, to specific grievances actually cited by rebel leaders and their followers to justify their protest.[1] The responses of those who supported these movements were not based on conscious perceptions of global trends or general processes of culture clash and sociocultural transformation. They were rooted in discontent that arose from the participants' personal experiences and grievances which resulted from the conditions under which they lived their everyday lives. Nevertheless, given the general contexts of culture contact and change in which this discontent arose, their grievances can best be analyzed by means of the theory of relative deprivation. Of all the approaches to social protest proposed in recent years, none is as well suited as the concept of relative deprivation for situations of change like those under consideration. As a result of European colonialism, new groups, ideas, objects, and organizational patterns were introduced into non-Western societies, where they altered and threatened the positions of previously established indigenous groups.[2] In these circumstances, significant numbers of individuals and whole groups among the colonized came to feel that a gap existed between what they felt they deserved in terms of status and material rewards and what they possessed or had the capacity to obtain. This perception of a discrepency between expectations and capacities led to a sense of deprivation,[3] which was both relative and collectively experienced. Individuals and groups compared their status and abilities to those of others, or, equally important, to those that existed (or were thought to have existed) at an earlier time. In this process the element of change was critical, for "change itself creates discrepancies between legitimate expectations and actuality, either by worsening the conditions of the group, or by exposing a group to new standards."[4] Because the stress and frustrations that accompanied these feelings of relative deprivation were sufficiently intense and shared, they produced collective protest movements designed to ameliorate strain by closing the gap between the participants' expectations and their capacities.

The theory of relative deprivation is also well-suited to the comparative study of social protest because it is sufficiently broad and flexible to allow for significant variations in the causes which give rise to different movements. The historical contexts or sociocultural situations that produce feelings of relative deprivation vary greatly. Economic demands may be central in one case but far less important in another than threats to religious beliefs or social status. Although some scholars have criticized Aberle's development of the theory of relative deprivation as too narrowly materialistic, the concept can in fact be effectively applied to a wide range of potential sources of discontent, including declining individual and group integrity, loss of self-esteem, and the violation of long-cherished customs and relationships. In the movements considered in this study, the advance of the colonial order did not just impose a greater degree of political control or heavier economic demands, it raised questions of legitimacy, ethics, and social norms that impinged on every aspect of the colonizeds' lives. By means of the theory of relative deprivation, it is possible to relate and compare these disparate sources of unrest and collective protest.

Although those who deal with the causes of violent protest movements have typically divided these grievances into economic, political and social compartments, these categories are inappropriate for a number of reasons. To begin with, dividing human activities into spheres is an arbitrary process that distorts the multifaceted nature of most institutions, thinking, and modes of behavior.[5] To take a specific example, what label can one give to the head tax that was a major source of the discontent behind the Saya San rebellion? Should it be termed economic, since it deprived the peasant of income at an inconvenient time of the year, or political, because it was imposed by the colonial administration? The question is further complicated because payment of the head tax in Burman times had been a symbol of sovereignty and legitimacy. The Burman peasants' refusal to pay the levy amounted partly to a rejection of British claims to be their rightful overlords. The question of legitimacy in turn was linked to both social and religious issues because for Burmans a legitimate ruler was by definition a devout Buddhist, a defender of the faith and a patron of the monastic order or *Sangha*.

Many other examples of this mingling of the different aspects of human enterprise could be cited. Disputes over land tenure have social, religious, and psychological implications that extend far beyond the obvious factors of production and subsistence. The displacement of elite groups has also had multifaceted effects because these groups have simultaneously played economic, social, political, and religious roles. The participants in the movements under study did not make the sort of distinctions that are implied by the use of categories derived from the experience and perceptions of European peoples. The Maori or Matumbi did not neatly compartmentalize the religious and the secular or the military and the civilian. Religion was all-pervasive, and in times of stress all able-bodied men were warriors. Javanese peasants did not relate to their indigenous rulers in merely political ways; among other things, the king functioned as administrator, military commander, custodian of Javanese culture, and mediator between the forces of the cosmos and the terrestrial realm. The complex intermingling of different aspects of the societies under study meant that changes resulting from colonization could not be confined to one sphere or level of society. What began as seemingly minor alterations often set off chain reactions that shook the very foundations of the colonized societies.

Colonial Bureaucracies and Elite Displacement

Through war, co-option, or gradual replacement, the advance of the European colonial order invariably resulted in severe challenges to precolonial African and Asian elite groups. Alien European bureaucratic ideals and institutions were substituted for political systems that had been sanctioned by generations of use and acquiescence. With the new systems of administration came foreign personnel—both European officials and their immigrant, non-Western subordinates. The most direct and immediate effect of this process was to remove the indigenous lords or gradually to demote them to puppet status. The European colonizers attempted to transform local chiefs and village headmen from representatives of local interests into government functionaries. This process of bureaucratic extension, which has been seen as a major cause of peasant rebellions in Europe and China in earlier periods,[6] took divergent forms and had widely varying effects in different colonial societies. The degree and nature of elite displacement among colonized peoples varied according to the strength of indigenous political institutions, the willingness of colonized leaders to cooperate with their new overlords, and the extent to which the Europeans needed administrative assistance.

In the areas under study, there were three main patterns. First, in Lower Burma, the British colonizers assumed direct administrative control and initially replaced central and later local indigenous officials. Second, in Java, the colonizers sought indirect control through co-opted, indigenous elite groups. In Chota Nagpur the Europeans also ruled indirectly, through Hindu and Muslim nobles and landlord groups who were considered alien by the Mundas and other hill-dwelling peoples. In the Matumbi and Ngindo areas of German East Africa, indirect rule through indigenous elites comparable to that found in Java was combined with administration by alien, Swahili-speaking functionaries brought in by the colonizers. Finally, in New Zealand, indigenous leaders continued to control semiautonomous enclaves, but their authority was eroded as the strength and viability of their societies as a whole declined. Although there was some blending of different patterns in each of these areas, elite displacement was a major cause of each of the protest movements under consideration.

Konbaung political control over Lower Burma had never been extensive, but whatever had existed was abruptly ended after the British annexation in 1852. The Governor General of India in distant Calcutta became the new arbiter of the region's fate. Burman nobles and administrators either died resisting the British advance or fled into the Dry Zone, which was to remain under Konbaung control for several more decades. Although Burman settlers in the Delta may have felt continuing loyalty to their former sovereign in Mandalay, they now paid their taxes to and received orders from British administrators and their Western-trained Indian subordinates. Then, following the conquest of Upper Burma in 1886, the Konbaung monarch was deposed and the Burman kingship and court were consigned to oblivion. Although the available evidence regarding the fate of Burman nobles and government officials is scanty, most appear to have died in resistance efforts or to have retired from public life.[7] In many cases it is probable that they sought refuge in monasteries, as often happens in Theravada Buddhist Southeast Asia.

In Lower Burma the British attempted to extend and intensify the control exerted by the central administration over local affairs. In the Delta, where central control under the Konbaungs had been intermittent and loose, British efforts to establish ongoing regulation of village affairs were both highly innovative and deeply disruptive.[8] Until the 1880s, the British were content to leave local leaders in charge of the indigenous system, which was based on circles of hamlets rather than village units. After the widespread disturbances in the rural Delta that accompanied the annexation of Upper Burma in 1886, British officials were determined to remake local government on the basis of Indian and what they believed to be Burman precedents. Artificial village units were pieced together from the original circles of hamlets. Organic social units were dismembered and made into increasingly lifeless cogs in the machinery of colonial government. Local leaders were transformed into headmen, who were appointed by British administrators and expected to act in the government's interests rather than on behalf of their fellow villagers. From the government's viewpoint, these changes meant that taxes would be collected and censuses taken more effectively. For the majority of the Delta's peasants, the shift struck at one of their chief sources of protection: the collusion of local leaders whose position rested on community approval. Headmen lost prestige, status, and contact with most of their fellow villagers. These local officials would later become major targets of rural nationalist agitators, particularly during the anti–head tax campaigns of the mid-1920s.[9] During the Saya San risings rebel assaults were frequently directed against the homes of village headmen, who were regarded as traitors and informers and who possessed most of the firearms available in rural Burma.[10]

The Dutch preferred to co-opt Javanese administrators and all but the most implacable nobles and princes rather than to remove them. In the territories they formally annexed, the Dutch retitled Javanese officials and left them in power, while gradually reducing their privileges and functions.[11] In the princely states, the Dutch left the old nobility in power and the Javanese administrative system largely intact. In the decades preceding Dipanagara's rebellion, however, there was a rapid erosion of the position of the princes and nobility and of indigenous political institutions as well. This deterioration was caused largely by continuing Dutch annexations of Javanese-ruled territories and Dutch determination to gain effective control over the internal affairs of both Yogyakarta and Surakarta. As in the case of princely support for the great Sepoy rebellion in India in 1857–1858,[12] one of the key sources of the growing discontent of Dipanagara and the nobles who supported him in revolt was the persistent Dutch effort to whittle down the size of the states carved from the dismembered kingdom of Mataram. By the end of the eighteenth century virtually the entire outer ring of provinces of the old Mataram empire had been lost to the Dutch. In the first decades of the nineteenth century successive Dutch and British regimes began to lay claim to the provinces neighboring on the fragmented central core. After Sultan Sepuh's abortive resistance in 1812, the courts of Yogyakarta and Surakarta (the latter because of its collusion in Sepuh's schemes) were forced to cede several major provinces, including the valuable and strategic Kedu region bordering both princely states on the north. In 1824, the Dutch forced both states to "lease" certain lands to the colonial government for thirty years. The heads of the two states correctly suspected that temporary rental meant permanent annexation. In the same year the Dutch further alarmed the Javanese nobility by proposing further additional territorial concessions.[13]

Javanese fears for the very existence of the princely domains appeared to be confirmed by the actions and attitudes of Dutch officials. Most ominous was the careless comment by Governor-General van der Capellen to some of the highest officials at the court of Surakarta that it would be best if their state were ruled directly by the Dutch, like the previously annexed regions of Banten and Cheribon.[14]

The loss of fertile and heavily populated provinces like Kedu struck at the very foundations of the Javanese state system and the ancient world order of the Javanese elite. Nobles and administrators were supported mainly by apanage grants, which consisted primarily of rights to draw tribute in produce and labor services from the village populations of specified areas. The shrinkage of territory controlled by the rulers of Yogyakarta and Surakarta meant a decline in the land and manpower resources available for the maintenance of their retainers and administrators. This dilemma was exacerbated by the need to find support for officials who chose not to remain in areas annexed by the Dutch and by the continuing increase in the number of noble claimants and their retainers. Because a Javanese noble who reduced the number of his dependents or cut back on his sumptuous living standards faced a severe loss of prestige, new ways had to be found to wring additional revenues from sources of limited or declining potential.[15] These methods involved a variety of administrative abuses, increasing demands on the population remaining under Javanese control, and land rentals to Europeans and Chinese. (I will discuss these patterns in some detail when I consider the grievances that led peasants to give widespread support to Dipanagara's revolt.) The losses in political power, income, and prestige suffered by the nobility as a result of Dutch annexations were compounded by a deep sense of humiliation felt by proud Javanese leaders like Dipanagara, and growing concern among the Javanese ruling classes generally for their survival. These fears and frustrations were clearly reflected in the extensive support that Dipanagara received from both the court nobility and regional officials during the early months of his rebellion.[16]

The diminution of Javanese-controlled domains was paralleled by an equally threatening Dutch infiltration of the administrative systems of the princely states. In the first decades of the nineteenth century, the Dutch Resident's control over internal affairs steadily expanded, and the last vestiges of Javanese autonomy were slowly undermined as the Europeans forced numerous concessions and regulations on the princes. All important appointments were made subject to Dutch approval, and they not only selected but ruled in collusion with the chancellor or *patih*, Danureja IV, who was the pivotal official in the Yogyakarta bureaucratic hierarchy. The importance of the Dutch effort to form alliances with nobles in high office and rule through the chief minister as a cause of the 1825–1830 rebellion is illustrated by Dipanagara's intense hostility toward the puppet chancellor, Danureja. The chancellor sought to exclude Dipanagara and other high-ranking nobles from active roles in the government and was notorious for favoritism and blatant corruption.[17]

Beyond bureaucratic appointments, Dutch Residents and their assistants also became involved in revenue operations, mediated intramural disputes among the nobility, and approved all important decisions. Their influence even extended to matters of court dress, protocol, and ceremonies. The Javanese nobility found this interference particularly offensive, for they were highly sensitive to outward symbols of rank and deeply committed to their ancient religiopolitical rituals and beliefs.[18] The full extent of the control exercised by the Dutch by the 1820s could be seen in their ever-increasing role in determining the royal succession. They not only dismissed all claims that Dipanagara might have had to the throne, but formally proclaimed in the regulation of 1822 that, during the period of guardianship for their infant nominee, authority in Yogyakarta would be concentrated in the hands of the Dutch Resident. Dipanagara and those who supported him were openly hostile to Dutch officials at court and their Javanese allies, contemptuous of these factions for the way they dominated the Sultan to further their own designs, and implacably opposed to innovations that the Europeans had introduced into the courts.[19]

Although the *desa* or village unit in central Java remained intact, in contrast to the customary circle in Lower Burma, Dutch annexations and inroads into the upper levels of Javanese administration had important repercussions at the local level. As we have seen, diminished sources of revenue forced the courts and Javanese regional officials to make ever greater demands on the peasants for produce and labor services. The key figures in the fulfillment of these demands were the *bekels* (literally village heads), or deputies of the regents and nobles who held apanage grants. The *bekel* was responsible for the actual collection of taxes and the mobilization of labor services from the village populations under his master's control. Although he was traditionally drawn from the landowners and notables of the village or locale for which he was responsible, the *bekel's* demands on behalf of his superiors increasingly alienated him from the village community in the decades before Dipanagara's revolt. Frequently outsiders were appointed *bekels* to counteract local sanctions and prevent collusion.

In addition, Danureja and other Dutch puppets at court exercised growing influence on the appointment of regional and local officials, naturally favoring those who had demonstrated a willingness to cooperate with the agents of the Netherlands Indies government.[20] These shifts not only weakened longstanding patron-client relationships that had been essential to village harmony and functioning but also violated the time-honored principle that the *desa* community should avoid as much as possible contacts with the state and its agents.[21] In the days just before the outbreak of hostilities, Dipanagara received assurances of support from village and local leaders in the area of his residence. He complained to them of the disturbing decline in village administration in recent decades. Throughout the revolt his major source of support would be peasants, organized collectively on the basis of village units and directed by their customary *desa* leaders.[22]

The British colonial overlords in Chota Nagpur practiced a different form of the indirect rule that the Dutch imposed in Java. Because centuries of exactions by a Hinduized court and its alien landlord retainers had reduced the indigenous leadership to subservience, the British were forced to rely on lowland immigrants for control rather than on Munda headmen. The precise fate of local Munda leaders in the pre-British period is not recorded, although it is clear that many of their functions were usurped by servants of the landlords who had little concern for the interests of the Munda cultivators.[23] It is probable that some died in localized and futile efforts to resist the encroachments of outsiders, but the great majority gradually sank in status as the village freeholders declined as a group. The British policy of supporting the Raja and the Hindu and Muslim landlords (because of an apparent lack of alternatives rather than by preference) left the Mundas leaderless and virtually defenseless. A precolonial elite survived and prospered, but that elite was the oppressor rather than the legitimate representative of the Munda people. Occasionally, as in the Kol risings of 1831–1832,[24] Munda leaders emerged, but their careers were ephemeral. British backing for the alien landlords mean that rebels were quickly, often brutally, repressed. When a man appeared with the personal presence and manipulative skills of Birsa, the Mundas greeted him with intense devotion. Their longtime craving for effective leadership explained their response better than missionary grumblings about the fickleness and credulity of ignorant tribals.[25]

The Germans ruled east Africa through both forms of indirect control discussed above. They sought in some areas to turn indigenous leaders into agents of their foreign government. In other areas, their rule was exercised through officials called *akidas*, who were recruited primarily from the Swahili-speaking peoples on the coast. The form of control in the Matumbi area differed from that in the Ngindo. Perhaps because the Matumbi hills were closer to the coast and the colonial capital at Dar es Salaam and because the local leaders of the Matumbi were growing strong enough to provide a serious threat to German control, the Germans sought to introduce *akidas* extensively in the Matumbi homeland. In the more remote Ngindo areas the Germans strove to identify and prop up local leaders, whom they called *jumbes*. The *akidas* were as alien and as ignorant of Matumbi customs as were the Germans. In fact, memories of Swahili slaving expeditions into the interior made the Matumbi even more hostile to the *akidas* than to their distant German superiors. This hostility was intensified by the *akidas*' practice of having their dictates enforced by despised *ruga-ruga* mercenaries, who had once served the slave traders. Unfettered by supervision or any sense of duty, the *akidas* were (as even German officials had to admit) corrupt, insensitive, and inefficient administrators. As rivals of the indigenous leaders and as overseers of much hated forced cultivation schemes, the *akidas* were major sources of the discontent that gave rise to rebellion. Once hostilities began, the *akidas* were one of the main targets of rebel assaults.[26]

In contrast to the policy adopted in the Matumbi hills, the Germans attempted to administer the Ngindo people of the Liwale region through their own leaders.[27] The colonizers sometimes replaced the *jumbes* (a label that they rather indiscriminately applied to village and clan heads alike) with more cooperative clients, but more often local leaders remained in positions of responsibility in return for services rendered to the colonial regime. These services included tax collection, mobilization of forced labor, and cooperation with itinerant German officials and mercenary troops. The *jumbes* found these arrangements highly unsatisfactory. To begin with, they were paid poorly or nothing at all. Higher officials and mercenary soldiers treated them contemptuously and frequently humiliated them in front of their own people. For the most trivial reasons, *askaris* (or regular African mercenaries serving the Germans) could have the hapless *jumbes* publicly flogged. Further, a *jumbe* was expected to provide without compensation food, clothing, lodgings, and (if requested) women for *askaris* who passed through their villages. The violation of their women by Nubian and Somali mercenaries was particularly offensive to the Ngindo because their customary procedures for gaining wives were complicated and costly. Their usual response to adultery included violent reprisals.[28]

Jumbes' services to the alien Germans and their allies rendered their authority suspect in the eyes of their clansmen and fellow villagers. Matumbi and Ngindo chiefs and clan leaders had customarily been chosen on the basis of merit and local considerations and were expected to act wholly in the interests of their kinsmen or fellow villagers. The *jumbes* were caught in the middle—between the Germans who maintained them in office but treated them poorly, and their own people, whose expectations and demands they were unable to fulfill. A number of German officials attributed the outbreak of the Maji Maji risings to an elaborate *jumbe* plot. Although their belief has been shown to be without factual basis, it is indisputable that village and clan heads made up a majority of the leaders of the early outbreaks. Throughout the rebellion, they provided whatever semblance of coordination and organization that existed in all but the Ngoni areas in the southwestern interior.[29]

Although the new weapons, tools, and crops introduced by the Europeans enhanced for a time the power and prestige of a number of adventurous and able Maori chiefs, the coming of the whites to New Zealand generally resulted in a decline in the position of the chiefs, which was one aspect of a process of gradual tribal disintegration. Inadvertently, Christian missionaries were far more instrumental in undermining the chiefs than were white settlers or the British colonial government, whose role was largely indirect. The new tools and methods of production and exchange, introduced mainly by traders and missionaries, posed direct challenges to customary knowledge, skills, and rituals traditionally monopolized by the chiefs and *tohungas* or religious experts. As

Maharaia Winiata argues effectively in the following passage, many of these abilities and practices became irrelevant, with critical consequences for Maori leaders:

The Pakeha [white man]-originated commodities were devoid of age and history, the association with mythology and sentiment, that were part of Maori culture. The alien goods were surrounded at first with their own appropriate techniques, but no specialized knowledge or ritual skill was needed, apart from the general information available to the rank and file of Maori society. The changes in tribal diet—meat and vegetable—led to a gradual decay of ritual in forest lore and agriculture and a consequent minimizing of the ritual functions of the leaders.[30]

The missionaries themselves displaced the chiefs by providing alternative sources of authority as mission stations became centers of Maori Christian communities in the 1830s.

Because the missionaries were the main mediators between the Maoris and the technologically superior European world—acting as prime sources of European goods, techniques, and medicine—they were looked upon in many cases as "god-heros." They not only converted but came to dominate numerous Maori chiefs.[31] In assaulting fundamental Maori institutions and practices, such as war, slavery, and polygamy, the missionaries further weakened the chiefs' control over tribal affairs. With the coming of peace, the chiefs lost key roles as war leaders and chances to accrue prestige through military exploits. Monogamous marriage deprived them of kinship and intratribal links that once bolstered their power. Above all, the abolition of slavery created a new group that rejected their old status and resented customary deference to their former masters, both chiefs and free warriors.[32]

The growing demands by white settlers for Maori lands and the colonial government's furtherance of these aims placed additional handicaps on the chiefs. When rival and secondary chiefs and *hapu* heads defied tribal custom and their chiefs' and tribal councils' sanctions by selling land without tribal consent, the sales were more often than not approved by the colonial government. Land claims and sales led to bitter intratribal disputes and tensions that often nullified the chiefs' control over substantial numbers of their fellow tribesmen. In the Waikato and Taranaki areas in the southwest of the North Island, the chiefs were bitterly divided over land practices and other issues. These quarrels contributed substantially to tribal breakdown, which had gone as far in the Taranaki as anywhere among the Maori. It was no accident that the

Maori King movement was concentrated in the Waikato and that the Pai Maire movement arose and flourished in the Taranaki.[33] Because European political control had never been effectively extended to tribal areas, the Maoris were faced with a situation in which their indigenous leaders and organizations were increasingly ineffective but no workable substitutes had been developed.

A Question of Legitimacy

The impact of colonial administrations extended far beyond their most apparent effects on indigenous leaders at different levels. The colonial order also posed challenges for indigenous ritual and religious experts, the institutions and beliefs that they represented, and the very legitimacy of existing sociopolitical systems. Variations in the nature and degree of European penetration into different areas made for variations in the seriousness of the European challenge in these related spheres. In German East Africa indigenous religious leaders and belief systems were the least threatened, although the displacement of local leaders called into question the legitimacy of the new system. British disrespect for revered symbols of authority and neglect of key religious institutions in Burma were major sources of the discontent that led to widespread rebellion, as was the Dutch threat to put an end to the rule of Muslim princes in central Java. For both the Mundas and the Maoris, the challenges of the colonizers were part of a configuration of factors that threatened their very identity and continued existence as distinct peoples. Despite these variations, all of the societies considered saw the European colonizers as alien and illegitimate overlords who had imposed and maintained their rule by force—either directly with European troops or indirectly through indigenous allies or imported non-European mercenaries.

Despite the assertions of a number of contemporary German observers to the contrary and the extensive participation of seers, healers, and other magico-religious experts in the Maji Maji disturbances,[34] there is little evidence that the position of religious leaders, at least among the peoples who mounted the early insurrections, was as yet seriously threatened by the penetration of colonial rule. Missionaries and mission stations were the objects of rebel attacks on a number of occasions; however, the missionaries were targeted as white Europeans and as agents of the colonial establishment rather than as rival political or religious leaders.[35] At

the time of the rebellion the missionaries had gained very few converts among peoples like the Matumbi and Ngindo, having had, in
fact, little or no contact with the great majority of them. Hence,
Christian teachings had no influence on Maji Maji ideology.[36] The
key roles played by seers like Kinjikitile and his younger brother,
Nyangumi, and by healers and religious experts more generally
indicate that they held a yet unrivalled hold over the peoples who
supported the revolt. It is also important to realize that most of
these peoples had little exposure to European technology or European goods, either in the period of conquest or in the early decades
of German rule. Therefore, key grievances arising from elite displacement among Matumbi or Ngindo rebels mainly involved challenges to the authority of their village chiefs and clan heads, but
these challenges clearly raised the underlying issue of legitimacy.
In the place of local men selected on the basis of merit, who exercised authority sanctioned by popular (and by extension, ancestral)
approval and consecrated by ancient rituals, the Germans sought
to substitute hated alien functionaries or co-opted, and thus suspect, indigenous leaders. The Maji Maji risings were in part a rejection of this attempt and a desperate effort by clan and village
leaders to preserve their positions of political, military, and social
predominance. In this attempt they were supported by the local
ritual leaders who had customarily confirmed them in their positions of authority, and oracles, like Kinjikitile, who shared the
belief system which legitimized their rule.[37]

In Burma the British made little effort to perpetuate long-
established state links to the Theravada Buddhist monks who were
the guardians of the religious traditions of the great majority of
their colonial subjects. In the precolonial era Buddhist *pongyis* or
monks both supported and limited the power of Burman monarchs.[38] In turn Burman rulers were expected to protect and patronize Buddhist institutions. Burman monarchs were required to
build and maintain pagodas and monasteries, endow Buddhist
scholars and educational centers, and appoint ecclesiastical pri-
mates and councils to settle disputes and maintain discipline within
the *Sangha* or monastic community. During the period of British
rule, government support for Buddhist institutions and monks
was greatly reduced. Not only was state financial backing negli-
gible but the government no longer placed its executive authority
behind the decisions of the Buddhist primate and his council. This
loss of support and the fact that the primate's decisions could

be challenged in civil courts led to serious divisions and a decline in the discipline of the *Sangha*.[39] Because of this erosion in monastic supervision, large numbers of violence-prone and unruly pseudo-monks or "political pongyis" emerged to become deeply involved in the anticolonial and anti-Indian agitation of the 1920s and 1930s.[40]

In conjunction with growing disruption in the *Sangha*, Buddhist monastic education, which had traditionally been central in the socialization of Burman youths, fell on hard times. British efforts to combine Western and monastic education failed. The potential for professional advance offered by Western schools greatly diminished the demand for monastic education among Burmese elite groups, though rural Burmans continued to attend monastic schools where they were available.[41] The dangers to Buddhist institutions and religious groups were particularly apparent in Lower Burma, where most of the outbreaks which made up the Saya San revolt occurred. In the pre-British period Buddhism had never been as well-established in the southern frontier provinces as in the Dry Zone heartland. In the colonial era extensive commercialization and the concentration of Western education and influence in Rangoon and other Delta urban centers seriously impeded the firm establishment of the monastic order. At the village level in many parts of the Delta frontier, numerous observers noted the paucity of monks and monastic schools and the neglect of ritual festivals and traditional pastimes, like the Burmese *pwe* or theatrical entertainment.[42]

To the Burmans, the colonial regime's failure to protect and patronize Buddhism, which was (and is) "both the symbol and essential ingredient of their national identity,"[43] was but one more indication that the British were alien and illegitimate overlords. British ignorance of and disrespect for Burman traditions was also demonstrated by the fate of the royal palace at Mandalay, which colonial troops plundered in 1886 and the British later made into a social club. In doing so they desecrated the key symbol of Burman political legitimacy. The Burmans viewed the palace as sacred. It was a microcosmic representation of Mount Meru or the center of the Burman (and Hindu-Buddhist) universe, where the ruler communed with the gods and spirits who regulated the cosmos. In the precolonial period, possession of the palace was essential to the monarch's claims for obedience and loyalty from his people.[44]

The importance of the British neglect of Buddhism and the traditional Burman symbols of political legitimacy as a cause of the

Saya San rebellion can be shown in a number of ways. Substantial numbers of Burman monks (both bonafide and pseudo) actively participated in nearly all of the major risings. Buddhist monasteries served as meeting places for those plotting the rebellion and occasionally as rebel headquarters after hostilities began.[45] Saya San's claim of royal descent and his use of traditional political symbols, as well as the recruiting speeches, proclamations, membership oaths, and postrebellion trial testimony of the rebels amply demonstrate their intense concern for legitimacy and the well-being of the Burman sociocultural order. Saya San and his lieutenants repeatedly called upon the Burman people to rise up and overthrow the "infidel," the "heretic" colonial overlords, and to restore the monarchy in order to safeguard their precious Buddhist heritage.[46]

In Java growing Dutch encroachments on the power of the indigenous lords who remained formally independent led to great apprehension among religious leaders at different levels of Javanese society and among the subject population as a whole. For the Javanese their ruler was far more than a sacred king or defender of the Islamic faith. The Sultan or Soenan was regarded as the sole link between man and the cosmos, and as such essential to the maintenance of harmony between the heavenly and terrestrial realms. He was responsible for the fertility of his kingdom, the prosperity of his subjects, and the order and tranquility valued so highly by the Javanese.[47] The military men and merchants who served as Governors-General of the Netherlands Indies were hardly meaningful substitutes. They showed little inclination to promote Islam, which in a highly eclectic blend with various strains of Hinduism and Buddhism was the religion of the great majority of the Javanese people. In fact, the advance of Dutch power threatened a potential separation of religious and political, sacred and secular authority. These distinctions were alien to all Islamic societies in which the *ummat* or community of believers encompassed all aspects of human activity and the Western concept of the "state" was alien. Thus, the advance of European colonial control meant that conquered or annexed areas were lost to the *Dar-ul-Islam* and reverted to the *Dar-ul-Harb*, or land of war.[48] No group in Java resisted Dutch expansion more tenaciously than Muslim holymen, *ulama* (scholars), *kyais* (teachers), and *hajis* (those who had made the pilgrimage to Mecca).[49] In Prince Dipanagara these diverse groups found a patron and defender.

Long before the outbreak of the rebellion in 1825, Dipanagara had gained a widespread reputation as an ascetic and an intensely devout student of Islam. In the years before the revolt he had also strongly opposed the spread of European ideas and organizational forms among the Javanese nobility and criticized the growing influence of infidel administrators at the princely courts. In the view of Dipanagara and many Javanese nobles, such alien influence was the main cause of the dissolution, immorality, and rampant corruption that had so seriously sapped the strength of Mataram and was continuing to weaken the princely states. Dipanagara's commitment to Islam was so marked that a number of writers have argued persuasively that he revolted against the Dutch mainly because they would not acknowledge him as *pantagama* or "head" of Javanese Islam and not because of their alleged moves to deny him the throne of Yogyakarta.[50] Under Dipanagara's leadership rebellion was sanctified as a holy war that would reestablish just rule in Java. His followers recognized him not only as Sultan but also as the supreme regulator of religion on Java. In his proclamations and pleas for support from the nobility and the general populace, Dipanagara emphasized his belief that he was the leader of a holy crusade to drive the infidel Dutch from Java. In all stages of the revolt he received strong support from the *ulama, hajis,* and other Islamic leaders. The Dutch repeatedly singled out these groups for their fierce and fanatical attacks on government columns and fortifications. The holy war, however, was not in defense of Islam per se, but Islam as part of an ancient Javanese cultural complex that Dipanagara and his supporters believed to be in mortal danger because of the Dutch advance.[51]

Although Hindu mystic-saints may have won some converts among Mundas dwelling in the lowland approaches to Chota Nagpur in the precolonial period, the highland peoples as a whole resisted conversion to Hinduism or the other creeds of lowland invaders. Despite the Mundas' continuing adherence to their ancestral beliefs, however, the power and influence of the *pahans* or village ritual specialists declined as repeated sacrifices to Munda ancestral and community spirits failed to bring relief from the demands of alien overlords. Centuries of oppression and repeated defeats at the hands of their enemies nurtured doubts among the Mundas as to whether their gods were as potent as those of their adversaries. The strong initial Munda response to the conversion efforts of Christian missionaries was in part an extension of the Mundas' search for additional supernatural help against the lowland invaders.[52] This quest was also evident in the Birsa rebellion and a number of earlier movements. Birsa not only attacked the old gods as impotent, he attempted to introduce rather large doses of Christian *and* Hindu practices and beliefs.[53] The adoption of certain aspects of foreign religious systems was not an indication of Birsa's willingness to compromise with the lowlanders. On the contrary, Birsa borrowed to strengthen his people for the struggle to drive their alien overlords from the highlands. Birsa and his followers allowed no legitimacy to the claims of the Hindu Raja and his Hindu or Muslim landlord-retainers. They had not conquered the Mundas; they did not share, or even respect Munda culture; and their long rule had resulted only in mounting burdens and degradation. Rejecting both their Indian and British overlords, the Birsites consciously sought to resurrect the ancient symbols of indigenous Munda authority.[54]

The Maoris' whole complex of customary rituals and beliefs was threatened by the agents and products of industrial England. Because their religious experts or *tohungas* (*tohunga ahurewa* or *t. matatuhi*) and chiefs were extremely interdependent, the dilemmas faced by chiefs and tribal units applied with equal intensity to the custodians of Maori religious tradition. The *tohungas*, who were normally of high birth and often kinsmen of important chiefs, met powerful rivals in the Christian missionaries. The missionaries considered the beliefs on which the *tohungas'* social positions and self-esteem were based to be mere superstition and tried to eradicate them. As representatives of a civilization vastly superior in technological and empirical knowledge, the missionaries came into the contest with seemingly insurmountable advantages. In their medical knowledge and greater immunity to epidemic diseases, their scientific understanding, their literacy, and their possession of a wide range of skills important to the Maori, the missionaries and their God were demonstrably more powerful than Maori ritual experts and their sacred spells. Because the Maoris judged their gods' power by their ability to influence events in the earthly realm, the Christian God and his knowledgeable emissaries threatened to displace the *tohungas* and the old religion. The *mana*, or aura of inner strength and power, of the *tohungas* and chiefs dimmed as the all-pervasive Maori beliefs in *tapus*, or ritual prohibitions and sacred objects and persons, weakened under missionary assault.[55] Therefore, even though Te Ua Haumene's new faith, the Pai Maire, included strong elements of Christian doctrine and ritual, it was readily accepted by many Maori *tohungas* as a counterweight to Christianity. The *tohungas* saw it as a means of restoring status and influence undermined by missionary successes. Te Ua's prophecies promised supernatural assistance to neutralize the powerful Christian God, and the *tohungas* revived old battle chants and rituals to bolster the Maori in a bloody struggle that often took on aspects of a holy war.[56] For the adherents of the Pai Maire sect, however, the cause went deeper than defending Maori sociopolitical systems and the religious beliefs that permeated them. The issue was the very survival of the Maori people. The relentless advance of the white settlers, the collapse of their customary world order, and, most ominously, their diminishing numbers all made the Maori feel that they were on the edge of extinction.[57]

Displacement, Legitimacy, and Relative Deprivation

Although there were significant variations in the nature and extent of the displacements caused by the advance of colonial rule in different areas, this process resulted in a form of deprivation that was common to all of the peoples considered. Colonized groups found that positions of leadership and prestige were increasingly closed to them and that the posts they were allowed to retain no longer conferred the influence and social esteem that they had in the precolonial era. As new modes of organization and behavior were introduced, surviving indigenous leaders and the colonized peoples as a whole began to feel that "people did not behave as they should, or as they once did. . . ."[58] Confronted with the technological superiority and continued dominance of alien overlords, the colonized peoples began to doubt the viability of customary political systems and modes of organization. Ideologies and institutions that had once given the roles of indigenous leadership groups meaning and justified their claims to command came to be viewed as outmoded and untenable.

More apparent than deprivation relative to past conditions was the sense of immediate deprivation felt by displaced or co-opted elite groups toward the colonial agents who replaced them or usurped their powers. Very often the main rivals of indigenous leaders were not European administrators but alien African or Asian subordinate officials, Christian missionaries, and native men of low status, who were willing to cooperate with the new rulers. Because the Europeans were unable to supervise these groups effectively, their governance inevitably spawned disruptions and discontent. In each of the cases considered, European attempts to extend administrative control over colonized peoples resulted in makeshift systems that groped clumsily in a nebulous zone between collapsing indigenous institutions and new bureaucracies in formation. In this middle ground corruption and oppression thrived and the welfare of the subject populations as a whole was sacrificed to the ambitions of a few.

It would be absurd to contend that indigenous leaders had never exploited their subjects in the precolonial period. It is fair to argue, however, that the burdens of the ruled were considerably diminished by a sense of cultural identity with their overlords and the existence of reciprocity in the master-subject relationship (however lopsided). Above all, precolonial elites simply did not have the technological or organizational capacity to interfere extensively in local affairs. As the control of colonial bureaucracies increased and local leaders, who might have buffered the impact of change, were shunted aside, the subject peoples' ability to resist steadily declined.

Making the Colonies Pay: Land, Labor, and Taxation

One of the most cherished principles of dedicated European imperialists was succinctly summarized in the notion that "the colonies must pay." How to measure success in this regard was a matter of dispute, and debates raged in parliaments and in print about whether colonies were in fact profitable investments and, if so, for whom. Although these questions were never convincingly resolved, advocates of overseas expansion agreed that colonies should provide outlets for goods and investments and raw materials for industrialized or industrializing western European (and North American) nations. At the very minimum, the returns should offset the costs of conquest, administrative "reform," communications development, and the other essentials of the *mission civilisatrice*. The proponents of these ideas ranged from expansion-minded politicians struggling to persuade skeptical legislators to support further colonial adventures to theorists like Arthur Girault who argued that the Europeans had a duty to humanity to seize and exploit the underdeveloped lands and resources of "less advanced" peoples.[59] Establishing colonial administrative and judicial systems amenable to the needs of laissez-faire capitalism was essential to the goal of making the colonies pay. However, these measures and the resulting displacement of indigenous regimes were only a prelude to more far-reaching transformations that would more directly effect the welfare and daily lives of the mass peasant base of colonial societies.

Although the actual techniques and institutions used by the Europeans to mobilize labor and extract resources varied widely, they all led to increased demands on the colonized peoples and further eroded their customary practices and relationships. In the societies that gave rise to the prophetic rebellions under study here, a continuum of extractive systems can be identified, with labor tribute arrangements at one pole and highly monetarized economies based on smallholders at the other. In each case there was a blend of different systems, falling on a line somewhere between the extremes. Labor tribute arrangements tended to occur in relatively heavily populated core regions like central Java and the Matumbi hills, where there were well-established indigenous social structures and less European colonial penetration. Peasant smallholder-based systems, on the other hand, occurred in sparsely populated frontier zones like Lower Burma, where precolonial social patterns were not so firmly entrenched and thus were more easily altered to meet the needs of overseas colonizers and the European-focused, global capitalist economy.

The forced cultivation scheme, introduced by the Germans into various parts of German East Africa beginning in 1902, was an excellent example of a system designed to produce cash crops for export through the use of labor that remained locked in the predominantly subsistence sector of the colonial economy. For the Germans, who were one of the most industrially advanced of the imperialist powers, to resort to techniques characteristic of pre-industrial Iberian or Dutch expansion into heavily populated zones of the Americas or Asia is at first glance odd, but there is a ready explanation. There was a severe shortage of able manpower willing to take up posts in German east Africa or the German overseas empire generally. Because of the very limited number of available administrators, soldiers, and settlers, the Germans had concentrated their activities in east Africa in the north of the colony along the Pangani river valley. Consequently, few bureaucrats or planters were left to direct extraction efforts in the potentially productive south. The forced cultivation scheme, modeled after a similar system used in parts of Togo, required only a handful of German administrators.[60] Under the scheme, the colonial regime compelled certain peoples in the southeast and other areas to set aside a portion of their fields (an average of 2.5 acres per village) for the production on a communal basis of cash crops like cotton, sesame, and peanuts. The cultivators turned this produce over to representatives of the colonial government, who supervised its transport to the coast for export to overseas markets. German officials who favored the scheme argued that it would be minimally disruptive to the colonized peoples. They also predicted that it would become a major source of revenue for the colonial administration and suggested that it would stimulate the production of tropical products needed for industries in Germany itself.

Like much that the Germans attempted in east Africa, the forced cultivation scheme was applied without adequate supervision and in ignorance of indigenous customs and needs. Consequently, it was carried out clumsily and at times brutally. Although regular wages were supposed to be paid to the cultivators who worked the government plots, the money was either not provided at all or was offered in such small quantities that African laborers "contemptuously refused" it.[61] In the Matumbi hills, the hated Swahili-speaking akidas acted as overseers under a handful of German officials. The akidas' ready resort to floggings and threats to meet their quotas made it appear that opportunities to enslave the peoples of the interior, that had previously eluded the coastal peoples, were being realized under German rule. Among the Ngindo and other peoples where the akidas had not yet been established, jumbes and other local leaders were saddled with responsibility for the scheme. If they resisted, they were replaced; if they went along, they lost the trust and support of their people. In the heavily populated area occupied by the Matumbi, the scheme was especially resented because land and labor time formerly devoted to food production were sacrificed to grow export crops whose sale brought little or no benefit to the cultivators.[62] Material losses were compounded by the overseers' harsh treatment and the humiliation of freemen who in some areas were forced to work side by side with slaves. A number of ex-laborers later recalled, "Your back and buttocks were whipped and there was no rising once you stooped to dig." For many, the only wages were the welts on their bodies.[63]

Forced cultivation—particularly of cotton, which was the most demanding of the crops introduced—more than any other single cause was responsible for the initial outbreaks of the Maji Maji disturbances among the Matumbi and Ngindo peoples. The correspondence between the presence of the forced cultivation scheme and the areas where early risings occurred was total,[64] although the movement later spread to peoples not yet affected by the labor tribute system. Before the revolt some of the peoples who were to support it refused to pick cotton. Many of them traveled to the oracle at Ngarambe to complain to Kinjikitile of their oppression under the system and to seek remedies. The first outbreaks of violence in the Matumbi areas were sparked by orders to begin picking cotton, and in many cases the rebels' first action was to uproot cotton plants on government plots.[65] In the early days of the revolt, cotton fields, European planters, and Arab overseers were the main targets of rebel assaults. Several of the rebel leaders in both the Matumbi and Ngindo areas had suffered personal losses as a result of the forced cultivation scheme. Captured rebels or survivors of the disburbances frequently cited the abuses of the forced labor system as their sole reason for deciding to join the Maji Maji movement. To them, it was better to "die and have done with," than to continue to labor for alien overlords under harsh conditions and without payment.[66]

In Java, tribute demands were also the cause of widespread peasant unrest which burst into violence when Prince Dipanagara decided to resist the Dutch openly. Unlike their African counterparts, Javanese cultivators did not resent tribute demands as such, for they had paid tribute to indigenous overlords for centuries. Their discontent arose from the escalation of exactions of both produce and labor services far beyond the limits set by longstanding custom. As we have seen, the Javanese nobility were forced to make sharply increased demands on the peasants as Dutch annexations shrank the areas still under Javanese control. Indigenous and alien tax farmers gained more and more control of affairs at the village level. Once-free peasants were virtually reduced to the status of corvée laborers as Javanese nobles and administrators circumvented customary limits on taxes and service demands. Village notables had once protected the cultivators, but now they sided with their overlords or were replaced. *Bekel* overseers competed fiercely for the lucrative opportunities offered by supervising labor mobilization and produce extraction. Once in control they inflated quotas to get maximum returns for themselves before they were replaced by higher bidders. With the princely administrative systems riddled with corruption and staffed by disheartened nobles, these travesties of customary lord-subject relationships went unchecked. Most of the hard-pressed princes and their retainers saw no other choice.[67]

In some areas of the princely states, another pattern on exacting tribute took hold in the decades before Dipanagara's rebellion: the renting of apanage holdings to Europeans and Chinese. Although Javanese lords had begun to lease small portions of their tribute holdings for limited periods of time to Chinese merchant-landlords in the last half of the eighteenth century, only in the decade before the outbreak of the 1825–1830 rebellion did European officials also become involved.[68] Several Dutch administrators used their political influence to obtain long-term rental contracts on sizable estates, which they frequently shared with business associates and old friends. In return for substantial cash advances and annual payments to Javanese nobles, European and Chinese lessees became the virtual lords of large numbers of Javanese villagers. The new lords channeled the long-standing tribute services of these peasants into the production of coffee and other export crops. There is some disagreement about the overall effects of the system, but it is clear that it was established almost wholly to further the interests of a handful of foreign investors and that there were virtually no checks on their demands or supervision of their running of the rented estates. Javanese cultivators greatly resented their exactions because they both disrupted food crop production and were made in the name of aliens who had no legitimate claims to peasant services.

Because of abuses associated with the land rental system, it was abolished in 1823, two years before the beginning of Dipanagara's rebellion.[69] Because of the way in which the abolition was carried out, however, it intensified discontent and contributed to rebellious sentiment rather than reducing these as one might expect. The Dutch shifted the burden of the costs involved in the abolition of the rental system to the already hard-pressed Javanese nobility and ultimately their peasant subjects. Dutch officials insisted that the advances paid by European and Chinese lessees to Javanese nobles be remitted with interest. They also demanded that the leaseholders be remunerated by the Javanese for improvements to leased holdings and any losses that resulted from the sudden end of the rental system. Since most of the Javanese lords who rented their apanage holdings had long since spent the lessees' advances in an effort to maintain an aristocratic life style that belonged to an earlier age, they had little hope of complying with the Dutch demands. To make matters worse, the Dutch carried out the abolition without any attempt to assuage the feelings of the rulers of Yogyakarta and Surakarta. These princes complained that the Dutch decision violated contractual agreements, made a mockery of their claims to sovereignty, and humiliated them in the eyes of their retainers and subjects.

Some leaders, like Dipanagara, had long been opposed to the rental system and were therefore initially pleased when it was abolished. Soon, however, the excessive demands of the ex-renters and the domineering, almost contemptuous, attitude of Dutch officials during negotiations with the princes further alienated and angered the Javanese nobility. The abolition regulations disrupted the already badly battered fiscal systems of the princely states and heightened the pervasive sense that the end of the old order was drawing near. The extent of the indignities and impoverishment inflicted on the once-proud Javanese princes is perhaps best illustrated by the need of the guardians of the young Sultan of Yogyakarta to sell household articles on the open market to meet Dutch demands for compensation.

An additional burden that fueled discontent among both the nobility and the cultivating classes was provided by the toll network that straddled road and river systems in the princely states.[70] Less than a decade before Dipanagara's rising, the Dutch gained full control of the many toll stations of central Java which had long been operated by indigenous regimes. In part because they did not have the manpower to staff the stations themselves, the Dutch farmed them out to Chinese collectors. The Chinese were allowed to run them as they pleased as long as their agreed-upon quotas were met. The lessees in turn parcelled out their toll stations to relatives or the highest bidders, who were invariably Chinese. The result was a tiered network with additional charges for merchants and travelers built into each new level of an expanding system. With virtually no Dutch supervision and free of Javanese jurisdiction, the Chinese not only multiplied the number of toll stations but also rapidly raised the rates they charged on passing travelers, livestock, and trade goods. After 1817, toll rental contracts were limited to one year, but this measure merely drove the leaseholders to squeeze all they could from the defenseless population before they had to relinquish their station to another bidder.

The tollkeepers gave Chinese traders cut rates, whereas Javanese merchants had to pay exorbitant charges that greatly reduced their ability to compete. Toll costs also drove up the price of food and other products, especially in the court centers. The tollkeepers humiliated Javanese nobles by roughly searching their baggage and retainers to insure that all were fully taxed. Peasant women were occasionally abused and were regularly forced to pay duties on the children they carried on their backs. Although Dipanagara never specifically mentioned the toll system as one of the grievances that drove him to rebellion, it was certainly one of the chief causes of the sufferings of the "little people" that he drew attention to in his early correspondence with the Dutch.[71] More critically, the toll system in combination with increased taxation engendered the widespread peasant discontent that transformed Dipanagara's call to rebellion into such a formidable challenge to Dutch dominance. Throughout the disturbed provinces, rebel bands burnt down toll stations and murdered tax collectors. They also attacked the houses of the hated *bekels* and of indigenous administrators loyal to the Dutch. A number of Dutch officials observed sardonically that the rebels spared the colonial government the bother of abolishing the toll system and replacing unpopular local officials.[72]

Munda cultivators faced much more direct threats than did the Javanese or Matumbi and Ngindo to their continued control of village lands that had been cleared by their ancestors and had been their source of livelihood for centuries. Beginning in the 1790s, the Hindu and Muslim landlords of Chota Nagpur, backed by the might of Britain's growing Indian Empire, began to increase their demands on Munda agricultural communities.[73] Despite British regulations to the contrary, they required labor services and periodic "gifts" in money or produce from the villagers. At the end of the nineteenth century, government officials estimated that the average Munda cultivator was compelled to provide at least fifteen days of labor per year for the landlord. In some areas, including those where support for the Birsite rebellion was most pronounced, Hindu and Muslim lords claimed the right to demand all of the services they "felt necessary" from the Mundas. In certain cases this amounted to compulsory labor on the lords' lands on every other day. Most landlords levied cesses on special occasions, such as local festival days. They also demanded additional payments from Mundas who owned fruit trees and livestock or for services no longer provided by the landlords, such as the procurement of salt or mail delivery. Everywhere in the Munda areas where alien landlords had imposed their control rental rates increased sharply. Because there was no meaningful government supervision and because of the ignorance and resulting ineffectiveness of judges in the civil courts, the amount of rent and services extracted by the landlords from Munda cultivators depended largely on the relative strength of each party in local contests. Consequently, the landlords' take varied widely. It was generally highest in districts where the breakdown of Munda society was the most pronounced. This situation led to periodic outbreaks of local violence and endemic hostility between landlord and cultivator, both of which increased in the decades before the Birsa rising.

In addition to mounting rent and service demands, a second and even more serious threat to the Mundas appeared in the second half of the nineteenth century—the possibility of the complete loss of their lands to alien intruders.[74] In the British period Munda cultivators became peripherally involved in the cash-nexus market economy that was slowly gaining a foothold in the Chota Nagpur highland frontier. Increasingly Mundas paid their rents in cash rather than produce. In doing so they became more and more dependent on Hindu and Muslim moneylenders for loans to purchase farm implements or to tide them over the slack season. The vagaries of an uncertain monsoon, poor and undependable yields, and Munda ignorance of the meaning of loan contracts and consequent improvidence contributed to widespread indebtedness. Debts led to court actions instigated by merchants or moneylenders and, in many cases, to the alienation of Munda lands. Families and at times whole villages were displaced. One of the least discussed but most ominous trends in the late nineteenth-century Chota Nagpur was the substitution of Hindu for Munda tenants. Landless Hindu cultivators often agreed to pay higher rents than the Mundas, who bitterly resented making any payments on lands that their ancestors had occupied for centuries. At the same time the Mundas were forced further into market involvement by the colonial government's reservation of vast forest areas from which the highland peoples had customarily obtained free fuel, building materials, and lands for grazing or new settlement.

The Birsa rebellion was clearly an outgrowth and in many ways the culmination of centuries of Munda protest against the exactions of alien overlords. Many contemporary observers saw a link between Birsa and the Sardar movement of the 1880s and 1890s, whose adherents had by court action and force attempted to break the landlords' hold. In his recruiting speeches Birsa promised that rents would be abolished, that the forests would again be open for Munda use, that Mundas would again hold their lands free, and that all of the money in the world would turn to water.

Birsa's disciples repeatedly justified their calls for violent action by citing landlord exactions, land alienation, and the economic distress of the Munda people.[75]

In contrast to the extractive system which developed in Chota Nagpur, where the Mundas faced a blend of tribute and cash rent demands and a baneful involvement in the marketplace, the Maoris in New Zealand were confronted with an advancing tide of European settlers who sought the outright control of their ancestral lands. By the mid-1850s, many Maori leaders were grimly determined to prevent the further alienation of their people's lands, which came to be viewed as the central symbol of their identity as a people. More than any other cause, land alienation to European settlers led to the bloody wars of the early 1860s. Maori setbacks in these struggles led in turn to the rise and spread of the Pai Maire movement.

It was no accident that the Maoris focused on the land issue in their long overdue confrontation with the colonial government and immigrant settlers. The Maori treasured the land as their "mother" —the source of their sustenance and tribal prestige. As one prominent authority has observed:

To the settlers land was money; but to the Maoris it was life itself and more. It is impossible to exaggerate their love for their tribal lands, scene of a thousand ancestral deeds or ancient legends which were recounted endlessly and in loving detail in the houses of learning and on the village *marae* [greens].[76]

In the colonial period the extensive involvement of Maoris in cash crop production for the European settlements and overseas export greatly increased the real economic worth of their lands. In the early decades of contact, they had willingly given up their claims to large tracts of land in exchange for guns, blankets, and baubles. As European settlers began to immigrate in large numbers, however, the Maoris came to recognize the possibility that they might soon resemble—in the words of one of their most influential chiefs, Wiremu Kingi—"sea birds with no resting place."[77] Consequently, they grew increasingly reluctant to part with their ancestral holdings.

The Maori leaders who led the campaign to end the sale of tribal lands faced obstacles so formidable that peaceful approaches to the European settlers soon proved untenable.[78] Despite guarantees in the treaty of Waitangi that Maori land rights would be protected by the colonial government, from the early 1840s British administrators pursued policies that promoted the alienation of large tracts to European settlers. They also set aside additional areas as government reserves. Through most of the period from 1840 to the early 1860s, government officials alone were allowed to buy land directly from the Maoris. Although this policy achieved a semblance of control over land sales and in some cases protected the Maoris, it generally worked against their interests. Badgered and bribed by determined settlers, government agents generally promoted Maori land sales. Agents frequently recognized offers by individual Maoris that clearly violated tribal custom. The government bought the land for a pittance and resold it to European settlers at much higher prices. The margin of profit was supposed to go into a fund to finance education, communications development, and other benefits in the Maori areas. In fact, few of these profits were channeled into projects promoting Maori welfare. Understandably the Maoris came to equate government demands with settler desires for their lands. This supposition appeared to be confirmed by the fact that the so-called protectors of the Maori "aboriginals" were also the chief government purchasing agents of Maori lands. Not surprisingly most of the land which the Maoris sold found its way into the hands of the European settlers.

Maori dismay at government duplicity and the unchecked advance of the settlers was further aggravated in the late 1850s by a serious depression in the export market for agricultural produce. This slump was the first major setback for many Maori subtribes or *hapus* which had so eagerly participated in the market economy that the Europeans had extended to New Zealand. It also increased European demands for land, because many European settlers shifted from grain production to sheep grazing, which was vastly more land consuming.[79] Maori setbacks and frustrations came to a head in the late 1850s in a dispute over the sale of land in the Waitara area of Taranaki. A minor chief offered a large tract of land for sale over the opposition of most of his tribe and his superior chief. Government ignorance and miscalculations in handling this dispute triggered a decade of wars that began in 1860.[80]

Land losses were the key grievance that drove the Maoris to open warfare, and land confiscation·, as reprisals for Maori outbreaks were a direct cause of the Pai Maire movement that emerged from early Maori defeats. As many writers have argued, the confiscations were exactly the worst measure the colonial authorities could have adopted in their efforts to pacify the Maoris. They merely confirmed Maori suspicions that the Europeans were out to destroy them completely.[81] Grievances related to the land question dominated the causes for rebellion cited by adherents of the Pai Maire movement in speeches at the mock trial of the captured missionary, Volkner, and in recruiting rituals and rebel war chants, which linked the preservation of ancestral lands to the very existence of the Maori people.[82]

Despite repeated official denials[83] grievances related to land tenure and taxation were also important determinants of the widespread support that Saya San's rebellion received from Burman peasants in the early 1930s. Government arguments that the rebellion broke out before the Great Depression had begun to affect Burma's economy seriously, ignored severe agrarian problems that had been growing in intensity and scale for decades.[84] More than in any of the other cases considered, the crisis in Burma was the crisis of a market economy based on smallholder production. Lower Burma, where most of the risings were concentrated, was the epitome of a laissez-faire, capitalist-colonial enclave. Despite the great efforts of British administrators in the late nineteenth century to build a peasant proprietor-based system that would secure the welfare of the great majority of the population, no effective safeguards had been built into the system to cope with market fluctuations or other dislocations. Because British administrators failed to encourage effectively the diversification of the Delta's growing economy, it proved extremely vulnerable to the vagaries of the world market. The Delta's rice-export, monocultural base also meant that economic disruptions would have unfavorable effects on most sectors of the colonial society. Therefore, when cheap, unoccupied lands began to run out in the 1890s and market slumps and rice millers' cartels began to reduce cultivators' returns, the small-holder system gradually gave way to an economy dominated by milling and shipping interests, landlords and land speculators, rice merchants, and moneylenders. Well before the first outbreak of the Saya San disturbances, chronic indebtedness, land alienation, and the spread of tenancy had deprived a substantial portion of Delta cultivators of their land, their hopes for advancement, and the profits of their labors.

Although no district figures for agrarian debt were regularly compiled in the decade before the Saya San rebellion, a special enquiry committee estimated that the total debt of the Burmese peasantry had grown to between 500 and 600 million rupees by

1929. The plight of individual cultivators was indicated by special surveys taken by the same committee. They revealed that less than 30 per cent of the indebted agriculturists in Lower Burma could repay their loans within a year of the season in which they were taken. Of the remaining cultivators in debt, 55 percent owed amounts ranging from one-half to the total value of their holdings, while 15 percent had debts which exceeded the total value of their holdings.[85] The heavy indebtedness of the Burmese peasant often caused him to lose his land through foreclosure on the mortgage which he had used as security for loans. As credit tightened in the late 1920s in response to worsening market conditions, the number of foreclosures rose sharply. By June 1930, 21 percent of the crop-producing land of Burma was in the hands of nonagriculturists. In the Lower Burma districts where major Saya San risings were concentrated, the incidence of alienation was considerably higher, averaging 31 percent. In addition, serious anti-Indian assaults accompanied the rebellion in districts where large tracts of land had been alienated to Indian moneylenders.[86] Because many peasants rented land from other agriculturists, the percentage of land actually worked by tenants exceeded that which had been alienated. The average amount of land for the whole province of Burma let at full, fixed rents was 27 percent, while the average for Lower Burma districts involved in the Saya San disturbances was over 50 percent.

Living and working conditions among tenants and laborers in the Delta also fueled the discontent that enabled Saya San to forge a major rebellion. A government enquiry in Lower Burma in 1924 revealed that the tenants in the Tharrawaddy District, where the initial risings took place, were among the most oppressed in Burma. It was found that rental rates in the district were among the highest in the province, approaching 50 percent of the gross output in the townships that first rose in revolt. The report also revealed that Tharrawaddy landlords seldom gave remissions in bad years and that they manipulated rent collections in order to extract the maximum rates from their tenants. In the neighboring district of Insein, where the revolt spread rapidly after the first outbreaks in Tharrawaddy, rents were nearly as high as in Tharrawaddy and relations between landlords and tenants were extremely tense. In the Dedaye area of the Pyapon District, where one of the largest risings of the Saya San rebellion occurred, the rent rates were second only to Tharrawaddy.[87] It is important to note that these observations were made in the first half of the 1920s during a short-

term upswing in the export market that generally improved economic conditions in the Delta. In the last half of the decade world
demand and the price for rice again declined, so that the situation
of smallholders, tenants, and laborers in Lower Burma can only
have worsened. In the Dedaye area of Pyapon, a high percentage
of the cultivated land was lost to Indian moneylenders during the
1920s. Many of the villagers who supported the major rising in this
area were deeply in debt to these moneylenders and two of the
main leaders were former tenants who had been ejected by Indian
landlords.[88]

As the economic position and standard of living of the cultivating classes of Lower Burma deteriorated, there was growing
resentment among peasants of taxes imposed by the colonial government. In the late nineteenth century, decades of growth and
general prosperity, taxes took only a small share of the cultivator's
income. As the cultivator's income declined and the demands of
moneylenders and merchants mounted, however, taxes became an
increasing burden, even though the actual rate of tax increases
scarcely kept pace with price inflation in the early decades of the
twentieth century. Interestingly, peasant opposition to taxation in
Lower Burma was focused on the head tax, which was a pittance
compared with the share of their income claimed by land taxes.
Among landless laborers, who had no property to be taxed, this
response was understandable. It is less comprehensible among
small landholders struggling to make ends meet or among the
growing number of tenants who paid the taxes on the lands they
worked. Part of the explanation lies in the fact that the Burmans
had traditionally regarded the payment of the head tax as an ac-
knowledgement of the legitimacy of the government that collected
it. In addition, peasants especially resented the head tax because it
was levied in the months before the harvest when they were most
pressed for money. Thus, to pay it they often had to borrow and go
more deeply into debt.[89]

The strong resistance to this particular levy was to some extent
a sign of the growing political awareness and militancy of the Burman peasantry in the 1920s and 1930s. The village associations or
Wunthanu Athins, which were established by the General Council
of Burmese Associations beginning in 1921 as part of an effort
to broaden the base of the Burmese nationalist movement, seized
on the head tax issue as a means of inciting peasant agitation
in many areas. Athin-sponsored, antihead tax campaigns, which
erupted in the mid- and late 1920s, led to confrontations between

government troops and peasants in a number of Delta districts. In several places government troops brutally suppressed antitax campaigns by burning villages and forcibly removing their peasant supporters.[90] A number of writers have argued that Saya San's decision to begin plotting rebellion was made when a special inquiry that he headed on behalf of the So Thein branch of the GCBA revealed police excesses committed in the repression of the antihead tax campaigns.[91]

Rebel leaders and their supporters often cited taxes and the economic plight of the cultivating classes to justify their violent protest. On the eve of the Tharrawaddy rising, the peasants of the affected townships presented the acting Governor of Burma with a petition that listed a number of complaints including the burden of the capitation tax, widespread indebtedness and land alienation, and the worsening condition of the great majority of the rural population.[92] In a speech which reportedly incited the Dedaye rising, Saya San denounced the high taxes that continued to be levied despite the general depression of the paddy market. On other occasions he declared that the coming struggle would be for the "prosperity of the nation" and a means by which "poor people" might escape the "trouble and misery" that had resulted from the price slump and burdens like the head tax.[93] Rebel leaders linked revolt with the head tax issue in proclamations in many districts and in postrebellion trial statements made regarding their motives for joining the movement. A number of Saya San's lieutenants sought to recruit followers by promising that there would be lower taxes and that debts to Indian moneylenders would be cancelled if the revolt succeeded. Several government officials readily conceded that taxes and economic conditions generally had contributed to the rapid spread of the rebellion.[94] In the new kingdom that Saya San promised to establish, landlords, taxes, debts, and market fluctuations would be unknown and an imagined precolonial age of arcadian bliss would be restored.

Extraction, Ethnic Hostility, and Relative Deprivation

In recent decades something of a consensus has emerged among students of revolutionary movements that sheer oppression and grinding poverty do not necessarily drive men to rebellion. Though they may join spontaneous food riots or commit criminal acts, people who face starvation are too busy just surviving to plot the overthrow of governments or to formulate blueprints for alternative social orders.[95] The movements considered here support this proposition and the assertion that the potential for violent social protest corresponds to relative rather than absolute deprivation. None of the groups which supported the rebellions under study was reduced to starvation or total impoverishment, but all had suffered significant declines in their social standing and economic well-being. The Matumbi, Ngindo, Mundas, and Javanese experienced deprivation relative to conditions in the precolonial period, when the absence or weakness of central administrative control meant that the exactions of local and town-based elites were relatively light and frequently evaded. In each of these cases European colonial overlords, through the application of superior military and communications technology, were able to increase the demands made on their peasant subjects in terms of labor services and the amount of produce extracted. Under colonial rule, economic frameworks oriented to self-sufficience were retained, and the Europeans acted indirectly through intermediaries, both indigenous and immigrant non-Europeans. Peasant resentment resulted in part from new or excessive demands, but equally important were changes in tribute exactions which brought the cultivating classes only increased burdens and no meaningful material or status rewards. Mobility was generally downward for peasant groups, and they frequently labored under conditions that blatantly defied indigenous notions of reasonable demands.

The Maori and the Burman peasant experienced deprivation relative to two previous states—an idealized precolonial past and a period of relative prosperity during earlier stages of colonial rule. Those Maoris who survived the disastrous initial decades of European contact enjoyed in the early 1830s a period notable for their successful participation in the European-introduced market economy, and their apparently profitable adoption of aspects of Christian thought and European organizational patterns. This period of growth and adjustment was followed by a serious erosion of Maori gains beginning in the mid-1850s, when market outlets for their crops contracted and the tide of European settlement swept relentlessly across their ancestral lands. For the Burmans the period of solvency and economic gain was considerably longer than for the Maoris, extending roughly from the 1860s to the late 1890s, and the breakdown of the smallholder economy of the Delta was also more gradual. The Burman decline, however, accelerated in the years just before the Saya San risings. A majority of the Burman cultivating classes lost their solvency and the lands that they or their ancestors had claimed from jungle wilderness. They were also deprived of the opportunities for economic and social advance that had developed in the highly mobile society that grew up in the early decades of colonial rule, when able landless laborers could rise to the status of large landholders.[96] Thus, for both the Maori and the Burmans their setbacks were doubly disappointing. They had adjusted to new socioeconomic orders, but these seemed increasingly to work against them for reasons which they could not be expected to comprehend fully. In making their initial adjustments, they had weakened or sacrificed much of the precolonial order. As their positions worsened, they came to view the exchange of customary for imported systems as unsatisfactory.

Although the systems of extraction employed and the nature of the dislocations engendered varied in each of the cases considered, the end result in all instances was similar. Colonization led to serious disruption of the village units and kin-linked systems that regulated the lives and set the standards for the great majority of the colonized peoples. Despite recent well-argued objections to the frequently assumed view that the customary peasant village was characterized by communal harmony and contentment,[97] there is little question that the advance of the colonial order severely weakened, and in some cases destroyed, peasant mechanisms for maintaining community cohesion and security. In all cases local leaders were co-opted or replaced by outsiders amenable to the dictates of the central authorities. Thus the local community lost the buffers against outside exploitation that it had once enjoyed as a result of its effective autonomy and the strong bargaining position of local leaders vis-à-vis government functionaries. Among the Matumbi and Ngindo, the clans that comprised their pivotal social institution were rent by divisions. They were also severely weakened by suspicions of their leaders, whose prestige declined as their military outlets were curtailed and their ability to protect their kinsmen diminished. Different challenges had similar effects on the Maori tribal and *hapu* units and the Munda village communities, whose weakening position can be traced primarily to the increasing inability of local leaders to regulate land tenure. In Lower Burma once viable kinship-linked hamlets were replaced by arbitrarily demarcated village units. Customary checks on individual behavior and enriching and integrating religious ceremonies lost their meaning in villages over much of the Delta where the population was ethnically diverse, multi-religious, and highly mobile. The local unit fared best in central Java, but even there attempts by outside agents to displace or co-opt leaders and regulate land tenure signaled the beginning of a period of perilous transitions.[98]

Community cohesion and social control mechanisms were the most seriously weakened in New Zealand and Lower Burma, where there was extensive involvement in a market economy. New standards of success and achievement, which stressed competition and accumulation, gradually supplanted customary values that placed a premium on mutual help, minimum subsistence for all community members, and in-group solidarity. The sentimental and social significance of land faded, as it came increasingly to be regarded as a commodity to be bought and sold.[99] As long as the market demand held and cultivators could obtain consumer rewards and attain higher status by devoting their leisure time or extra man hours to market production, these new relationships and measures of morality and behavior were rarely questioned. When the market slumped and the flow of material rewards slackened, the peasant was left stranded between badly battered customary norms that could no longer effectively regulate community affairs, and bits and pieces of an alien, new order that lacked meaningful standards for social interaction.

The peasants and indigenous elites of the societies considered here also experienced deprivation relative to benefits gained by the alien agents of the colonial order. In this regard, non-European immigrants were in all cases, but the Maori, resented as much as or more than the actual European overlords. These groups and not just the Europeans played major roles as the agents of culture contact and accelerated change.[100] Their prominent roles in the colonial systems under study and the fact that they were singled out as major targets of rebel assaults call into question the emphasis placed by many writers on the anti-European character of social protest in colonial situations. This emphasis is rooted in a simplistic view of colonial systems that failed to take into account the power and influence exercised by non-European immigrants as well as by indigenous allies of the European overlords.

Swahili *akidas* were the immediate and direct oppressors of most of the peoples who initiated the Maji Maji movement. They gave the orders, administered the floggings, and openly enjoyed the fruits of the cultivators' labors; and they either fled or paid with their lives once the revolt was underway. In Java, Chinese merchants and toll keepers were major targets on rebel assaults. In Chota Nagpur, Hindu and Muslim landlords and policemen, and not British administrators, were the main culprits in the eyes of the rebellious Mundas. In Burma anti-Indian riots in Rangoon pre-ceded the Saya San rebellion, and after the initial outbreaks, com-munal disturbances spread across the rural Delta and into Upper Burma. Indian landlords, merchants, and moneylenders were fa-vorite targets, but impoverished Indian tenants and laborers, who were highly resented because of their competition for scarce jobs, were also beaten and killed.[101] In New Zealand, European settlers posed more direct threats to the Maori than non-European interme-diaries might have done. The settlers, particularly landless squat-ters and the urban poor, made no secret of their contempt for the Maoris, whose resentment of their mistreatment by government officials was heightened by frequent allusions to their "savage natures," "grotesque" customs, and the alleged filth of their bodies and settlements.[102]

As these examples illustrate, the "racial" or ethnic hostility that has often been associated with revitalization movements among colonized peoples[103] is inseparably linked to the fact that in colo-nial societies power was monopolized by and most of the economic benefits went to the European rulers and their immigrant, and at times indigenous, allies.[104] All of the rebellions considered aimed at ending this state of affairs. This goal was to be pursued not through gradual reform or the extensive adoption of attributes that had made for European dominance but by the violent destruction of the colonial order and its agents. The fact that in every case the condition of the colonized peoples appeared to be steadily worsening gave credence to the argument voiced by rebel leaders that immediate and decisive remedial action must be taken. In the colonial context, the ruled could act quickly and decisively only through violence.

THREE

An Absence of Alternatives

Cultural confrontations and sources of deprivation similar to those described in the preceding chapters could be found in many, if not all, European colonial societies. Deprivation is widespread and its existence does not necessarily lead to social protest.[1] Therefore, in evaluating the factors that have given rise to prophetic rebellions, a number of additional questions need to be posed. These questions concern the leaders, techniques, and events that transformed amorphous discontent into directed protest movements. Why were prophetic and millennial solutions adopted? Why did dissident groups turn to violence? How did the rebels' leaders mobilize and organize them for revolt? These closely related problems have often been neglected in studies of revitalization movements or confused with attempts to identify causes for discontent. Each of the remaining chapters will be devoted to an analysis of the issues raised by these questions. Before turning to that analysis, however, potential alternative responses need to be examined because the mode of expression that was adopted by dissident groups was to a significant degree determined by the absence of other viable options. Although the alternatives to prophetic rebellion that I will examine by no means exhaust the conceivable options available to the discontented, they represent the major avenues of grievance redress that were actually explored in one or more of the areas under study. I will consider other alternatives, like banditry and nonmillennial violent resistance, when I deal with the question of why force was ultimately employed by the groups in protest.

In all of the cases considered, protest options available to aggrieved groups were limited by their lack of traditions of large-scale political organization and popular agitation above the village level. Even in societies like those in Burma and Java, where there had been considerable centralization in the precolonial era, a person's self-identification and loyalties were primarily locally focused, personalist, and based on kinship ties. Popular political participation was present in differing degrees in all of the societies considered, but it was confined primarily to one's village or kin unit. Although all the peoples considered, except those who supported the Maji Maji revolt, had some sense of broader ethnic and cultural identity, this had not resulted in precolonial institutions promoting sustained or widespread mass mobilization or even interregional awareness. The Europeans' manipulation of particularistic allegiances both facilitated their conquest and proved an essential prop for the colonial regimes they established.

Since the great majority of potential recruits in each case were disgruntled cultivators, barriers to mobilization were compounded by a number of obstacles which have been associated with peasant societies in general. The peasant's deeply entrenched ties to a particular plot of land or his dependence on a particular patron-landlord; his sense of belonging primarily to family, kin, and village units; and his suspicion of all that lay beyond the village perimeter had to be overcome if substantial scale were to be achieved in these movements of protest. The peasant's potential for mobilization was also limited by what has been termed the "tyranny of his work,"[2] which was tied to the seasonal routine of the cropping cycle. If the cyclical pattern of planting and harvest were altered or disrupted, starvation could and often did result for both the peasant and his dependents. The importance of this obstacle can be dramatically illustrated by cases of peasant-based armies of resistance or rebellion which have simply melted away when the time came to return home for planting or harvest.[3]

Though these obstacles were formidable, too much can be made of the peasant's "limited horizons" or his lack of contact with events beyond his village or kin group. In all of the societies considered—and in fact in peasant societies generally—local and regional markets, itinerant merchants and craft specialists, oracle and temple centers, and intercommunity marriage links combined to provide channels through which news was transmitted and reactions conveyed. In addition, geographical and in some cases vertical mobility on the part of peasants increased their contacts beyond their home villages. Among the Maori and Mundas, missionaries and mission stations also provided centers for disseminating news. When the rebellions considered occurred, however, these channels of communication had not yet given rise to ongoing organizations or effective methods by which peasant sentiments could be voiced and peasant needs satisfied. These had yet to be developed, and the nature of colonial administrative responses and the absence or ineffectiveness of Western-educated, indigenous elite groups had much to do with a reliance upon millenarian modes of expression.

Unresponsive Bureaucracies

However much colonial bureaucrats may have professed and even sincerely believed that they acted mainly in the interests of their colonial subjects, with rare exceptions they proved incapable of understanding or responding effectively to their needs. In part this inability can be attributed to vast cultural differences between ruler and subject, which prevailing notions of European superiority in the era of high colonialism gave the European civil servant little impetus to surmount. In addition colonial administrators were by definition committed to global political and economic systems geared primarily to the interests of the colonizers and only incidentally to those of the colonial peoples. As the cases examined have amply illustrated, the Europeans also very often ruled through immigrant minority groups or co-opted indigenous elites, whose interests were best served by European indifference to and ignorance of local affairs. In colonies such as New Zealand where there were substantial numbers of vocal and influential white settlers, the ability of European administrators to respond decisively to the needs of the indigenous peoples was perhaps the most severely impaired. The inability of colonial bureaucracies to respond effectively to the problems of their non-European subjects forced even well-meaning administrators to concentrate on the detection and suppression of resistance and unrest, rather than acting to remedy the grievances which had given rise to it.[4]

In each of the cases considered the reasons for colonial administrative impotence varied, although a number of central patterns can be discerned. A sheer lack of trained manpower was critical in German east Africa, Java, and the highlands of east-central India. German administrators in east Africa were both individually inexperienced and collectively lacked a body of precedents, policies, and traditions that older imperialist powers like Britain and France had built up through decades of experience. Neglect of the southeast, combined with regulations like that forbidding German administrators to sleep away from district headquarters without permission, left the Germans profoundly ignorant of the customs and desires of the peoples they claimed to rule. This ignorance made them oblivious to the impact of the policies which they formulated largely in response to external demands.[5] Thus, there were no knowledgeable or trusted district officials to whom the aggrieved Matumbi, Ngindo, or other peoples could appeal. Virtually all contact with the colonial regime was through Swahili *akidas* or

mercenary *askaris*. The colonized peoples regarded these intermediaries as alien and corrupt oppressors from whom no hope of a
fair hearing, much less effective action, was to be expected on their
behalf.

In Java the transition to a new generation of career officers in
the first decades of the nineteenth century contributed to a growing insensitivity on the part of the Dutch to Javanese customs and
an inability to intelligently supervise affairs in the princely states.
With regard to the origins of the Dipanagara rebellion, these failings
were exacerbated by the frequently noted ineptness, and at times
corruption, of many Dutch civil servants who were given key positions at the court of Yogyakarta in the decade prior to the revolt.[6]
For Javanese princes and administrators, on the other hand, effective authority and determined action were steadily diminished.
They struggled to function within a political system that was increasingly controlled by outsiders, riddled with excessive corruption, and routinely manipulated by self-seeking Dutch, Chinese,
and indigenous officials. The dispossessed or cheated found that
customary relationships, Islamic laws, and indigenous (*adat*)
regulations were all dead ends. The Dutch cared little for these
potential avenues of redress, and concerned Javanese princes and
officials no longer had the power to give them meaningful executive support. As noted in chapter 2, Dipanagara and those who
shared his views were deprived of effective power by the machina-
tions of the Chancellor Danureja and his clique. Dipanagara's
relations with Dutch officials were at best strained. Dutch courts,
like that established at Semarang for the adjudication of disputes
related to the toll system, provided virtually no avenues of redress.
They were expensive, time-consuming, and run on legal principles
that were alien to the Javanese—noble and peasant alike.[7]

In Chota Nagpur the British attempted to maintain a system of
indirect rule, with many of the same unfortunate results found in
German East Africa and central Java. In Chota Nagpur, however,
the indigenous landlord elite maintained its power and preroga-
tives more successfully than did the Ngindo *jumbes* or Javanese
nobility. They were able to frustrate virtually all attempts on the
part of the British to improve the conditions of the Mundas or
other highland groups.[8] Not only did the British confirm the positions of the Hindu and Muslim adversaries of the Mundas, they
also brought in additional administrators, judges, and policemen

from the lowlands. The collusion of these immigrants with the Raja and landed elite of Chota Nagpur was both natural and highly profitable. The British left local administration and police control largely in the hands of the landlords and their retainers, although a nominally independent constabulary was finally established in 1863. Civil and criminal courts were introduced in the early decades of British rule, but these consistently served the interests of the landlords, who could afford the lawyers and timely bribes that insured victory over any cultivator audacious enough to bring suit. Since the legal statutes themselves heavily favored men of property and alien judges were notoriously ignorant of conditions in the hill frontier areas, court hearings were frequently reduced to farcical parodies of the Western judicial process. Individual Mundas did not have the resources to engage in prolonged litigation. When they banded together, they invariably fell into the clutches of fast-talking barristers from Calcutta, who took their money and then performed poorly in court (leading one to suspect that they too had been bought off). Thus, the Mundas often lost their lands or rights and fell deeply into debt as a result of legal actions. They understandably came to view the courts as "instruments of oppression (rather) than justice."[9] Their reverses served only to intensify their bitterness and frustration. The strong hold maintained by the Raja and the landlord elite over the police, administration, and judiciary in Chota Nagpur made a mockery of British legislation pertaining to the area. Despite several much-touted inquiries, elaborate legal codes, and volumes of regulations, the colonial administration had taken virtually no effective measures to bolster the position of the Munda cultivator in the century before the Birsa rising.

In New Zealand a combination of settler influence and official duplicity and ineptness were largely responsible for the adversary relationship that dominated the contacts between colonial administrators and the Maoris during the years of crisis from the late 1850s through the 1860s. The ill-effects of the misguided land policies discussed above were exacerbated by the fact that the colonial regime spent little on educational, economic, or political institutions which might have eased the Maoris' adjustment to the European-dominated order. The administrative departments in charge of Maori affairs remained understaffed, and their employees were poorly paid, badly trained, and limited largely to petty functions.[10] As a result, the Maoris had little opportunity to master the wide range of skills that were essential if they were to compete successfully with the white settlers. The pitiful share of the colonial budget devoted to Maori improvement contrasted ironically with the large share of government revenues contributed by the Maoris in the 1850s. In the middle of that decade, for example, the Maoris paid an estimated 50 percent of the customs revenue and provided most of the land revenue. Yet, on the average, less than 5 percent of the colonial budget was set aside for projects in Maori areas.[11]

In New Zealand, as in Algeria and other colonial societies where there were sizable European immigrant minorities, European settlers strove to dominate the administration and to monopolize parliamentary outlets. The legislature was from the outset the pre- serve of the white settlers; it acted more as a lobby promoting settler interests in British official circles than as a body representing the peoples of New Zealand as a whole. Before the 1860s, the Maoris had no seats in the legislature, no votes in elections, and little say in policy formulation. When Maori leaders attempted to draw attention to their peoples' needs, they were given scant respect by government officials. In the mid-1850s, for example, Winemu Tamihana, an intelligent and well-educated Maori chief, traveled to the capital at Auckland to present his proposals for the creation of a Maori parliament to the governor. The petty offi- cials who arranged the governor's appointments refused to allow Tamihana to see him or any other important leader. They rudely dismissed the influential chief with mutterings about "bloody savages."[12]

The government also failed to keep its frequent promises to set aside secure reserves for the Maoris. Although European officials made some contributions as mediators of Maori disputes in the 1840s and 1850s, the government did not establish adequate judi- cial or police agencies in the areas of Maori settlement. The Maoris were subjected to alien laws that they could not read, much less understand. Efforts to introduce self-administration among the Maoris were frustrated by settler opposition, official indecision and ineptitude, and a persistent refusal by the Europeans to allocate the necessary resources to these projects.[13]

Despite the existence of an adequately staffed and well-trained bureaucracy in Lower Burma, the British colonial regime failed to prevent the disintegration of the smallholder-based export economy which had been so carefully fashioned in the late nineteenth cen- tury. Commitment to a laissez-faire political economy and the opposition of powerful mercantile and landlord interest groups explain in part why the government failed to bolster the sagging position of the Delta cultivating classes in the early decades of the twentieth century. Inertia and a dearth of tested remedies also played a role. In addition, as many volumes of government documents amply testify, most British officials either did not recognize or refused to admit the gravity of the crisis which overtook Burma. After the failure of efforts between 1890 and 1914 by a handful of knowledgeable revenue officials to pass legislation to protect the cultivating classes,[14] the government of Burma did virtually nothing to avert the breakdown of the rice economy and Delta society as a whole. As in Chota Nagpur and New Zealand, the Western-style legal system dutifully installed by the colonial overlords offered little solace for cultivators and urban laborers. These groups were too poor to afford lawyers and court fees and ignorant of their rights and how to protect them. Power and influence were held by Western and Indian rice mill owners and merchants and by Indian and Burmese landlords and moneylenders who benefited from the weak position of the laboring classes. The colonial bureaucracy continued to function impressively by standards set in the late nineteenth-century boom decades. As a handful of critics argued at the time, however, it had become a rigid and unresponsive machine unable to comprehend or alleviate the sufferings of the peoples it was supposed to govern.

The Failure of Constitutional Agitation

In only two of the five cases examined was it possible for aggrieved groups to seek relief through constitutional agitation. At the time of the east African and Javanese rebellions, legislatures, vernacular newspapers, and Western-educated nationalist elites had not yet come into being. Techniques of constitutional agitation such as economic boycotts and mass rallies were still unknown. Although the nationalist movement had already taken root in India at the time of the Birsa disturbances in the late 1890s, it was largely irrelevant to the Mundas. Indian nationalism was and would remain concentrated in the lowlands, spearheaded by Western-educated Hindu and Muslim elite groups. Up to the time of the Birsa revolt, these groups had shown scant interest in the plight of even the lowland cultivators, who were their coreligionists and potential base of mass support. It is not surprising then that they displayed no concern whatever for the welfare of distant Munda "aboriginals." During the "study club" phase of nationalist development, the lawyers, landlords, and schoolteachers who made up the bulk of the membership in political organizations in India were mainly interested in promoting their own rights and socioeconomic advancement.[15] The Sardar movement, which was the focal point of Munda constitutional agitation in the decades before the rise of Birsa, relied in part on petitions to the government and widely publicized court cases to dramatize landlord abuses. The Sardars, however, did little to advance the Munda cause, because of poor and inexperienced leadership, lack of familiarity with European procedures and institutions, overstated demands, and a haphazard use of force that alienated potential supporters among both the Christian missionaries and European colonial officials.[16]

Rebuffed and cheated by the colonial authorities and excluded from the New Zealand legislature by the white settlers, the Maoris became acutely aware of the pressing need for unity and political organizations to represent their interests. This awareness gave rise in the late 1850s to the Maori King movement. The chief aims of the Kingites were to forge ongoing intertribal links through an elected king and a representative assembly that would formulate policy and bargain for the Maori people as a whole.[17] The founders of the movement were mainly mission-educated chiefs who both imitated European institutions (king and parliament) and drew upon Maori precedents, such as the *runanga* or traditional assembly of the subtribe which was to be expanded into a transtribal delegate assembly. The Kingites initially made their demands, which were focused on issues related to the loss of Maori lands to European settlers, in petitions to and audiences with government officials. Its founders viewed the movement as one that would employ peaceful persuasion and constitutional maneuvers, rather than violence or threats of war. However, the realities of communal hostility and power politics in the colony frustrated their intentions.

Many colonial officials feared the Kingite party, denounced it as treasonous, and demanded that it be put down with force. Others ridiculed Maori attempts to adopt European techniques and dismissed them, in the words of the bungling Governor Gore Browne, as "child's play."[18] In the face of such opposition Maori efforts made little headway. Government officials continued to sell Maori lands to European settlers, and the colonial legislature became even more strident in its demands and effective in wresting concessions from weary colonial officials. Equally ominously, the Kingite efforts to unite the Maoris failed; the tribes split into factions of those who supported and those who strongly opposed the movement. Earlier divisions between individual *hapus* and tribes were enlarged into hostile multitribal confrontations. Intermittent violence between Kingite and anti-Kingite factions erupted in the decades before the outbreak of the Waikato wars. In part, the Pai Maire ideology was designed to bridge these differences, but its failure was dramatically demonstrated by the considerable assistance provided by anti-Kingite tribes in the suppression of the Maori risings of the 1860s.

Due to the fact that the Saya San rising was the latest of the movements considered here to occur, the potential for successful constitutional agitation was the strongest in the Burman case. By the first decades of the twentieth century, well-established nationalist organizations led by articulate and influential Western-educated Burmese landlords and professionals had emerged in Rangoon and other urban centers. There were also legislative bodies in which Burmese representation was steadily growing, numerous vernacular newspapers, and abundant precedents and some direct support from the larger nationalist movement in India. As noted in chapter 2, some factions of Burmese nationalists had begun to campaign for rural support in the early 1920s. Saya San himself had for a time been a member of one of the splinter parties of the General Council of Burmese Associations. Many of the leaders of the local risings that made up the Saya San movement were members of the nationalist-inspired village *wunthanu athins*. Finally, one of the key motivations among those who supported Saya San's rebellion—the defense and restoration of Buddhism—was also a rallying cry of the major nationalist parties. Despite these promising developments, before the 1930–1932 outbreaks Burmese nationalists had achieved virtually nothing in the way of social reform or relief for the agrarian classes. The administrative inertia discussed above was partly responsible for the meager results of nationalist agitation, but the most fundamental cause was the character of nationalist leadership and organization in the decades before the rebellion.

Although Burmese nationalism had begun to move beyond the "study club" stage by the 1920s, its base remained primarily urban and limited to a small percentage of the colonial population. Except during brief flurries of popular unrest, most nationalist leaders were too embroiled in constitutional issues and bitter factional fights to give adequate attention to the problems that concerned the great majority of the people. Their lack of concern for peasant problems is strikingly illustrated by their failure to seriously consider, much less pass, any agrarian legislation until after the Saya San rebellion. Although dynamic *pongyi*-politicians like U Ottama and U Wizaya were able to generate considerable mass enthusiasm, they had neither the coherent programs nor the organizational backing needed to effect significant reforms. Their fiery political styles and the adulation they received from crowds of peasants and laborers rendered them suspect in the eyes of more moderate Burmese nationalist leaders, who dominated the administrative and legislative positions open to the colonized.[19] Although *pongyi*-politicians and the leaders of the *athin* organizations strove throughout the 1920s to arouse the consciousness of Burman agriculturists and to organize them for effective agitation, their efforts met with little success. Antitax campaigns were repressed, petitions were conveniently lost in the maze of the colonial bureaucracy, and seemingly endless proposals for agrarian reform came to nothing. *Pongyi* and *athin* agitation finally served only to heighten peasant frustration and resentment by arousing expectations that neither group had the means to satisfy.

Reform efforts by many Burmese urban politicians were also discouraged by their vested interest in the status quo. Some leaders were landlords or the heirs of landlords, rice brokers, and moneylenders. Others depended on Indian mercantile interests for financial support for their splinter parties.[20] Whatever the reasons, Burmese nationalism and constitutional agitation provided so little relief for the cultivating classes in the 1920s that Saya San left one of the most radical nationalist factions—the So Thein GCBA—to mount a very different sort of movement from that envisioned by urban politicians. His call to revolt and millennial transformations attracted many peasant representatives of the only meaningful nationalist network that had been established at the village level, the *wunthanu athins*.

No Refuge in Christ

In two of the cases considered, the Munda and Maori, discontented groups sought the help of Christian missionaries in their efforts to cope with alien invaders and their imports. In Chota Nagpur the Mundas flocked to first Lutheran and later Roman Catholic missionaries in the belief that these men, whom they regarded as the guardians of the innermost secrets of white power and technological mastery, would share their secrets and help the Mundas to overcome their ancient Hindu and Muslim adversaries. Many contemporary observers commented on the clear connection in the Mundas' minds between conversion to Christianity and the struggle against the Raja and the landlords. This association was encouraged by both Protestant and Roman Catholic missionaries, who were aware of the oppression of the Mundas and sympathetic to their cause. The missionaries' support, however, was severely limited in most instances by their abhorrence of radical tactics and fear of the social unrest Munda agitators might create. Repeated missionary retreats into pious platitudes when violent confrontations threatened disenchanted the more determined Munda agitators and sent them in search of more potent allies. Ultimately, radical Munda factions like the Sardars became openly hostile to the missionaries and Munda converts who remained faithful to Christianity. Birsa and his adherents sustained this hostility despite their adoption of certain Christian beliefs and practices. They denounced Christianity as the religion of their oppressors' allies and overlords and made mission stations and missionaries major targets of the violent assaults that were to usher in the new order.[21]

Like the Mundas, many of the Maoris turned to the missionaries in search of skills that would enable them to cope with the bewildering changes that were transforming their island home. As representatives of a demonstrably more powerful god, the missionaries threatened to completely supplant the traditional Maori magico-religious practitioners or *tohungas*. However, as rebuffs at the hands of the colonial authorities multiplied and the contest with the settlers turned against them, many Maoris began to question the value of missionary assistance and to suspect that the prime loyalty of European missionaries was to other Europeans. Like the Melanesians who rejected Christian teachings for the promise of the return of their ancestors with an abundance of European goods or "cargo,"[22] the Maoris began to feel that the missionaries were not truly sharing their most potent secrets with their faithful converts. How else could they explain their continued reverses despite their worship of the Europeans' god? This suspicion was reflected in Te Ua Haumene's promise that adherence to the Pai Maire cult would bring legions of angels to teach the technical skills that the Maoris viewed as a key source of European dominance.[23]

Maori suspicions were further aroused by the fact that many missionaries openly advocated further European settlement and used their influence to facilitate the sale of Maori lands. One of the staunchest European proponents for more land concessions was the Reverend John Whitely, who had both converted and instructed the young Te Ua. The vehement opposition of many missionaries to the Kingite movement turned the doubts of many Maoris to open hostility. Maori feelings were epitomized by a contemporary anecdote which related that when the missionaries came to New Zealand they pointed to the heavens telling the Maoris to pray; while the Maoris did so, European settlers crept in and stole the earth from beneath their feet.[24] Although many of these charges were unfair to numerous missionaries who sincerely sought to promote Maori interests, the Kingites and other defiant Maoris seldom made distinctions. All of the missionaries preached a Christian morality and justice that bore little relationship to the reality of Maori contacts with the Europeans. The final break for many tribes, particularly those supporting the Maori King, came during the Waikato wars of the early 1860s, when many missionaries openly sided with the European settlers and British military forces. Some missionaries went so far as to spy on the Maoris. Others blessed the armies that marched on Maori villages and conducted services in thanksgiving for government victories. Not surprisingly, missionaries were among the victims of Pai Maire assaults, and Maoris who refused to apostasize were among the most resolute opponents of those in rebellion.[25]

Despite variations with regard to the obstacles that blocked alternative avenues of grievance redress, the groups under consideration all lacked the social and economic standing that would have given them a share of, or at least access to, political power. They had no effective ways *within the colonial system* to influence policy decisions or stimulate much-needed reforms. Displaced elite groups were by definition excluded from effective power. Co-opted leaders could do little more than obey the dictates of their superiors. Colonial officials viewed some groups, such as the threatened religious leaders of the colonized peoples, with open hostility and suspicion. The peasants, due to the erosion of local cohesion and autonomy, had even less to say in determining their destiny than they had had in the precolonial period. Unable to simply flee, as their ancestors would have done in the face of similar oppression and disruptions, the peasants endured and waited for the deliverance that their traditions told them must come.

FOUR

Prophets and Millenarian Visions

One of the standard arguments of scholars seeking to explain the occurrence of millennial movements is that they arise in societies with a tradition of such movements, or in those that have historically demonstrated a strong propensity for millenarian solutions to major crises. Initially, I assumed that this argument could explain why the disgruntled groups under consideration, finding other alternatives for the redress of their grievances blocked, turned to millenarian expression. This line of reasoning, however, proved problematical in a number of ways. A close examination of the five movements in question revealed that the assertion that millenarian expression is adopted because there is a tradition of millenarian expectation is at worst tautological and at best ex post facto. Although there were well-developed millennial currents and a succession of previous prophetic figures in three of the five areas examined—German East Africa, Burma, and Java—millennial-prophetic elements in the thought systems of the two remaining cultures were much less apparent. In Chota Nagpur and New Zealand, ideas (both indigenous and imported) and predilections that could be molded into millenarian ideologies were present, but they were diffuse and inchoate. In these cases prophetic figures consciously fashioned millenarian ideologies, which were then elaborated by their followers. In these movements, as well as the others under study, a millennial tradition alone was not enough to explain them. In each, an essential role was played by a prophetic figure who molded millennial tendencies into a persuasive ideology.

The importance of prophetic figures in leading deprived groups to turn to millenarian modes of protest may provide a solution to one of the problems that has long vexed students of revitalization movements: the failure of these movements to occur in cultures and under conditions that appear to be fertile ground for them.[1] Most of the thought patterns that have been seen to predispose diverse peoples to millenarian expression were (and are) widespread in preindustrial, prescientific cultures. Longing for a past golden age, a preoccupation with stability and consensus and an abhorrence of disruption and overt dissent, a protective rather than critical attitude toward time-honored beliefs, a time concept involving the sense that the world is winding down and must be periodically rejuvenated—all have been shown to be characteristic of numerous cultures that have undergone the shocks of European colonial expansion.[2] Yet on the basis of the evidence now available, it is clear that many, perhaps a majority, of these cultures did not respond in a prophetic-millenarian idiom. On the basis of the cases that I have examined, I would argue that to a large degree the explanation of these negative cases lies in the fact that deprivation and millennial thought tendencies are not in themselves sufficient to produce sustained social movements. Popular discontent and millenarian tendencies must be amalgamated and articulated either by a prophetic leader (or leaders) or by prominent figures in established socioreligious organizations, such as cult-shrine networks and secret societies.[3] Though prophetic leaders do not necessarily proclaim millenarian visions, in the great majority of known cases prophets have been central to the process by which diffuse millennial ideas have been forged into ideologies capable of generating sustained protest movements (as opposed to spontaneous and ephemeral outbursts of resistance).[4] Therefore, in the following discussion of the rise of prophetic figures, which I view as *the* critical determinant of the mode of protest expression adopted by the groups under consideration, I will focus on the relationship between these leaders and the millennial thought currents that they personified and that were critical to their ability to gain a following among disgruntled groups. The life of each of these prophets will also be examined for personal attributes and experiences that contributed to the intensity with which they reacted to their own misfortunes, as well as the ways in which their setbacks reflected more general sources of discontent. Beyond their attraction as exponents of millenarian ideologies, the appeal of these leaders must also be related to their individual personalities, backgrounds, and careers.

Five Prophets and the Promise of Salvation

DIPANAGARA: PRINCE AND SAVIOR-KING

Of the five prophets considered in this study, the life and character of Prince Dipanagara are by far the most abundantly documented.[5] Not only did he dictate a detailed autobiographical account of the events leading up to his rebellion, but as a major figure at the court of Yogyakarta his activities and attitudes were discussed and recorded by Dutch officials beginning decades before the Java War of 1825–1830. From the outset his life was exceptional, even for a prince of the ruling house. He was born in 1785, the eldest son by an unofficial wife of the man who was to become the third ruler of the kingdom of Yogyakarta. Courtly traditions relate that his great-grandfather, the brilliant leader who had founded the dynasty in the mid-eighteenth century, had predicted that Dipanagara would someday attempt to bring the Dutch to ruin. He had added significantly, however, that he could not foresee the final outcome of Dipanagara's efforts. The aged Sultan also later entrusted the care of the child to his wife, Ratu Ageng, and thereafter his great-grandmother took charge of Dipanagara's upbringing. Ratu Ageng, who was noted for her piety and devotion, was appalled at the increasingly immoral and irreligious tone of courtly life after her son (Dipanagara's grandfather) became Sultan. For this reason, and to protect the infant Dipanagara from court intrigues, she left the palace at Yogyakarta and took up residence at an estate house called Tegalreja. There Dipanagara passed the formative years of his youth, semiisolated from the court and surrounded by Muslim mystics and religious teachers who journeyed to Telgareja to enjoy his great-grandmother's patronage.

After Ratu Ageng's death when Dipanagara was still a small boy, he continued to live at Tegalreja, appearing at court only on special festival days. Alone, except for the servants who cared for him and the holymen he continued to support, Dipanagara developed into a deeply religious and introspective youth. Although the sons of Javanese nobles were routinely given some religious training at the age of seven or eight, Dipanagara's education went far beyond the smattering of Arabic and the rote repetition of Koranic texts that was standard at this time.[6] Though his religious mentors cannot be identified with precision, they inspired Dipanagara's deep commitment to the syncretic, highly mystical variant of Islam that was characteristic of religious schools in central Java. Thus Dipanagara gained the extensive religious training and youthful commitment that has been common to many prophets in the Islamic tradition.[7] In this respect Dipanagara differed substantially from his princely brothers and cousins, who had only a veneer of Islamic learning and were embroiled from their childhoods in the politics at court. His training and mystical inclinations were given full expression in youthful pilgrimages to the holy places of central Java

Prince Dipanagara. Source: François de Stuers, *Mémoires sur la guerre de l'île de Java de 1825 à 1830* (The Hague, 1833). Reproduced by permission of the British Library.

and in solitary meditation in caves and grottoes that provided welcome refuges for the sensitive and restless prince. During these wanderings Dipanagara experienced the first of several visions that convinced him that he was a man with a special mission, visions that would later give credence to his prophetic claims. The supernatural figures who appeared to him also prophesied impending political upheavals that were soon to draw him into court intrigues for the first time.

A detailed account of the complex power struggles for dominance in Yogyakarta between various factions of Javanese nobles, the Dutch, the British (between 1811 and 1816) and then the Dutch again, is not necessary for the purposes of this study. However, a number of issues and confrontations that deeply affected Dipanagara should be mentioned in connection with his emergence as a prophet of rebellion. Although a prince, Dipanagara was the off-spring of an unofficial wife. This meant that even though he was the eldest son of the third Sultan, Radja, his younger brother, Djarot, who was the eldest son of an official wife, had the strongest claim to succeed to the throne of their father. There are conflicting views regarding Dipanagara's attitude to succession, but I find most convincing the arguments that he openly acknowledged the validity of Djarot's superior claims and that he did not covet temporal power. He knew that British promises to elevate him to the throne (which were allegedly made during the period of turmoil that surrounded his grandfather's removal from the throne in 1812) would have done little to establish his legitimacy in the eyes of the Javanese nobility or the peasantry. In any case, both the British and the Dutch chose to ignore the promises. The British elevated Djarot to the throne after Radja's sudden death in 1814; and the Dutch later recognized Menol, Djarot's infant son, in 1822.

Dipanagara's growing discontent arose not primarily from having been refused the throne but because the chancellor, Danureja, and his clique undermined his influence as a senior prince at the court, debased time-honored customs, and sought to humiliate him and his supporters. Dipanagara may well have been somewhat resentful over being denied the throne in 1822, but the Dutch heaped insult upon injury by relegating him to the position of one of four guardians of the infant Sultan. Dipanagara had hoped to be appointed sole regent and was deeply disturbed by the fact that one of the guardians was a firm ally of his acknowledged enemies. Even after he had withdrawn from the court in anger, however, he did not claim that he had been deprived of the throne. Although his followers proclaimed him Sultan after hostilities were under way and he assumed many of the trappings of a Javanese monarch, Dipanagara's major demands remained the removal of Danureja and his clique and Dutch recognition of his right to be the supreme arbiter of religious affairs on Java.

Beyond the formal rebuffs received by Dipanagara at the hands of hostile courtiers and the Dutch, there were further frustrations that were less tangible, but contributed significantly to his decision to become a rebel leader. As a prince and a man of considerable judgment, strong opinions, and administrative ability,[8] he was repeatedly drawn from the calm of his refuge at Tegalreja into the factional fights at court. He was increasingly involved in personal confrontations with his enemies. On these occasions, angered by his growing impotence and the petty insults of his rivals, Dipanagara frequently lost his temper, even to the point of striking antagonists like Danureja. To a man of Dipanagara's pride, sensitivity, and self-awareness and to a prince raised in the Javanese courtly tradition, these losses of self-control must have been deeply mortifying. Years of striving to gain self-control and composure through the practice of meditation and asceticism seemed undone by a few moments of anger. His failure to have his counsel heeded could only have increased his sense of frustration and self-doubt.

After Djarot's death in 1822, Dipanagara's solution seems to have been to withdraw from court to his retreat at Tegalreja. This course of action, as he was well aware, only made further confrontations inevitable. The refusal of so prominent a prince to appear regularly at court amounted to a rejection of the Sultan's legitimacy.[9] He may well have anticipated that his enemies would not permit such an affront to pass unnoticed, and indeed they did not. Further quarrels with Danureja and his Dutch-backed clique at the court resulted in open hostilities between Dipanagara's followers and his enemies. Dipanagara was declared a rebel, and his flight from Tegalreja began nearly five years of bloody warfare.

Dipanagara's high birth, his outspoken condemnations of continuing Dutch penetration and internal decay in Yogyakarta, and his close ties to many nobles and the local officials on his estate all guaranteed substantial support for his decision to defy the Dutch-dominated court. The prince's enduring appeal, however, and his ability to gain widespread support among the peasantry and the regional lords of the outlying provinces rested mainly on their acceptance of his prophetic claims. His followers believed that Dipanagara was the *Ratu Adil*, the long-awaited savior-king who was the central figure in a syncretic complex of millennial beliefs that had been invoked by Javanese rulers and rebels for centuries.[10]

Even before the first waves of Hindu-Buddhist influence began to affect Javanese cultural development in the first centuries A.D., the inhabitants of the island displayed great reverence for men who through occult practices were able to gain great magical powers which could be used for the benefit of other men or to inflict great sufferings upon them. The assimilation and transmutation of Hindu-Buddhist concepts produced a heightened sensitivity among the Javanese to stability and tranquility and the disruptive effects of change.[11] It also resulted in a time sense that was based on a belief in the repeated and cyclic creation, decline, and destruction of the universe. As the world aged, it became increasingly more corrupt and men grew more wicked. In the final era of dissolution (*Kali Yuga*), kingdoms and social order collapsed and men reverted to savagery and bestial practices. Gradually, in part as a reflection of the successive rise and fall of Javanese dynasties, the notion of a *Ratu Adil*, or "Just King," became implanted in Javanese thinking. It was prophesied that the *Ratu Adil*, righteous and invincible, would appear in times of dissolution and drive away the forces of darkness and disorder. He would then restore the pure, harmonious order associated with the early stages of the Hindu-derived time cycle. As successive waves of Buddhist and Hindu influence were transmitted to Java by Indian merchants, monks, and scribes, the idea of a savior king was embellished by various currents of Hindu-Buddhist eschatological thought which focused upon the coming of *Erucakra*, or the restorer of order. These themes were further enriched by the prophecies associated with the semi-mythical twelfth-century Javanese monarch, Jayabaya, and Balinese eschatological writings.[12] During the centuries of the spread of Islam in the Indonesian archipelago, beginning in the late thirteenth century, an additional prophetic-millennial strain was added in the guise of the promised *Mahdi*, the defender and purifier of the faith and precursor of a utopian age for the Muslim faithful.

Long before the first European contacts with Java, these beliefs in various combinations had been regularly invoked by Javanese rulers to bolster their legitimacy or extend their domains, as well as by rival claimants, dissident nobles, and disgruntled holymen. In times of dynastic crisis and social unrest, prophetic figures and their millenarian visions often provided the nuclei for new kingdoms and the basis for restoring sociocultural equilibrium. The rise of Dutch power on the island resulted in changes that were particularly unsettling to the Javanese who so treasured harmony, order, and stability. In response the incidence of prophetic-millenarian outbursts increased, reaching a peak (insofar as the existing records allow us to determine) in the nineteenth and early twentieth centuries, when European influences first began to alter Javanese society in depth. Numerous prophetic figures, exhibiting varying combinations of the prophetic themes outlined above, emerged in the centuries before Dipanagara's revolt, and the succession of prophetic figures continued through the struggle for independence to the present day. Millennial expectations were particularly effective in generating peasant support for anticolonial revolts, because they were deeply rooted in the village or "Little

Tradition" of Javanese society. As Dutch dominance increased, an additional theme became more and more prominent in Javanese resistance movements: the Muslim concept of the holy war.[13]

Despite considerable ambiguity and contradictions in the available sources, it seems clear that Dipanagara regarded himself and was widely accepted as a savior in the *Ratu Adil* tradition.[14] In his *Babad*, or autobiographical history of the events leading up to his rebellion, Dipanagara describes the series of visions that began when he was a young man. On a number of occasions he was visited by such revered figures as the Goddess of the Southern Ocean (*Ratu Kidul*) and the Muslim holymen (*walis*) to whom the conversion of Java to Islam was attributed. In these encounters he learned of the great sufferings and struggles ahead and was told that he would someday be king. He also records that he was addressed by many titles, which included *Erucakra* or "Just King," Lord of the Faith, and Khalif of the Prophet of God. Both the supernatural figures who appeared to him and the titles they bestowed reflected the complex blending of different religious and millennial traditions that characterized Dipanagara's message and Javanese culture generally. On the eve of the rebellion he conferred with his religious advisers regarding the appropriate moment to declare himself the *Ratu Adil* and to begin the holy war against the Dutch infidels. During the struggle he assumed numerous titles which indicated that he was the promised savior-king and the head of the Islamic faithful on Java. These claims were widely accepted by both his noble and peasant followers as well as by the Muslim religious figures who flocked to his standard. In part the fierce devotion demonstrated by many of his adherents, even long after his cause was clearly lost, can be attributed to their belief that he truly was the *Ratu Adil* come to fulfill one stage of the *Jayabaya* prophecies.

SAYA SAN: FROM NATIONALIST AGITATOR TO FUTURE BUDDHA

Like Prince Dipanagara, Saya San emerged as a protest leader in a culture imbued with an ancient and deep current of salvationist-millennial longing. Saya San's ability to draw upon the many aspects of this tradition in his attempts to gain followers was critically influenced by the many and varied occupations which he took up in the years before he embarked on his career as prophet and protest leader.[15] He was born in 1882 in Shwebo, one of the core districts of the Dry Zone, the heartland of the Burman people. The district had played a major role in the precolonial era as a major source of troops for the armies of Burman monarchs and as a refuge for bandits, rebels, and dynastic rivals. When Saya San was a small boy, the British annexed Shwebo, along with the remaining portions of the Burman kingdom, to their Indian Empire. It is probable that he witnessed, or at least heard tales of the long resistance waged by guerilla bands in Shwebo and neighboring districts against the new overlords. Princely pretenders, Buddhist monks, and so-called *dacoit*, or bandit chiefs, led these bands, and many armed their followers with magical charms.

As a young man, Saya San moved from district to district supporting himself as a fortune teller and *se saya*, or Burmese medical practitioner. He also developed an interest in alchemy and probably led or at least belonged to one or more of the *gaings*, or cult-sects, that were (and are) widespread in Burmese Buddhist society.[16] Through these pursuits he gained an extensive knowledge of beliefs concerning animist or *nat* spirits and the occult and protective aspects of Buddhism that would later serve him well as a leader of protest. Although the available records do not indicate the date or place, Saya San entered a Buddhist monastery and apparently remained long enough to become a *pongyi*. In the 1920s, he drifted down to the town of Moulmein south of the Delta,

Saya San after His Arrest. Source: Ba Maw, *Breakthrough in Burma* (New Haven, 1968). Reproduced by permission of Yale University Press and the British Library.

where he was convicted of running illegal lotteries. During this same period he was also accused of and tried for murder but was acquitted. In 1924, he joined the nationalist General Council of Burmese Associations, where he remained a peripheral figure for some time. When the GCBA broke apart in the following year, however, Saya San joined the radical So Thein splinter group and soon became deeply involved in nationalist agitation. He attended annual conferences and spoke to numerous *athin* groups. In 1928, he headed a special inquiry into police abuses, which as I have noted, may have influenced his decision to prepare the Burman peasantry for rebellion.

At the time of the 1930–1932 disturbances, Saya San was nearly fifty years old, a slender, rather short man who was said to be slow and deliberate in speech. His initial appeal was largely personal and limited to fellow radicals within the So Thein GCBA. His fervently held and frequently expressed convictions that British colonial rule was oppressive and could only be ended by violent revolt gradually attracted followers among the leadership of the village *athins*. His appeal to large numbers of Burman peasants, however, and his ability to incite them to open rebellion against their British overlords, was rooted primarily in his claims to fulfill the millenarian expectations that long had permeated Burman society.

Saya San proclaimed, and in all probability came to believe, that he was the *Setkya-Min*, the Burmese equivalent of the *chakkavatti* (Hindu: *chakravartin*) or universal emperor. According to Burman tradition, the *Sektya-Min* was (and is) a powerful and benevolent ruler who would appear at the end of Buddhism's age of decline—which could easily be interpreted to mean the era of European colonial dominance. He would restore the *Dhamma* (world moral order, literally, law) and prepare mankind for the coming of the Embryo or Future Buddha (*Buddha Maitreya*). When all had been made ready, the *Sektya-Min* would become the Future Buddha and renew and fulfill the dispensation of the *Gautama Buddha*, which had been largely forgotten. His reign would usher in an age of bliss when:

The totality of Burma's people shall be made happy through an abundance of gold and silver and gems. [And the] people of the entire world shall equally become Buddhist [in] religion . . . the people of the land will practice the Law, and the ruler will have the ideal royal virtues . . . people will be pious, freed from illness and shall have peace of mind and body. Numerous beings will achieve Nirvana.[17]

Belief in these prophecies, often mingled with eclectic and esoteric cult ideas,[18] was extant in Burman culture centuries before European colonialism began to take its heavy toll on indigenous institutions and thinking. Burmese monarchs, like Alaungpaya, (literally, Embryo Buddha), the founder of the last Burman dynasty, proclaimed themselves *Maitreya Buddhas*. After successive British conquests and annexations of Burman territory, many prophets arose claiming to be *Sektya-Mins* come to rescue the faithful from the alien British overlords. In the colonial period, these claims were supplemented by appeals to the peasants' belief in the return of a just Burman king or prince (*minlaung*) who would drive away the European heretics and restore monarchical rule and an idealized pre-European order, free from disruption and oppression.[19]

In its basic ideology, Saya San's rebellion was much the same as many previous localized risings in which Buddhist monks, princely pretenders, and perhaps *weikzas* or cult magicians had proclaimed themselves *Sektya-Mins*. He too stressed his commitment to Buddhism and the restoration of the monarchy. He issued proclamations under the title of *Sektya-Min*. He bestowed the name of *Buddha Raja* (king) on the palace-city that he founded in the forest; and he frequently employed rubies (one of the traditional symbols of the *Sektya-Min*) in the royal ceremonies and dress that were also designed to further his claims to legitimacy. Rumors that the *Sektya-Min* was about to appear were widespread in the months before Saya San's rising, and after his first coronation his followers prayed that he might become the Future Buddha.[20] Saya San's own sincere belief in his special mission is clearly indicated by entries in his diary noting the miraculous occurrences that accompanied both of his coronation ceremonies. He related that after the first coronation the rays of the (*Gautama?*) *Buddha* shone on the pagoda where the ceremony was performed and twin suns appeared in the sky. After the second ceremony in the Shan States, the clapping of hands could be heard for over twenty miles.[21] Clearly Saya San believed himself to be something more than a mortal king.

KINJIKITILE: ORACLE OF REBELLION

Of the five prophets examined in depth in this study, we know the least about Kinjikitile Ngwale, the instigator of the Maji Maji rebellion. The German sources tell little more than that he was a "medicine man" and anti-German agitator and that he was hanged for his seditious preaching on 5 August 1905, shortly after the outbreak of the first Maji Maji risings.[22] Gilbert Gwassa has provided patches of further biographical information, but even in his relatively detailed essays, Kinjikitile remains a mysterious figure who seems to spring into prominence and then be brutally removed by the Germans.[23]

According to Gwassa, Kinjikitile was of peasant origins and had only recently migrated to the village of Ngarambe in the northwest Kilwa district where he established his oracle. Practically nothing is known of his early life, but he seems to have possessed considerable knowledge not only of the Matumbi but also of related peoples like the Ngindo and Zaramo. For reasons that are not recorded, he seems to have come into conflict with the Germans, and this may well have influenced his decision to arouse resistance against them. On the basis of later oral testimony, Gwassa estimates that Kinjikitile was middle-aged at the time of the rebellion, tall, and an eloquent speaker. How he came to be accepted as an oracle is not known, but he clearly was trained in the esoteric arts of a Matumbi-Ngindo diviner and medical practitioner. This knowledge was essential to his rise to a position of widespread influence. It also provided key ingredients in the ingenious ideology of salvation and revolt by which he was able to incite resistance by a remarkably large number of disparate peoples.

Millenarian themes in the thought systems of the Matumbi, Ngindo, and neighboring peoples were more amorphous than among the Burmans or Javanese. These themes were also not as clearly related to the fortunes of political regimes as the notions of the *Ratu Adil* and the *Setkya-Min*. Definite statements about the nature and importance of these beliefs in the pre-Maji Maji period are difficult to make, because neither Kinjikitile nor any other leader of the revolt left behind autobiographical evidence like that provided by Dipanagara's *Babad* (chronicle) or Saya San's diary. Further, insofar as I am aware, little work has been done by anthropologists or students of religion on the belief systems of either the Matumbi or the Ngindo.[24] Thus, in constructing the ideological background of the millennial themes expressed in the Maji Maji movement, I have had to rely heavily on inference from anthropological and historical evidence provided by studies of other African peoples, particularly those of Bantu-speaking central and east Africa, which appears to me to have validity for the Matumbi, Ngindo, and their neighbors. Wherever possible, I have made use of evidence relating to groups like the Zaramo who actually supported the Maji Maji.

As Robin Horton and other authors have argued,[25] in sub-Saharan African and similar thought systems it is imperative that all human misfortune be explained. To suggest coincidence or admit ignorance of the causes (and implicitly the cures) of vital occurrences such as droughts or personal accidents is to concede serious deficiencies in and perhaps the bankruptcy of the group's unified and unrivaled thought system. Thus social disorders and personal setbacks, like those experienced by the Matumbi and Ngindo in the first decades of German rule, had to be explained and cures had to be sought. The admittedly scanty evidence available suggests that the Matumbi, Ngindo, and other peoples to whom the Maji Maji cult spread believed that one of the most important causes of their adversity was sorcery or witchcraft. These peoples in turn concluded that powerful medicine and rituals were needed to counter the pernicious effects of these sources of human suffering. Sorcery is one of the African diviner's most prominent explanations for illness or misfortune. There had also been a profusion of antisorcery cults in the tumultuous decades of the nineteenth century, and these cults continue to the present day. These movements had spread among the peoples of German East Africa from the west (particularly from the Congo region) and the south. They had often coalesced about prophets or healers, who were sometimes chiefs intent on extending their power base. These men claimed the power to eradicate sorcery and thus restore order and eliminate suffering. Millenarian expectations were thus associated with antisorcery campaigns whose adherents believed them capable of entirely eradicating evil from the world through the exposure and elimination of its source, witchcraft.[26] When these beliefs were linked to the basic African concept that the passage of time results in an ever-increasing corruption and disorientation of the world and that periodically the world must be renewed,[27] the basis for a powerful millenarian ideology had been laid.

The available evidence indicates that these millennial elements were contained in the Maji Maji ideology. Among the Ngindo and a number of other peoples to whom the movement spread, the antisorcery and all-purpose curative aspects of the cult and its medicine water (*maji*) appear to have been initially its most appealing aspect. For peoples whose life patterns and cultural systems had been disrupted and threatened by the influx of new ideas and external demands, the medicine promised a "new world . . . a world without evil." Different peoples thought that the medicine had powers that ranged from preventing famine and sickness to protecting ripening crops from wild pigs.[28] In his role as religious expert or *pundi*, Kinjikitile, the prophet-founder of the Maji cult, was viewed as a "killer and hater" of the sorcerers who had brought so much misery to the peoples of the Rufiji river complex. His antiwitchcraft powers were thought to be enhanced many times as a result of his being possessed by the mighty Hongo spirit, who had been sent to Kinjikitile by the superior divinity, Bokero.[29]

As his reputed possession by the Hongo spirit suggests, Kinjikitile drew on additional thought traditions in his efforts to forge an ideology of resistance that would extend beyond the Matumbi and Ngindo peoples and provide a basis for unity among diverse ethnolinguistic groups. Widespread belief in his possession gave evidence that his followers linked him with powerful deities who had long been revered as sources of fertility and regulators of rainfall and riverine waters—the guardians of the essence of life itself. These themes were clearly associated with the serpent imagery of the Bokero-Hongo cult, with the location of Kinjikitile's oracle near a great pool, and with the use of a water-based medicine as the key symbol of the Maji Maji movement. They also represent thought currents that Kinjikitile knew to exist among other peoples of the Rufiji river complex, as evidenced by his attempts to establish links with the Kibesa oracle upriver and the strikingly similar snake cult of the Zaramo, who were one of the first peoples beyond the Matumbi-Ngindo heartland to join the Maji Maji movement.[30]

Kinjikitile also drew on the deeply rooted veneration for ancestral spirits exhibited by the Matumbi, Ngindo, and most African peoples. Clan leaders who journeyed to Kinjikitile's oracle at Ngarambe were shown their ancestors as evidence of the prophet's great powers, and rebel parties going off to war invoked the blessings of their ancestral spirits.[31] Whether or not Kinjikitile consciously and explicitly molded the complex ideology that Gilbert Gwassa has attributed to him, it is clear that there were longstanding ideas and traditions in southeast German East Africa that could arouse millenarian expectations and lend appeal to a prophetic figure. These could be and were harnessed to a widespread protest movement aimed at reversing many of the changes set in motion by European colonial penetration.

BIRSA: MUNDA PRODIGY

Although the Mundas of Chota Nagpur had a long tradition of resistance to foreign invaders of the highlands, there is little evidence that their responses had involved millenarian or prophetic

Birsa. Source: S. Sinha, *Life and Times of Birsa Bhagwan* (Ranchi, 1967). Reproduced by permission of the British Library.

beliefs until the rise of Birsa.[32] There were millenarian tendencies in Munda mythology, such as the longing for the lost golden age mentioned in chapter 1, but these had not given rise to prophetic figures. Even in the case of Birsa, millenarian expectations were vague and the ideology of his movement eclectic and fragmentary. Somewhat ironically, Birsa built that ideology as much (or more) on the thought of the Mundas' lowland adversaries as upon indigenous myths and beliefs. Explanations for this apparent contradiction can be found in Birsa's childhood and adolescence and the educational influences that shaped his thinking as a young man.[33]

Birsa Munda rose to prominence from lowly origins. He was born in the 1870s as the fourth son of an impoverished peasant family from the village of Chalkad in the Tamar Thana of Chota Nagpur. His parents' inability to support their many offspring forced them to send Birsa to his aunt's home in another village. Deprived of parental affection and unwilling to suffer the indignities, including beatings, which his uncle inflicted upon him, Birsa fled back to his parents' village. They had apparently found the means to support him in the interval, because it is known that Birsa attended a vernacular school in his home village where his superior intelligence was quickly recognized. Perhaps with financial assistance from other villagers, his parents found the means to send him to a more advanced school in the town of Burja. At Burja he became a Christian and was baptized with the name David. He soon advanced to a larger mission school, where he came into close contact with European teachers for the first time. The European missionaries found Birsa a precocious youth, but they also discovered that he was quarrelsome and restless. Arguments regarding the missionaries' attitudes toward the Sardar agitators caused Birsa to be expelled from school after several years' attendance, and he again returned to his home village.

After serving for a time as a domestic servant, he went to work for a weaver who lived near his village. His new employer was a devotee of the Hindu God Vishnu, and through him Birsa was introduced to a local *munshi* ("priest") named Anand Panre. Much impressed with Panre's teachings, Birsa soon became the *munshi's* disciple and was initiated into the ancient Hindu techniques of meditation and asceticism. During this period he was also exposed to the Vaishnava monk, Bombhani, who persuaded him to give up hunting and eating meat. For reasons that are uncertain, Birsa left his holyman-guru after some months and returned to his paternal village.

Birsa's refusal to remain with either his Christian or his Hindu teachers may well have been influenced by the fact that he grew up in an area that was a major center of Sardar agitation. He could not have been unaware of his people's oppressed condition, nor of the lowland invaders' responsibility for much of their suffering. His own deprivations may have caused him to emphathize even more intensely with his people's misery and to resolve to find ways to free them from their oppressors. Birsa is known to have lived for a time with his guru, Anand Panre, in the home of a wealthy Hindu landlord. The landlord's contemptuous exploitation of his Munda tenants made a deep impression on Birsa, which was later expressed in his diatribes against the alien landlords and his promise that when he ruled all land would be held tax and rent free.

After returning to his village, Birsa was initiated by an unknown person into the cult secrets and curing techniques of the *sokha* or Munda medical practitioner. Birsa soon began his own career as a healer but appears to have encountered opposition because of continuing financial problems and his attempts to spread non-Munda beliefs and practices. He was driven by hunger to dig up a local grave in order to steal jewels to buy food. A villager discovered the theft, and the village elders declared him an outcaste and banished him from the village. It was probably in this period of exile that Birsa received his first revelations. While walking with a companion in the forest during a thunderstorm, Birsa was struck by lightning. His companion related that, rather than killing him, the lightning transfigured Birsa's face and his skin changed from brown to glowing red and white. This incident was followed by a series of dreams, the content of which Birsa interpreted as injunctions for him to return to his people and rescue them from their misery. For unknown reasons, he was allowed to return to his village and again take up his practice as a healer.

Although Birsa renounced his Christian conversion, he continued to study Hindu sacred texts and to practice yogic meditation. He became increasingly critical of the spirit worship of his people, and his vocal assaults soon brought him again into conflict with village leaders. They blamed him for a smallpox epidemic that swept through his home area in the mid-1890s and drove him for a second time from his village. Shortly thereafter, perhaps because of his devotion to those stricken by the epidemic, he was allowed to return to his village where his growing reputation as a holyman and healer soon attracted crowds of Munda pilgrims. Birsa began to preach his new religion and declared that he was the "father of the world" come to save the Mundas.

Birsa strove in his teachings to reconcile Munda and Christian as well as Hindu beliefs. He ordered his followers to cease worshipping the village and ancestral spirits, which he claimed had failed them in their struggle against the lowland invaders. At the same time, he proclaimed Sing-Bonga, the Munda chief god and creator, the sole force that was worthy of veneration and able to assist his people. His prophecies of a great deluge that would destroy all but his followers and his warnings that the day of judgment was approaching were inspired by both indigenous and alien thought. The Biblical allusions are clear, but it is equally probable that Birsa (and especially his followers) associated these predictions with ancient Munda myths. These myths told how Sing-Bonga attempted to destroy man in a fit of rage by showering the earth with a terrible rain of fire. In his claims to have revelations from God and to be the savior of the Munda people, Birsa both consciously and subconsciously fused in a rather haphazard fashion the life of Christ, Hindu Vaishnava salvationist tendencies, and Munda legends relating Sing-Bonga's victorious struggle with the Vulcan-like Asuras who were scorching the earth with the heat of their furnaces. It is not certain how far his followers understood the underlying themes of his teachings. It is clear, however, that many of his supporters regarded him as God's special messenger, or as God himself (which he claimed to be), and as such capable of miraculous feats.[34]

TE UA HAUMENE: PROPHET OF PEACE

Although Maori mythology is well provided with legends of cosmic upheavals and god-like heros, like the story of Tane the bringer of light and custodian of occult knowledge,[35] none of them appear to have been consciously incorporated into Te Ua Haumene's teachings or the ideology of the Pai Maire movement. Although the rituals and practices of the Pai Maire were permeated with ancient Maori beliefs and techniques (see chapter 5), its millennial content was based almost wholly on transmuted Biblical eschatological ideas, both Christian and Jewish. As in the Birsite movement, this emphasis on the beliefs of the European invaders was largely determined by the prophet Te Ua's early and extensive contact with Christian missionaries and their teachings.[36]

Born into the Taranaki tribe,[37] Te Ua was enslaved and carried into captivity at the age of three by the Waikato who lived north of his homeland. The orphaned youth must either have escaped from his captors or have been freed by European missionaries, because it is known that some years after his abduction he was first exposed to Christianity and taught to read and write at the Methodist mission school at Kawhia Harbor on the west coast. Te Ua converted to Christianity during this period and gained a reputation as an astute student of the Bible, particularly of the Book of Revelation. After a number of years, for which we have little information except that he may have fought against the settlers in the early wars of the 1860s, he found his way back to his original home near Cape Egmont in the Taranaki. Despite his being literate and possibly a student of the magical arts of a Maori *tohunga*,[38] Te Ua had apparently gained little respect among his fellow tribesmen. His lowly status was indicated by the rebuffs that he suffered in a controversy that probably touched off his early visions and prophetic career. The quarrel focused on whether or not his fellow tribesmen should plunder a British ship that had run aground on Cape Egmont in 1862. After his counsel that his people should refrain

Te Ua Haumene. Source: Angus J. Harrop, *England and the Maori Wars* (London, 1937). Reproduced by permission of the British Library.

from plunder was contemptuously rejected, he became seriously ill and had his first visions.

The growth of his reputation as a seer and prophet began with a number of miracles that he was said to have performed during this period. His relatives and fellow villagers, believing him to be insane, carried him away from the village and bound him in chains, but Te Ua escaped from his shackles without assistance on three occasions. Reports of his supernatural powers spread among his tribesmen, but they persisted in their refusal to accept his counsel about the wrecked ship. His reputation was further enhanced, however, by a new revelation in which God ordered him to sacrifice his son in much the same manner as Jehovah had commanded Abraham to sacrifice Isaac. Depending upon the account chosen, Te Ua either maimed the boy and then·cured him or killed him and brought him back to life. The villagers who had been sent by his wife to rescue the boy witnessed these miracles and became his loyal disciples. Te Ua now began preaching in earnest and soon gathered about him a small band of followers who believed him to be an infallible prophet sent to save the Maori race.

Except for its reference to deep-seated Maori ancestral veneration in promising the return of all Maoris who had died since the
beginning of time, Te Ua's apocalyptic vision was couched wholly
in Judeo-Christian, Biblical terms. The god of deliverance was
Jehovah and his chief agent was the angel Gabriel. Legions of
angels, rather than the traditional Maori guardian spirits would
descend from the heavens to assist the Maoris in their struggles
with the Europeans. When all the tribes had been converted to the
new faith, the Maoris would receive the gift of tongues (a clear al-
lusion to the Pentecost) and thus the secrets of European learning.
They would be cured of all diseases, gain the power to retain their
ancestral lands, and receive many of the objects of European culture
that they so greatly admired. New Testament themes were mixed
with Old Testament millennial expectations, such as the recovery
of the lost kingdom, and the Maori people were strongly identified
with the Jews. Both were viewed as God's chosen people who
were being tested by sufferings and exile from their homeland.

There is wide disagreement in the available sources about the
fate prophesied by Te Ua for his followers' European adversaries.
Although one recent author has argued persuasively that Te Ua
envisioned a partition of the North Island between Maoris and
European settlers, there is also considerable evidence that his more
militant followers believed that the whites would be destroyed in a
great flood. If true, this latter prediction may have had its roots
either in the Biblical flood or the ancient Maori myth of Ruatapa
who, after quarreling with his people, destroyed many of them in a
deluge.[39]

Not only was the content of Te Ua's millennial vision predominately Biblical but the historical precedents for the Pai Maire cult
were movements that also had been heavily influenced by missionary teachings. In the decades before the emergence of Te Ua, a
number of prophets appeared among the Maori. They preached
that Christ was about to descend or they claimed various supernatural powers. During this period there was also a proliferation of
spirit contacts and curing cults based primarily on Maori religious
ideas. Some of these cults stressed the imminent return of the
Maoris' ancestors, a theme also woven into the more predominately
Biblical teachings of Te Ua.[40] The more widespread appeal of the
Pai Maire, compared with these earlier, more localized movements,
can be partly attributed to the worsening position and military
defeats suffered by the Maoris in the early 1860s. However, equal
stress must be placed on the abilities of Te Ua and his lieutenants

and the appeal of the ideology they forged. Although they seemed gibberish to contemporary European observers,[41] the beliefs of the Pai Maire were far more coherent and persuasive than any that had gone before.

The Roles of Prophets and Millennial Visions

As the Count de Tocqueville observed in his study, *The Old Regime and The French Revolution*, "Patiently endured so long as it seemed beyond redress, a grievance comes to appear intolerable once the possibility of removing it crosses men's minds."[42] Such a possibility, such a promise of escape from increasingly intolerable circumstances, was provided by the prophets and millenarian visions described above. Despite considerable variations, each case clearly demonstrates the close relationship between prophet and millennium. The prophet articulated and embodied millennial expectations: the millenarian vision in turn provided the basis of the prophet's appeal and authority. In each case, the prophets received their missions and messages from supernatural agents —Dipanagara in visions while in meditation, Saya San at his coronations, Kinjikitile during a night spent in the pool of the serpent-spirit Hongo, Birsa during a thunderstorm, and Te Ua in series of dreams. These revelations and the prophets' claims to be either divine or divinely-appointed redeemers gave supernatural sanctions to their decisions and transmitted a sense of legitimacy to their followers.

Though the overall millenarian visions were characteristically vague,[43] they conveyed a sense of supernatural concern for the sufferings and anxieties of the groups addressed and often dealt with the resolution of specific grievances. It was prophesied, for example, that all foreigners would be destroyed or driven away or that all taxes and debts would be abolished. Thus, millenarian prophecies became important vehicles for the articulation of the grievances of displaced leaders and peasant groups who had little access to the wielders of power and little experience in supra-village, popular agitation. Prophetic leaders and their millennial visions gave voice and hope to these discontented groups when other avenues of redress seemed closed.

Displaced indigenous leaders, deprived of their once-pivotal socioeconomic roles, quite naturally saw the destruction of the colonial order and the return of the indigenous as a way to recover their lost status. Because the displaced elite groups that dominated the leadership of the movements under study were mainly sacral-political or religious, the ideologies they espoused had a markedly magico-religious tenor. In all cases resistance was intimately linked to a desire to restore legitimate rule, which was by definition based on ancestral and supernatural sanctions that the alien and commercially-minded European overlords could not even pretend to possess. In one sense these movements can be seen as attempts to restore customary sacral orders that structurally and ritually were society-encompassing talismans attuned to the dictates of pervasive and responsive cosmic forces. The emphasis placed on the revival or assertion of ancient rituals and behavior in part represented attempts to build up cosmic support and magico-religious strength for the coming confrontations with the technologically superior colonial overlords.

The erosion or breakdown of institutions and customs that regulated the personal aspirations, behavior, and social interaction of colonized peoples also strongly influenced the mode of expression adopted. The adherents of these prophetic rebellions, like those of revitalization movements more generally, strongly desired to create or to restore meaningful social bonds and effective mechanisms for the regulation of human intercourse. New religious sects, independent churches, and millenarian upheavals have all embodied attempts to forge new networks of social dependencies. They have set forth new standards of exchange and reciprocity to replace those threatened or shattered by the advance of the European colonial-capitalist order.[44] Prophet and nascent social movement offered a protective shelter, a refuge from a world of decay, deprivation, and increasing isolation. They provided a locus of stability, certainty, and confidence in times of bewildering and disruptive change, and a sense of vision and purpose for a future that otherwise appeared perilous and uncertain. These movements also offered new measures of human achievement and personal morality. They provided the means for colonial peoples to recover their dignity and integrity that had been so badly battered by their lowly status and largely unsucceessful participation in colonial societies.[45]

Prophetic and millennial appeals found particularly strong acceptance among peasant groups, which formed the great majority of the rank-and-file supporters of all the movements considered. Beyond their deep attachment to the magico-religious assumptions upon which these appeals were based, peasant adherents saw in these movements a means of recovering the high degree of local autonomy, community cohesion, and security that they had enjoyed in the precolonial era. The power and demands of the colonial overlords threatened or seriously undermined all of these essential elements in customary peasant life. The technological and organizational regressions that colonial officials and many writers have associated with revitalization movements have been due in part to the conscious preference of their adherents for decentralized systems. In such systems, inefficient communications and feeble techniques for mobilization made for a high degree of local control and generally a lower level of extraction by groups outside the village.

As the movements under consideration demonstrate, prophetic ideologies are normally eclectic both temporally and culturally. They include elements drawn from past and present experience and contain visions of the future. They mix, often in incongruous combinations, aspects of the indigenous tradition and ideas derived from outside groups. As the cases under examination demonstrate, they can arise in sociocultural contexts where there is a rich prophetic tradition or where eschatological ideas have been introduced by outsiders. Whatever their content, they achieve widespread adherence only where there is extensive social disruption and deprivation.[46]

In both Java and German East Africa, there were well-established millennial currents. These two areas were also the least affected by changes engendered by European colonial penetration. Thus, the prophetic styles of Dipanagara and Kinjikitile and their millenarian ideologies were almost unaffected by European ideas or precedents. At the other end of the spectrum, neither the Mundas nor the Maoris possessed well-developed indigenous millenarian or prophetic tendencies. Among both of these peoples outside religions and ideas had made significant inroads, and customary gods and beliefs had been largely discredited by the continued successes of foreign invaders. Consequently, the prophetic-millennial themes contained in the movements mounted by both the Mundas and the Maoris exhibited strong foreign influences.

Burma is not so easily placed on this hypothetical nativist-syncretist continuum of prophetic-millennial expression. Colonial penetration in the Delta was the most pronounced of all the cases, yet Saya San's prophetic style and his eschatological vision were wholly derived from pre-European themes long present in the Burman cultural milieu. The resolution of this seeming contradiction lies in the fact that though the market economy and colonial bureaucratic institutions made deep inroads in Lower Burma,

Christian or Western thought had made progress only among a tiny urban-based elite and a number of non-Burman minority peoples. Burman Buddhism and cultural traditions retained a sanctuary in the Dry Zone of Upper Burma, which was annexed decades later than the Delta and was far less exposed to foreign influences. Burman peasants carried their ancient beliefs and customs to the Delta and continued to cherish them even though they might not always be able to translate them into proper monastic centers or properly observed rituals. Thus, millennial expectations retained a strong appeal for the peasant masses of an intensely colonized frontier society, which was from the peasants' point of view merely an extension of their fairly isolated Dry Zone heartland.

Although the mode of expression adopted by the dissident groups under study cannot be understood apart from underlying sociocultural contexts, the eschatological themes in their ideologies in some ways transcended specific historical circumstances. These beliefs exhibited patterns that may be regarded as norms of millenarian expression. The adherents of these movements anticipated far more profound transformations than the destruction of the colonial order. Victory over the agents of colonialism was merely a preliminary, but necessary, stage in the establishment of a new order that would be radically different from any that had gone before. Although there was often an appeal to past golden ages and honored precedents as a means of lending legitimacy to millennial prophecies,[47] the coming age of salvation would be beyond time and history and yet represent the culmination of both. It would be free of sin, suffering, and social injustice.[48] The promised kingdom of peace and bliss would be terrestrial in Norman Cohn's sense that it would come in the here-and-now rather than after death,[49] but it was clearly envisioned as a blend of material and spiritual, of this world and the supernatural. Only the faithful as a group would partake of its delights. The colonial overlords, their immigrant and indigenous allies, and all who refused to follow the prophet would perish or be driven away. In this sense, there would be a purging of alien or adversary groups, rather than the "role reversals" often postulated by scholars of revitalization movements.[50] These promises naturally served to reinforce group identity and solidarity.

The extent to which the promised utopia was imminent, another of the key millenarian characteristics suggested by Cohn, is debatable. Most of the prophets examined here were wise enough not to commit themselves to specific timetables. Birsa, who did cite a date for the deluge that was to usher in the millennium, was saved from humiliation by the timely intervention of the colonial authorities. He was able to claim that they had upset the cosmic processes.[51] More critically, all of the prophets insisted that there would be a period of strife and suffering before the millennium finally arrived. The world had to be cleansed and the faithful were the agents who had been divinely appointed to fulfill that task. All of the prophets except Saya San enjoined their followers to observe new and more demanding moral codes. These ranged from familiar prohibitions of drunkenness, lying, and looting to Dipanagara's attempts to restore *adat* (custom) and Islamic law an.ˇ Kinjikitile's attack on sorcery.[52] In all of the cases, tʰ e prophets or their followers eventually came to accept force as an additional means by which they could usher in the new order. This insistence on human activity and a direct assault on the existing social order suggests that Cohn's stress on the role of supernatural agents also needs qualification, at least for this type of movement. The prophet and his followers called upon supernatural forces, but the faithful themselves had to act to prepare the way for the promised millennium.[53] This emphasis on human initiative may explain why none of these movements, except the early Birsite when passive retreat was commanded, exhibited the abstention from work or destruction of property that frequently have been associated with revitalization movements.[54] The millennium was inevitable, but human struggle and further suffering were essential.

Whatever their derivation and form, these millennial expectations took on significance in their specific social contexts only when they were molded into a more or less coherent ideology and propounded by prophetic figures. Despite widespread deprivation and millennial tendencies, if there had been no prophet there would have been no large-scale or sustained protest movements in these particular places at these particular times. The key role of the prophet is probably best illustrated by Prince Dipanagara, for the Java War was in a very real sense his war. As one Dutch scholar has argued,[55] much the same conditions that led to nearly five years of rebellion in Yogyakarta also existed in the neighboring kingdom of Surakarta. In fact, Dutch influence on the court of Surakarta was even more pronounced than at Yogyakarta, and the amount of land rented to Dutch and Chinese entrepreneurs was even greater. In Surakarta there were also many toll stations, disgruntled nobles, and even frustrated claimants to the throne. The prophetic-millennial longings that underpinned revolt in Yogyakarta were equally pervasive in Surakarta. Thus despite important differences in the two courts, especially in their approach to the Dutch, if Dipanagara had been born into the royal house of Surakarta and matured under similar circumstances, the Java War of 1825–1830 might have originated there rather than in Yogyakarta.

What was true of the Java War was equally true of the other movements. The Saya San rebellion was aptly named, for it was because of his organizational skill and personal appeal that this outburst of social protest achieved a scale far surpassing the many risings that had gone before. Kinjikitile, Birsa, and Te Ua all pieced together ideologies and founded movements that provided outlets for the release of pent-up frustrations and offered channels of redress for longstanding grievances. Te Ua rose from the wreckage and disenchantment of the Kingite failures and Maori defeats in the wars of the early 1860s. Birsa offered persuasive leadership for a people jaded by centuries of defeats and futile resistance. Kinjikitile and his cult provided a focus and an ideology of resistance for the diverse and divided peoples of the Rufiji river complex and beyond.

The pivotal roles of these prophetic leaders in the movements under consideration demonstrates the importance of comparative analysis of their careers in order to identify factors that contribute to the formation of prophetic personalities more generally. Since five individuals is a rather small sample from which to generalize, I have supplemented the examples contained in this study with biographical data on similar leaders of movements in other areas.[56] I offer the following observations not as any rigid model of prophetic personality formation but rather as suggestions of patterns that seem to recur and might be tested by further case studies. From this sample a continuum of prophetic backgrounds emerges. At one pole are indigenous authority figures whose position is threatened by changes introduced by the agents of alien civilizations. The careers of Dipanagara and Kinjikitile are excellent illustrations of this pattern. Both emerged in colonial contexts where foreign influences were still relatively peripheral and indigenous institutions and thought patterns had not been eroded as severely as in areas like New Zealand or Lower Burma. Dipanagara and Kinjikitile, as well as leaders like Muhammad Achmad and many Amerindian prophets like Handsome Lake and Tenskwatawa, epitomized roles that were highly revered in their respective societies. Because the indigenous sociocultural order was still largely intact and the European presence not yet overwhelming, the locus of power still rested in indigenous institutions and roles. Leaders who occupied these positions emerged as defenders of the customary, precontact cultural order and as champions of those groups who were being displaced or threatened with severe status loss from the growing control of outsiders.[57]

At the other pole of the continuum are men of low birth, who are exposed to a high degree to alien but dominant civilizations. On the basis of my sample, this is the more common background for prophetic protest leaders. Leaders of this type have neither an established place in the precolonial order nor avenues for advancement in the colonial setting. For able and ambitious men like Saya San, Birsa, Te Ua, Chilembwe, or many of the prophets discussed by Peter Worsley, this situation produced both frustration and determination to achieve positions of status and respect. The assumption of prophetic roles made it possible to fulfill these aspirations in situations where other avenues of advance seemed closed. Their exposure to both the indigenous and foreign sociocultural systems allowed them to function as "cultural brokers."[58] With varying degrees of effectiveness, they participated in and were able to interpret both systems. They drew on both for their ideologies, leadership styles, and modes of organization. Because they arose in societies where the impact of colonial contact had been far more profound than in Java or German East Africa and the locus of power was shifting or had shifted away from indigenous leaders and positions, the prophets' success in bridging the gap between two worlds was vital to their ability to mobilize large numbers of supporters.[59] They had to demonstrate a capacity for dealing with the dominant Europeans and their ideas and institutions to gain widespread support in their own societies.

Differences in their historical contexts placed different demands on each of the prophetic types. Prophets who rose from indigenous elite groups responded to well-established models of behavior and drew their ideologies from long-established millenarian beliefs. In their person and actions, they had to correspond to their peoples' image of what a prophet was, what he would promise, and how he should behave. Prophets of the cultural broker type responded to quite a different challenge and in many ways had to demonstrate a good deal more creativity. They had no well-established, or at least still viable, models on which to pattern their behavior or base their ideologies. They themselves had to fashion ideologies and develop prophetic styles that would be convincing to those groups to which they hoped to appeal. They had to earn the legitimacy that was inherent in the positions occupied by prophets who rose from indigenous elites. To be successful, prophets of the cultural broker type had to determine and select, whether consciously or intuitively, those elements of the indigenous culture that were still viable and then to combine them effectively with key aspects of the European colonial order. Prophets from elite origins could be more certain that their indigenous ideas and modes of behavior would have strong appeal and had less need to take into account those of their European adversaries.

Although the messages and methods of prophetic leaders reflected important differences in their situations and personal backgrounds, it is possible to distinguish a number of common patterns in their lives. Each of the five prophets examined in depth was well educated by the standards of their societies and each had been extensively exposed to esoteric, magico-religious beliefs and healing techniques. Although some illiterate prophets have arisen,[60] prophetic figures ranging from the Taiping leader, Hung Hsiu-ch'üan, to the Brazilian messiah, Antonio Conselheiro, demonstrate the importance of education, particularly religious education, in the formation of prophetic personalities. Mission educations played formative roles in the lives of many prophets who have arisen in colonial situations; Islamic prophets frequently have emerged from Muslim brotherhoods or schools run by *shakyhs, hadjis,* or mystics.[61] However much culture brokers such as Birsa, Hung, Simon Kimbangou, and Te Ua drew on foreign ideas and examples, they had to formulate their millennial ideologies and develop their prophetic styles in the cultural idiom of the peoples whose support they sought. Thus, initiation in the cult secrets and religio-magical skills of their respective cultures was essential to their success. Knowledge of these ancient and revered arts enhanced their standing among their people and validated their claims to special powers and contacts with the supernatural.

As well as having exceptional educational backgrounds, prophetic leaders have frequently been well-traveled individuals with extensive exposure to the agents of dominant alien groups. Travel developed their awareness of the widespread dissatisfaction of colonized peoples. It also restructured their sense of identity, which came to extend far beyond the continued boundaries of village, kin, and locality that often restricted the scale of protest among colonized peoples. Some prophetic leaders like Kinjikitile had only limited contacts with the colonial overlords, but most gained some familiarity with their future adversaries' ideas, institutions, and material achievements. Even for leaders like Dipanagara or the Sudanese Mahdi, whose prophecies and movements were little affected by foreign models, these contacts proved important. Beyond acquiring personal grudges, the prophets came to know something of their enemies' weaknesses and how to exploit them and of their strengths that had to be counteracted. Prophetic leaders from lowly origins—like Saya San, Ngo Van Chieu, Apolinario de la Cruz, Birsa, Te Ua, Simon Kimbangou, and the many visionaries described by Peter Worsley—gained an aura of achievement from participation in the educational-religious or political-military institutions of the European colonizers that was vital to their success. Achievement in the white man's world compensated to some extent for the lack of legitimacy that was associated with leaders like Dipanagara, Handsome Lake, or Muhammad Achmad by virtue of their birth or position of high status in the indigenous society. The prophets' contacts with the Europeans seemed to indicate an ability to deal with the colonizers' material culture and organizational capacities that the subject peoples found so formidable. Prophets who had been soldiers or policemen might be credited with substantial knowledge of Western military technology and, by inference, of how to counteract it. Literacy, acquired by an aspiring prophet at a mission school, was also frequently seen as a sign of his capacity to master the secrets of the European overlords. In most instances, the very fact of literacy enhanced the prophet's standing since the ability to read and write carries something of a magical aura in predominantly nonliterate societies.[62]

Each of the five prophets studied in depth gained a considerable reputation as a healer, an attribute which many scholars have found closely associated with salvationist leaders in widely differing cultures.[63] Cures played critical roles in validating the revelations of Kinjikitile, Birsa, and Te Ua and in their success in attracting followers. Saya San's very name reflected his expertise in the arts of the *se saya*, or Burman medical practitioner.[64] His skills as a healer had a direct bearing on his followers' faith in the protective amulets and magical tattoos that were prominent in his efforts to mobilize followers. Although Dipanagara was never a medical practitioner as such, his adherents believed that he possessed miraculous healing powers. It was widely held that merely to touch his garments or eat the leftovers from his meals was sufficient to cure the most serious illnesses.[65] Cures were closely linked to the prophets' revelations and to their alleged invulnerability and ability to predict the future.

Most of the prophets examined in this study and many covered in my broader sample began their prophetic careers after severe personal setbacks. Like many of Eric Hobsbawm's "social bandits," who began their lives outside the law after being wronged by landlords or government officials,[66] official persecution or police actions often contributed to the emergence of prophetic leaders. Personal failures were also critical in many prophets' lives. Dipanagara failed to win the position of respect that he felt he deserved at the Yogyakarta court; Simon Kimbangou and Hung Hsiu-ch'üan both failed exams that were essential to their continued advancement; Te Ua failed as a tribal leader; Birsa's early prophesies proved false; Antonio Conselheiro was humiliated by his wife's infidelity; and Handsome Lake and Tenskwatawa lost the respect of their people after years of alcoholism. Physical illness often followed these personal setbacks and set the stage for the prophets' initial revelations. This pattern is illustrated by the careers of Te Ua, Birsa, Hung Hsiu-ch'üan, Wovoka, Handsome Lake, and Chilembwe, to list just the most prominent.

Despite significant differences in their cultural and personal backgrounds, prophets and millenarian visions played pivotal roles in each of the movements under study. Through these prophetic figures and their divinely inspired revelations, a belief in the efficacy of resistance and the possibility of escape from their troubles was born and nurtured among deprived, colonized peoples. Despair gave way to hope and confusion to a sense of purpose. Colonial systems that were once viewed as impregnable were confronted with opponents who would not withdraw in silence and who were willing to employ violence to achieve their ends.

FIVE

Toward Violence: Abortive Repression and the Rise of Secondary Leaders

Precipitants of Rebellion

One of the major deficiencies cited by critics of the theory of relative deprivation centers on the difficulty of gauging at what point frustrations rooted in the perceived gap between expectations and actual achievement will result in violent aggression.[1] Although this criticism applies primarily to the theory's predictive value rather than its explanatory potential, which is the quality of importance for this particular study, its validity must be admitted. Human beings are too complex, group interaction too unpredictable, and historical situations contain far too many interacting variables for the social scientist, using this or any other theory of revolution, to construct a fixed, calibrated scale measuring the intensity of deprivation multiplied by the number of persons experiencing it, and then declare that when point X is reached there will be violence. The expectations of different individuals and groups and the importance they attach to different attainments vary widely, and these are often impossible to determine with precision because of a lack of biographical data. Reactions to deprivation will also vary according to established societal norms for resolving individual dissatisfaction and group tensions.

Although attempts to arrange these variables systematically in order to predict when social violence will occur have not been convincing, it is possible to draw general conclusions about the sort of situations that have caused groups experiencing relative deprivation to resort to force to achieve relief. The nature of their deprivations and the absence or blockage of other channels of redress discussed above are obviously of critical importance. But for violence to break out, there must be precipitants, occurrences (or nonoccurrences) that actually spark the outburst of violence. In recent years there has been an unfortunate tendency among social scientists to play down the importance of precipitants on the ground that they are too unique and specific to warrant comparison or theoretical analysis.[2] This stance has led in some cases to neglect of factors that play a vital role in the transition from social unrest to violent protest. Although precipitants take on meaning only in conjunction with examinations of underlying historical contexts and specific grievances, the causal sequence is incomplete without them. In the cases of prophetic rebellion under study here, three interacting factors were the main precipitants of violent efforts to overthrow the existing order: (1) the decisions of prophetic leaders to lead their followers in rebellion; (2) the prophets' loss of effective authority over their followers to more violence-prone secondary leaders; and (3) the failure of the colonial authorities to take prompt action or their bungling of attempts at repression.

If (as I have argued) the Java War depended on Dipanagara's grievances and decision to rebel, that decision was made inevitable by the clumsy efforts of the Dutch to compel his obedience if not allegiance. Disgruntled by repeated rebuffs at the hands of the Dutch and his lack of influence at the court of Yogyakarta, Dipanagara retreated to his estate at Tegalreja. There is some evidence that Dipanagara and his closest followers then began to gather arms and prepare potential supporters to resist further encroachments by the Dutch,[3] but open rebellion was actually forced upon him by further insults from his rivals at Yogyakarta and bungled efforts to arrest him. His arch rival, the Chancellor Danureja, ordered a road to be built that at one point passed along the edge of Dipanagara's estate. The chancellor approved this route without seeking the prince's permission or even consulting him. Rightly perceiving Danureja's actions as an insult and additionally angered by the road builders' violation of an ancient grave site that lay in their path, Dipanagara resolved to resist. Thus the actions of an irresponsible official drove Dipanagara to an open breach he might not otherwise have risked. As his own account and the evidence of contemporary Dutch observers clearly indicate, he was a man plagued by self-doubts and indecision, so much so that one Dutch scholar has drawn elaborate comparisons between Dipanagara and Shakespeare's Hamlet.[4] He had been rebuffed many times before, the court's decline and peasant grievances had intensified for decades, and yet he had not acted. Danureja's measures and the confrontations that followed left Dipanagara with little choice other than violent resistance.

Peasant resentment over the additional labor service demanded of them for the building of the road and Dipanagara's longstanding popularity among the village population brought widespread support for his efforts to resist Dutch demands. After half-hearted attempts by the Dutch and court officials to negotiate a reasonable compromise and a tense and bloody struggle to replace road markers with spears and vice versa, the Dutch Resident, Smissaert, ordered troops to proceed to Dipanagara's estate and bring him to the court. Any lingering doubts Dipanagara may have had about initiating rebellion were rendered of no account. His incensed followers tried forcibly to prevent the government column from reaching the prince's residence. Fighting broke out and the ill-prepared government troops allowed Dipanagara to escape in the confusion that followed. They also managed to deliver another blow to hopes for a peaceful settlement by burning Dipanagara's residence. As news of the incident and the prince's open revolt spread, disgruntled princes, holymen, peasants, and bandit chiefs flocked to his standard. Thus began nearly five years of bloody civil strife.[5]

The available evidence suggests that the Maori prophet, Te Ua, did not intend his followers to use violence against their European adversaries. Te Ua himself was a gentle man whose background more closely resembled that of a Maori deacon than a warrior-chief. He called his new religion Pai Maire, which meant good and peaceful, and there is no evidence that he exhorted his followers to open warfare with the whites. His preachings stressed withdrawal, prayer, and peaceful preparation for the millennium that was at hand. He appears to have believed that the new faith would give solace and hope to the Maori people who had just suffered such heavy setbacks in the Kingite wars and who faced the confiscation of their remaining lands.[6] The sources do not indicate which of his followers first turned Te Ua's teachings to warlike ends, but the specific occasion has been described in detail in numerous works.[7] On 6 April 1864 a party of colonial troops and settler militia was burning deserted Maori settlements and crops near the town of New Plymouth in the Taranaki. The troops were commanded by a captain named Lloyd, who had only recently arrived in New Zealand and was not familiar with Maori war tactics. Lloyd and one of the detachments in the party blundered into a Maori ambush and were routed. Seven soldiers (including Lloyd himself) were killed; twelve others were wounded but fortunate enough to escape with their lives. No one bothered to record Maori casualties, but their losses were probably slight given the completeness of the surprise of their well-executed assault.

The victory, coming in the midst of a succession of Maori defeats, suddenly transformed Te Ua's movement in ways he had not envisioned. Although he had not ordered his followers into the fight, members of the Pai Maire movement had participated. Te Ua's lieutenants were quick to claim that the new faith had given them the strength to overcome the colonial armies. They moved to turn Te Ua's message of peace and goodness to warlike ends. The heads of Captain Lloyd and the other ill-fated soldiers were taken as trophies that proved the potency of the Pai Maire. Leaders like Patara Puakatauri and Kereopa carried the heads to many parts of the North Island in an effort to spread the movement to all of the Maori tribes. Maori magical beliefs and rituals were revived (see chapter 6), and the Pai Maire came to serve as the basis for a renewal of hostilities against the whites.

At one point the Government of India's handling of the prophet Birsa seemed the very ideal of preventive repression.[8] In 1895, after months of preaching and curing, six or seven thousand loyal Munda followers gathered in a great camp about Birsa's tent on a hill near the town of Chalkad. Birsa predicted that a flood followed by fire and brimstone would soon destroy all but the faithful who had gathered about him on the hill. When the holocaust failed to materialize at the appointed hour, the prophet explained that it had been postponed. Since his followers had abandoned their homes, neglected their crops, and sold most of their possessions to buy special garments that Birsa had instructed them to wear in preparation for the apocalypse, they were understandably disappointed and restless. Not surprisingly, Birsa's teachings suddenly became more worldly. For the first time he spoke of using force to drive the Mundas' oppressors from the highlands. Supernatural agencies alone, he decided, could not save the Mundas. Human struggle was required to prepare the world for the coming "age of gold."

After his followers threatened the Rajput notables of a nearby town and drove off some policemen who had been dispatched to keep Birsa's camp under surveillance, rumors spread that a general rising was planned in which all of the Mundas' lowland oppressors were to be massacred. At this point, the British decided that force must be employed if necessary to prevent potential, widespread violence. In a well-conceived tactical maneuver, a handful of British and Indian policemen crept into Birsa's camp late at night, gagged and bound the unsuspecting prophet, and ferreted him away to jail. His followers awoke to find their savior being carried away but could do little to prevent his arrest. Birsa was tried and sentenced to several years in prison, along with a number of his chief subordinates. Despite attempts by Sardar agitators to sustain resistance in his name, Birsa's removal appeared to have put an end to his movement. His devotees broke camp and despondently made their way back to their villages to salvage whatever crops and possessions remained.

The success of these early repressive measures were undone, however, when Birsa was released in the general amnesty during Queen Victoria's Diamond Jubilee in 1897. Embittered by what he believed to have been an unjust imprisonment and now totally committed to the use of force, Birsa disappeared for a time in the forest wilderness. After several months of hiding he began once again, this time clandestinely and with extensive support from the Sardars, to organize his people for a rising that was intended to drive the invaders from the highlands and usher in an utopian age.

Unlike the prophets Te Ua and Dipanagara, Kinjikitile advocated violent resistance for some time before his followers first came into open conflict with government forces. More than any other single element, Kinjikitile's determination and the great powers he displayed made violence inevitable. In a very real sense violence was his only option, for passive withdrawal or pacific sectarianism, which has been characteristic of numerous African revitalization movements,[9] simply would not have sufficed. Without violent action, the *akidas* and their exactions would remain, and the Germans would not long tolerate their subjects' refusal to cooperate with the forced cultivation schemes.

Despite ample warning, the Germans did virtually nothing to head off the rebellion that Kinjikitile preached with increasing boldness. Colonial officials watched bemusedly as crowds of chanting pilgrims from the Matumbi, Ngindo, and Zaramo areas made their way to Kinjikitile's oracle and then, fortified with his prophecies and war medicine, returned to their villages to await the signal for a general revolt.[10] The Governor-General said his staff in Dar es Salaam ignored the pleas of Arab *akidas* in the interior for assistance, despite the latters' reports that Matumbi and Ngindo villagers were refusing to work government land, uprooting cotton plants, and threatening the overseers with physical assault. Nearly two weeks passed between mid-July 1905, when these first warnings were telegraphed, and late July and early August when the first violence erupted. Although the Germans were quick to capture and hang Kinjikitile after the revolt was underway, it was too late. As he defiantly informed his executioners, his message and the *maji* medicine had already done their work.[11] The German administration's failure to move against Kinjikitile before violence erupted can be attributed to its overall ignorance of the peoples of the southeast. Government ineptness can also be traced to the Germans' failure to anticipate the political ends to which an ostensibly religious movement could be directed by peoples who did not compartmentalize human activities as did their European overlords.

More than any of the rebellions considered, that to which Saya San gave his name was carefully and consciously plotted by its prophet-instigator. As early as 1928, Saya San had resolved to oust the British and their Indian allies from Burma by force. He spent over a year secretly recruiting the followers and building the organization that was to carry out his plan. Although Saya San himself led only two of the eleven major risings that comprised the 1930–1932 rebellion, he visited seven of the eleven areas where the outbreaks occurred in the months before the revolt. On his tours he advocated peasant resistance to taxation and strengthening the *athins* or village political associations. At the end of 1928, he drew up plans for a rebel army and in early 1929 began to recruit peasant levees. He also conferred with a number of leaders who were to play prominent roles in major outbreaks in the lower Delta and the Dry Zone. The final preparations for the revolt were made during a meeting in mid-December at the town of Taikkyi in the Insein district. Delegates from several of the districts where major risings were about to occur were present at this secret conclave.[12]

In what was either a sincere attempt to give peaceful methods one last chance or merely a shrewd tactical maneuver by Saya San, a delegation of peasants and local leaders in the Tharrawaddy district presented a petition to the acting governor, Maung Gyi, on 22 December 1930. The document included a lengthy list of peasant grievances and suggested a number of possible solutions. Maung Gyi, who had no power to commit the government to reforms even if he had been so disposed, dealt with the petitioners in a curt fashion that made the futility of their appeals all too apparent.[13] On the night of the same day in the same district of Tharrawaddy, Saya San led his "armies" into battle for the first time. The rebels' early attacks on the residences of village headmen, the shops of foreign merchants, and railway stations were stunning successes. The British seem to have been taken completely off guard. These initial victories did much to lend credibility to Saya San's royal pretentions and claims of magical powers. The ranks of his followers swelled. Within weeks the British faced major risings, communal disturbances, and "bandit" activity over much of Lower Burma and in a number of places in the Dry Zone.[14]

Although the persuasiveness and organizational acumen of Saya San were decisive in determining that social protest in Lower Burma would be violent, the government's failure to act was also notable. As the reports issued during and after the rebellion indicated, Saya San's activities had been under surveillance for some time before the actual outbreaks of violence. As he was a known nationalist agitator of the radical So Thein GCBA and a former defendant in a murder trial, it is surprising that his activities were not taken more seriously. It is probable that government officials dismissed him as one of many "quack" magicians (as he is in fact labeled in a number of reports) or *weikzas* that flourish in the Burman cultural milieu. Perhaps they were simply too preoccupied in the months before the 1930–1932 rebellion with communal riots in Rangoon, the devastation caused by a severe earthquake, and an attempted prison break to give Saya San the attention which, in retrospect, he clearly deserved.[15]

Historians have long linked the failure of incumbent regimes to make effective use of the means of repression at their disposal to the outbreak of the so-called "Great Revolutions" of Europe.[16] In the movements examined in this study, the ineptitude of colonial regimes actually gave impetus to rebellion by either provoking prophetic leaders or providing opportunities for them to mobilize supporters. Government inaction or initial bungling also obscured its potential military might in the eyes of the colonized peoples. In many instances disgruntled groups saw government failures as signs of the great power of prophetic leaders and as a promise of their inevitable victory. Dipanagara's early escapes and recovery from battle wounds convinced his followers' that he was invincible and invulnerable.[17] Birsa's release from prison appeared equally miraculous. The massacre of Captain Lloyd's party, Saya San's early victories, and the early successes of the Maji Maji rebels all gave credence to prophetic claims of miraculous powers. These triumphs were seen as undeniable evidence, that despite their superior weapons, the colonial overlords had finally met their match.

Such successes were critical in all cases because efforts at violent resistance had previously only meant death and humiliation to the conquered peoples, no matter how courageously they fought. War, like appeals to the government, had been a futile endeavor. Centuries of Dutch involvement in the bloody dynastic struggles of the Javanese princes had resulted in the ever-growing strength of the former and the constant weakening of the latter. Current widely accepted notions of the essential gentleness and peacefulness of the Javanese bear little relation to their ancient martial traditions, which included regular tournaments at the court centers and frequent and often lengthy wars of succession and expansion throughout their history.[18] But bravado could not compensate for deep indigenous rivalries, poor organization, and inferior weapons. Thus, even as the Dutch global position deteriorated markedly in the eighteenth century, they became the dominant power on Java.

The Maoris, who were perhaps the most martial of the peoples considered here, had also found resistance to the Europeans a losing proposition. Outgunned and outnumbered on many occasions, they fought valiantly from their ingeniously constructed fortresses, but the sappers of the colonial armies soon reduced their defenses to rubble. The defeats of the Kingite tribes in the Waikato and Taranaki were a crushing blow that clearly prepared the way for the rise of the Pai Maire. The Maori could take little comfort in knowing that the British, who had much experience in the matter, found them the "grandest native enemy" they had ever encountered.[19]

Although there had been few direct confrontations between the peoples who initiated the Maji Maji rebellion and German military forces before 1905, peoples like the Matumbi and Ngindo must have known about the defeats suffered by powerful warrior kingdoms like the Hehe,[20] and thus of German military prowess. In this case, unlike the others, there had not been a direct test of strength, but there were plentiful examples that warfare alone would not suffice. A long succession of abortive Munda risings made a similar conclusion inescapable. The number of outbreaks that preceded Birsa's revolt is not known, but in the British period alone five major rebellions were recorded in just over a century, in addition to scores of local riots and disturbances sparked by groups like the Sardars.[21] Death and imprisonment were all the Mundas had to show for these attempts at violent protest.

In many ways the Burmans' violent collisions with the Europeans had been even more frustrating than those of the Mundas.

They too had a long tradition of resistance to foreign encroachments. The Burmans had been proud victors over their ancient Siamese foes and had won a series of ego-inflating victories over the expeditionary forces of the mighty Manchu dynasty of China. Unlike the Mundas, they had not known recent defeats, and thus their successive and decisive setbacks in the Anglo-Burman wars of 1825–26, 1852, and 1886 were humiliating and traumatic.[22] After each defeat there was widespread resistance by irregulars, whom the British lumped under the label of *dacoits* (bandits). Throughout the British period a current of unrest persisted despite British claims of the loyalty of the colonized and numerous accounts of the friendly and peaceful nature of their Burmese subjects. Unrest exploded into open rebellion periodically. The most serious outbreaks were led by Burman monks or pretenders to the empty throne of the vanquished Konbaung dynasty.[23] As in Java, millennial currents and resistance had previously been fused, but no one had combined the two as effectively as would Saya San.

In all cases but the Maji Maji, where the Matumbi and Ngindo were well aware of neighboring peoples' unsuccessful resistance, conventional warfare and nonprophetic rebellions had failed to prevent European colonial penetration. Irregular or guerilla resistance had also been tried in a number of areas, and in Burma and New Zealand it had given European-led armies considerably more trouble than conventional resistance. However, the guerilla war of the peoples under study was the particularistic, poorly organized, and uncoordinated variant that has an ancient lineage in many parts of the world. The commitment to a well-defined ideology, the cadre-based organization, the discipline and focus that have come to be associated with guerilla war in the twentieth century were lacking in all cases.[24] No Mao Tse-tung or Che Guevara emerged in the crisis situations considered in this study, and their models for guerilla war had not yet been formulated, much less tested. Prophetic figures rather than revolutionary strategists arose. Through deliberate choice or prodding from others, they combined violence with millennial visions and deeply-rooted traditions of magic (see chapter 5) to bring about the changes that they and their adherents believed essential.

Commanders for the Holy Wars

As each of the movements under consideration became more and more dominated by violent resistance, leadership shifted from the prophet-instigator to secondary leaders who sometimes shared authority with the prophet and in other cases usurped it entirely. These other leaders rapidly took effective control through their roles as propagators of the prophets' messages, as mobilizers and organizers of recruits, and as field commanders. Saya San and Birsa planned and personally supervised this delegation of power as part of their efforts to mount widespread protest movements. Dipanagara also placed relatives and gifted supporters in positions of power, but they gained greater control of the rebellion made in his name than he would have preferred. Te Ua clearly lost control of his disciples and faded from view as their calls for war supplanted his vision of salvation through divine intervention. Kinjikitile apparently sought to use his special messengers or Hongos to coordinate the resistance of the diverse groups to whom he directed his message. However, his untimely death and the weakness of links to the often distant groups who responded to his call frustrated his designs from the outset.

The different patterns of secondary leadership displayed by each of these movements strongly reflected the sociocultural contexts in which they arose. The most elaborate command structure was associated, not suprisingly, with Dipanagara's revolt.[25] Dipanagara and his advisors organized their followers in a manner which virtually duplicated the time-honored Javanese state structure. Dipanagara sought to establish a counter-court and state system in opposition to both those of Yogyakarta and Surakarta. He selected relatives and close supporters to fill the court positions and administrative offices that bore the titles, functions, and, whenever possible, the material and status rewards characteristic of Javanese kingdoms. He placed areas under rebel control in the hands of his loyal followers, who levied tribute for support in the time-honored manner. A hierarchy of officials extended from Dipanagara and his inner circle of adherents to regents in charge of rebel "districts" and below to loyal village heads and local notables. Dipanagara's problems of staffing this rather elaborate system were considerably reduced, at least in the early days of the rebellion, by the inclusion among his supporters of (according to Peter Carey's estimates[26]): more than half of the royal princes of Yogyakarta, most of the Sultan's bodyguard, forty-one of the eighty-eight *Bupatis* or court administrators who can be identified, and many regional officials and village leaders. Beside this hierarchy of command, which, of course, never functioned as neatly as it might appear on paper, were ranged allied but autonomous groups headed by Muslim holymen and religious teachers, as well as professional bandit chiefs.

Dipanagara's adversaries singled out two of his secondary leaders for special comment due to the critical roles they played in sustaining his rebellion. One, Alibassah Prawiradirdja or Sentot, was Dipanagara's able field commander. The second, Kyai Madja, served as Dipanagara's spiritual advisor and his self-proclaimed ideologue. The two men were from vastly different backgrounds. Sentot was the son of Raden Ranga, a Javanese nobleman who was killed in an earlier revolt against the Dutch. At the time of the outbreak of Dipanagara's rebellion he was still an adolescent of eighteen years. Despite his youth and small size, his great courage and talent for tactical maneuvers soon won him a position among Dipanagara's chief field commanders. Although other military leaders gained attention for their ability, the Dutch repeatedly singled out Sentot and his core of youthful followers as the best of the rebel fighters. Dipanagara himself admired Sentot above all of his followers.

Kyai Madja, whom many Dutch officials considered the driving force of the revolt, was originally a religious teacher from a small village near Surakarta. According to Dipanagara, Kyai Madja joined him only after hostilities had begun, though a number of Dutch writers have charged that Kyai Madja persuaded Dipanagara to revolt. Kyai Madja had a considerable reputation as a Koranic scholar and possessed what was reputed to be one of the best libraries of Arabic manuscripts on Java. He was highly emotional and intensely devoted to the defense of Islam. There is some evidence that he overplayed his role as Dipanagara's religious advisor, perhaps attempting to assume the position of arbiter of Islam on Java. Since this was the role that Dipanagara coveted for himself, it may have been the decisive difference among many that eventually resulted in a complete break between the two leaders. Their quarrels culminated in Kyai Madja's surrender to the Dutch late in 1828, well before the end of the rebellion.

The contributions of dynamic and gifted secondary leaders, like Sentot and Kyai Madja, were also critically important in other millenarian movements, of which the most notable are the Taiping rebellion in China and the Mahdist upheavals in the Sudan. The extensive areas covered by each of these movements and their long duration suggests a noteworthy two-way relationship between the emergence of able secondary leaders and the scale and time spans achieved by movements of this type.[27]

Although Saya San aspired to resurrect a dynasty that had once ruled over a state with a central court and a bureaucratic hierarchy, the secondary leadership patterns in his movement bore only the slightest resemblance to Konbaung precedents.[28] Although he was successful in his attempts to duplicate Konbaung physical and ritual symbols (see chapter 6), he was unable to establish a counter-bureaucracy as fully as did Dipanagara. Not only had he no personal experience of Burman courtly life; the model he drew upon had been defunct for nearly half a century. Unlike central Java, Burma had no body of disgruntled courtiers or regional officials to rally to Saya San's standard. These too had passed away decades before. Thus, despite his attempts to revive the old order, which played a vital role in attracting followers, the actual leadership of Saya San's rebellion came from two main groups: political *pongyis* and the leaders of village *athin* organizations.

Of some fifty-seven leaders of major risings whose backgrounds can be identified from postrebellion reports and trial proceedings, twenty-five (44 percent) were Buddhist monks. Although most were *pongyis* (monks who had spent a minimum of ten years beyond their initiation in the monastery), one was a *sayadaw* (head of a monastery) and five were *upesins* (monks who were full members of the Sangha but not yet *pongyis*). Second to the *pongyis* in the number of leaders provided were heads or members of village *wunthanu athin* organizations. They supplied twenty-four (42 percent) of the secondary leaders accounted for. Of these twenty-four, fifteen (63 percent) were presidents of local *athin* units and seven (29 percent) were officers. Since the *athins* were village-oriented organizations whose purpose was to involve the peasantry in the nationalist movement, it can be assumed that the majority of leaders from *athin* backgrounds were peasants. Other rebel leaders included former bandits, exgovernment officials, and two rice brokers. The predominance of *pongyis* and *athin* heads is not surprising because both of these groups represented institutions or organizations that still played effective roles in the lives of the peasantry. The *pongyis* sustained a long tradition of anticolonial agitation; the *athin* leaders turned from their urban-based organizers and techniques to much older, more deeply entrenched methods and beliefs. Both groups of leaders and their peasant followers fought for the restoration of a monarchical, autocratic, Buddhist kingdom, not a nation-state modeled after those of western Europe.

The diffusion of authority was virtually inherent in the circumstances under which Kinjikitile sought to arouse resistance to the Germans and their coastal allies.[29] Kinjikitile's close disciples carried his message and the *maji* medicine to ever more distant peoples, and these in turn made the pilgrimage to his shrine. Despite these contacts, effective leadership remained localized. Whether Kinjikitile would have been able to give the movement more unity had he lived or had more time to prepare cannot be known, but there are good reasons for arguing otherwise. Power among the Matumbi, Ngindo, and neighboring peoples of the core areas of the Maji Maji rebellion had never been centralized. Precedents for kingship and increased centralization were certainly known to these peoples because of their contacts with expansion-oriented kingdoms like the Ngoni and Hehe, but no institutional or organizational foundations existed in Matumbi or Ngindo society on which Kinjikitile could build a disciplined and coordinated resistance movement. The prophet had no way to assert close control over or to sustain continuous contacts with the groups that responded to his call to revolt. In a situation of crisis and confrontation, decision making and command devolved instinctively to the local leaders and clan heads who had customarily provided leadership. Indigenous religious experts buttressed the authority of these leaders through customary rituals and promises of magico-religious protection. In the Matumbi areas, clan heads organized rebel bands and led them into the field. Among the Ngindo the *jumbes* renounced their positions in the colonial hierarchy and called the village populations in their charge to war. Since military organization and coordination depended in both areas on the agreement of local leaders and clan heads, large-scale assaults or sustained campaigns were virtually impossible. Timing was haphazard and support unreliable. This adherence to particularistic authority, despite Kinjikitile's unifying ideology, provided ample opportunities for German repressive measures.

As in the Maji Maji resistance, it was perhaps inevitable that authority in the Pai Maire movement would revert to the level of the tribal and *hapu* chiefs and kinship leaders where it had customarily resided.[30] In contrast to Kinjiktile, however, Te Ua's weaknesses as a leader of protest and his own actions contributed substantially to the breakdown of whatever unity the movement had originally possessed. The attack on Captain Lloyd's party was the inevitable consequence of the usurption of authority in the Pai Maire movement by leaders who were committed to violent resistance to the Europeans. The details of this transfer of power from Te Ua to his warlike disciples is not known, but we do know that Te Ua himself chose the leaders who came to control the movement. In a special ritual (or rituals), which in part entailed the disciples smoking the prophet's pipe, the former assumed Te Ua's powers and went forth as the savior's messengers to all parts of the island. This transmission of power probably took place before the massacre of Lloyd's party, which marked the end of Te Ua's effective control.

Like Te Ua, most of his major disciples, such as Patara and the infamous Kereopa who instigated the murder of the German missionary Volkner, were "new men" or transitionals who had had significant contacts with European missionaries and settlers. Although many of these leaders transformed Te Ua's vision of reconciliation and peaceful coexistence into a gospel of violence and a war for survival, they too blended ancient Maori customs and ideas with Biblical teachings and European organizational forms and technology as they spread the new faith across the North Island. Both because of their often lowly origins and the highly localized nature of political power among the Maoris, it was essential for Te Ua's disciples to win over local leaders if they were to gain supporters for the movement. However, as they dispersed, the Pai Maire movement fragmented into localized risings led by tribal chiefs, *hapu* heads, and *tohunga* in the southern and eastern areas of the North Island.

Although the names of some of Birsa's closest disciples were recorded, very little is known about the social origins of these men. The available evidence indicates that many of Birsa's inner disciples had long been involved in the Sardar protest movement. Apparently these agitators saw in Birsa the strong leader that the Sardar movement had so long lacked. After Birsa's first arrest and release, when his teachings became increasingly oriented to rebellion, the Sardars assumed key roles as recruiters and organizers.[31] Because the Birsite revolt consisted essentially of a single violent clash (during which the prophet deserted his followers), there was little opportunity for a full structure of command to develop or for authority to diffuse as in the other movements considered.

The patterns of leadership outlined above bear on a number of points of contention associated with prophetic movements and peasant protest more generally. Although prophetic figures were essential to the initiation of each of the movements in question, only two of the prophets retained any semblance of authority throughout the whole time span of their movements. The violent phase of the Birsite disturbances was too brief for this control to be significant. Dipanagara remained the central symbol of the rebellion he had initiated, but he delegated both political authority and military control to his closest advisors. Te Ua lost control over his movement perhaps even before it moved into its violent phase, and the Saya San and Maji Maji disturbances continued even after their prophet-founders had disappeared from the scene.

Although four of the five prophets were peasants by birth, all had assumed different occupations and statuses before launching their careers as leaders of social protest. At the level of primary leadership, therefore, the evidence supports the assertions made by many writers that peasants tend to borrow leaders from other social groups when engaging in protest actions that extend beyond localized and short-lived outbursts of violence.[32] At the level of secondary leadership, however, village leaders and kinship heads who were primarily agriculturists and village-based religious specialists played major roles in protest mobilization and command in battle. The importance of these peasant and local leaders indicates a need to qualify our assertions about sources of authority in peasant protest movements to take into account complexities that result from the layering and diffusion of control. The vital roles of local leaders also supports the view that peasants fervently and willingly attach themselves to exceptional individuals among their peers. Such leaders are acknowledged by virtue of their practical skills, courage in conflict, and proven judgment. This view contrasts with the approach to peasant leadership associated with the concept of the "image of limited good," which has been seen as central to all forms of peasant activity. According to the "limited good" approach, peasants are reluctant to delegate authority to their peers or to assume leadership roles because of their fear of creating disruptive imbalances in the distribution of what is perceived to be a limited supply of status and material rewards.[33]

The cases examined indicate that the decisions of local community leaders can prove decisive in the spread of rebellion in agrarian societies. Headmen and village notables rallied common villagers and dependent laborers; chiefs and elders led their kinsmen into battle; and princely leaders like Dipanagara forged alliances with regional lords and bandit chieftains and through them mobilized complex hierarchical chains of subordinates extending to the village level. Thus the growth of widespread movements of anticolonial resistance was dependent upon the existence of longstanding patron-client ties between landholders and tenants, nobles and peasants, religious teachers and students, bandit leaders and their followers, and chiefs and elders and their subordinate kinsman.[34]

SIX

Mobilization: Symbol and Ritual, Talisman and Sympathetic Magic

In the early centuries of European overseas expansion, most of the peoples of Africa and Asia did not find themselves at a decisive disadvantage in comparison with the Europeans in military technology and organizational techniques. The initial European advantages in technology were selective and preponderantly oriented to the sea. Disease and geographical barriers and sheer numerical superiority permitted most Afro-Asian peoples to prevent extensive European penetration or to limit it to coastal and insular areas. Persistent manpower shortages, an awareness of their limitations in land warfare, and the nature of their expansionist aims also restricted European inland penetration in most areas. Beginning in the last half of the eighteenth century, however, and gaining increasing momentum throughout the nineteenth century, the Europeans' advantages in conflict with non-Western peoples became decisive in almost all categories of weapons and organization, on land and sea. The industrial revolution and its concomitant advances in military and communications technology broke down geographical and disease barriers and transformed simple numerical superiority, epitomized by the massed cavalry charges that were the backbone of many Asian and Sudanic African armies, into mass slaughter. Ironclad steamships and river boats, mobile and increasingly accurate field artillery, railways, machine guns, and general staffs made possible the conquest of vast areas of the globe. They also made it feasible to administer these conquests in depth and to bring about extensive socioeconomic transformations.[1]

The reactions of non-Western peoples to the demonstrated superiority of European arms varied widely, depending on their own level of technological and organizational development, the time period when intense European penetration (hence military confrontations on land) occurred, and their previous contact with the Europeans. Small-scale, relatively isolated societies, such as those found over much of east and central Africa or in Oceania, were apt, as Ndabaningi Sithole has expressed it, to be "overwhelmed, overawed, puzzled, perplexed, mystified, and dazzled."[2] Peoples like the Chinese and Japanese who had developed large-scale and highly sophisticated political and military systems and who had long been in contact with the Europeans were forced, however grudgingly, to admit Western technological superiority. This admission eventually led to demands for changes in their institutions and thought patterns aimed at closing the obvious technological gap.[3] Much of the sense of impotence and humiliation initially felt by colonized peoples can be traced to the awesome superiority that the Europeans demonstrated in material, particularly military, matters. From West Africa to Japan, large kingdoms and small found in the words of the ill-fated Vietnamese mandarin, Phan Than Gian: "Nobody can resist them. They go where they choose. . . . Under heaven, everything is feasible to them, save only the matter of life and death."[4]

As I discussed in the last chapter, all of the peoples who mounted the prophetic rebellions under consideration had been made acutely aware of European military capacity during the period of conquest and primary resistance. This awareness of the decisive edge possessed by the Europeans in the business of organized killing and the threat of their violent reprisals[5] was a major impediment to all forms of protest or resistance to colonial domination. It particularly obstructed efforts by the colonized to mobilize violent protest, which involved a much higher degree of personal risk than other forms of agitation. In the cases considered here, these obstacles were compounded by the problems involved in mobilizing widespread resistance among peasant groups, which were discussed in chapter 3.

Self-confident and persuasive prophets and their millennial visions played critical roles in allaying the doubts and fears of the groups whom they sought to recruit to their causes. In the ensuing conflicts, however, the Europeans still possessed a decisive edge. Therefore, further assurances and potent weapons were required to carry the faithful through the period of strife and suffering that was critical to the inauguration of the millennium. The specific techniques and devices employed by different groups to bolster their strength and neutralize the advantages of the Europeans and their allies varied considerably, but for the purpose of analysis they can be grouped under five general headings: (1) preparatory rumors and omens, (2) legitimating symbols, (3) rituals to establish solidarity and invoke supernatural assistance, (4) use of talismans, and (5) imitation of their adversaries' behavior or sympathetic magic. One additional technique, which varied in importance in each case, must also be considered—the resort to threats and force to recruit those whom all other appeals had failed to win to the cause.

Disaster and Rumors: Setting the Stage for Revolt

The peoples of societies like those under consideration, where there are beliefs in a constant interplay between supernatural and terrestrial forces, commonly regard natural occurrences as portents of events or great upheavals to come. They view drought and famine, volcanic eruptions or comets as reflections of turbulence in the heavens, which in turn is associated with periods of social disorder and moral decline on earth.[6] These occurrences frequently intensify millennial expectations and have often presaged the rise of prophetic figures.[7] Natural calamities clearly fostered an atmosphere receptive to salvationist movements in all but one of the cases examined in this study.

In Lower Burma a great earthquake in May 1930, which levelled buildings and took many lives in Pegu and other towns in the Delta, was widely interpreted as a sign that great upheavals were pending. To those who had been exposed to Saya San's fiery orations calling for rebellion, the earthquake seemed a confirmation of rumors that Saya San was the *Sektya Min* or Just King. In German East Africa, drought in some areas of the interior gave impetus to those who sought to spread the *maji* cult with its promise of the eradication of the sources of this and similar misfortunes. The famines and epidemics that struck Chota Nagpur in the period of Birsa's initial appearance as a prophetic figure and again after his release from prison not only heightened salvationist yearnings, they also gave Birsa opportunities to demonstrate his capacity as a healer and his great concern for the needs of his people.[8] In Java, famine, cholera epidemics, and volcanic eruptions were associated both with Dipanagara's visions and with key events in Yogyakarta in the years before the Java War. The rampant corruption of those in positions of authority, the debasement of highly revered customs and relationships, and the unchecked depredations of robber bands—all were closely linked in the Javanese prophetic tradition with the period before the coming of the *Ratu Adil*.[9]

Natural calamities and widespread social disorders proved fertile sources of rumors, which further heightened colonized peoples' sense of anticipation and frequently counteracted the all-powerful and invincible image of the European colonizers. Rumors also served to articulate long-repressed dissatisfaction and provided a way for prophets to test popular reactions to their salvationist claims and their calls to rebellion.[10] Long-held assumptions about the limits set on the lifespan of dynastic houses fed speculation in Burma and Java that the fall of the European overlords was imminent. In Burma it was also rumored that the deposed Konbaung dynasty would soon be restored. Not purely coincidentally, Saya San claimed to be the twelfth monarch of that royal house.[11]

Although rumors that the colonizers had lost battles in foreign wars, which have given impetus to revolts in many colonial areas,[12] did not figure in the movements under consideration, three of the prophets instructed their followers to spread the word that the Europeans would soon be destroyed or driven away. Prophetic leaders also consciously employed techniques certain to spawn rumors and thereby heighten the level of tension and anticipation. One of Kinjikitile's central organizing devices was a whispering campaign designed to spread the secets of the *Maji Maji* cult, which would undoubtedly give rise to a rash of anxious speculation. After his return from prison Birsa recruited his followers primarily at secret meetings held deep in the forest at night. This tactic was, of course, in part dictated by a desire to avoid rearrest, but Birsa must have been aware of the dramatic effect of these clandestine, nocturnal meetings held around great bonfires. A succession of curing prophets and mysterious sightings of returning ancestors prepared the way for Te Ua. After the ambush of the Lloyd party, Pai Maire organizors used the aura of secrecy and taboo that surrounded the messengers who carried the severed heads of Lloyd and his troops to all parts of the island to insure continued receptivity to their message.[13]

The Quest for Legitimacy

Although each prophet's appeal and his ability to mobilize widespread support were ultimately rooted in his personality, revelations, and millenarian visions, all of the prophets invoked additional institutional props, behavioral patterns, and rituals to enhance their legitimacy. In Burma, Java, and German East Africa these symbols were based almost wholly on indigenous, precolonial precedents. Among the Maoris and Mundas, foreign influences played important roles.

Perhaps the most elaborate attempt to gain legitimacy through the use of indigenous political-religious symbols was associated

with the Saya San rebellion in Burma.[14] Before both of the risings
that he personally led, Saya San presided over impressive coronation ceremonies, which were conducted insofar as possible in
accordance with customary Burman court protocol. Four queens
and chief ministers were present; one each for each point of the
compass, symbolizing his dominion over all of the regions of
the earth. Saya San mounted a lion throne, modelled after that
of the Konbaung monarchs, and brandished the traditional regalia
of a Burman ruler, including a white umbrella and the crown and
sword of victory. He bestowed titles on his chief followers, reviewed
his troops, and issued proclamations after the fashion of a newly-
crowned Burman monarch. He sat in regal splendor while his
followers prayed for his good fortune and offered their homage.

After the first coronation ceremony Saya San retired to the
palace that his adherents had built for him atop a hill in the forest.
The palace, which was built in imitation of structures that were the
actual and symbolic centers of precolonial Burman states, was essential to Saya San's efforts to achieve widespread acceptance of
his claims to legitimacy. In accordance with well-established precedents set by rival claimants and royal pretenders in the precolonial
era, as well as by a number of earlier rebels in the British period,
the palace was laid out in imitation of the classical Mt. Meru cosmic
diagram that has played such a prominent architectural role in
"Indianized" Southeast Asia. Beyond its legitimitizing functions,
the palace and the "royal city" of bamboo huts that surrounded it
provided a physical and symbolic anchor for Saya San's following
in a land burdened with economic depression, social and religious
decay, and widespread crime. Saya San's followers believed that
the palace and city were impregnable and invisible to all but the
faithful supporters of the new monarch.

Since Dipanagara was genuinely of princely birth, his assumption of royal titles and the other accoutrements of Javanese sovereignty arose from a need to demonstrate that he was the rightful
spiritual ruler of the Javanese, rather than an effort to establish the
dynastic links that so occupied Saya San. Dipanagara displayed his
concern for legitimacy repeatedly before, during, and even after
his rebellion against the Dutch and their allies. In the years before
the rebellion he made a number of pilgrimages to holy places and
sacred gravesites of saints and former rulers. He chose the sites
and patterned the pilgrimages themselves after precedents set by
earlier monarchs, like Sultan Agung who had ruled the house of

Mataram at the apogee of its power. On these trips Dipanagara paused frequently to pray and meditate, which did much to contribute to his considerable reputation as an ascetic and mystic. Whatever his personal motives may have been, many Javanese saw his practice of meditation as further indication of his worthiness to be Sultan. Meditation was (and is) associated in Javanese culture with the accumulation of great magical powers, which were frequently claimed by reigning potentates and rebel claimants to the throne. Dipanagara's mystical encounters with the Goddess of the Southern Ocean (Ratu Kidul) could also be seen by his followers as supporting his claims to the right to succession. Javanese rulers customarily sought to demonstrate their ties (often through symbolic marriage) with this most powerful figure in the Javanese spirit pantheon.[15]

Dipanagara's followers repeatedly asserted his claims to the throne of Yogyakarta. Dipanagara himself demanded that he be recognized as the supreme arbiter of religious affairs in Java in letters to his adversaries and proclamations to his followers during the rebellion. He bolstered these claims by founding his own court and palace-centers, bestowing offices and titles on followers who were in many cases of noble birth, and having himself proclaimed Sultan and *ratu paneteg santagama* (the king who stands as the supreme arbiter of religion). He displayed the splendid accoutrements of Javanese lords, including his personal *pusakas* (literally, ancient holy objects), some of which were said to have been given by the gods and to have great magical powers. Although Dipanagara himself dressed in the garb of a Muslim leader engaged in the holy war, he and his courtiers were surrounded by the gilded umbrellas, inscribed banners, and the pomp and ceremony befitting the entourage of a Javanese monarch.[16] Even after his cause was clearly lost and his once impressive counter-court had dwindled to a handful of local leaders, village religious teachers, and peasants, Dipanagara refused to deny the righteousness of his cause or renounce his claims to religious supremacy. He defended his actions and legitimacy in conversations with his captors and those who escorted him into exile. He also recorded his justifications for his descendants in his account or *Babad* of the events leading up to the Java War.[17]

Because the persons who initiated the Maji Maji rebellion had known no centralized bureaucracy or dynastic house in the precolonial era, they took their symbols of legitimacy from local leaders and symbols of authority.[18] Kinjikitile placed great emphasis on the role of the clan heads in his movement, but there appears to have been considerable tension between his necessary reliance on these leaders and his attempt to forge new, more encompassing symbols of legitimacy based on his role as prophet-diviner. This tension is clearly revealed by the ceremonies at his pool oracle, the major means by which Kinjikitile communicated his cult beliefs and message of revolt to local leaders.

On the one hand, Kinjikitile's claims to authority were based on the complex of millenarian cult beliefs outlined above in chapter 3. When pilgrims arrived at his oracle, a messenger would call Kinjikitile from his secluded residence. The prophet would appear suddenly and dive into the oracle pool to consult with the god Hongo before preaching to the pilgrims. During the consultations that followed, Kinjikitile would sit on a rock or raft in the pool, which physically symbolized his role as god-oracle. He and his servants also carried fly whisks as constant reminders to visitors of their exalted and sacred status. In these ways, Kinjikitile presented himself as an authority figure that transcended clan and ethnic boundaries.

The second form of legitimization rituals, however, stressed precisely the particularistic identities that the oracle-millennial complex was designed to subordinate. In the meetings at the oracle, Kinjikitile addressed his remarks and distributed his medicine to the clan heads of the pilgrim groups who had come to seek his assistance. The clan heads were permitted to communicate with their ancestors and were given sacred water from the pool. The prophet confirmed them as the commanders of the forces that, under Kinjikitile's guidance, were to drive off the foreign invaders. The authority of the clan leaders was also bolstered by the very fact of preparing for rebellion, since they again would assume their positions as military leaders, which had been one of their key sources of power and prestige in the precolonial period. Matumbi and Ngindo religious experts also reclaimed their vital roles as the celebrants of ceremonies initiating local groups into the cult, as well as those preparing the faithful for battle. In addition, the religious experts often served as messengers who were the main links between Kinjikitile and his followers and who spread the Maji Maji cult to peoples beyond the Matumbi-Ngindo heartland.

The tension between these two levels of legitimizing symbols is illustrated by one of the central physical standards of the Maji Maji movement, the ancestral shrine. At his oracle, Kinjikitile had his followers construct a shrine much larger than those used in household or village worship. Kinjikitile's shrine was intended to honor the ancestors of all of the faithful, regardless of their clan or ethnic identity. It was thus intended to unite previously divided, and often hostile, groups. Direct contact between Kinjikitile and his followers, however, was at best limited to a single meeting. Once the pilgrims departed from the oracle center, local leaders and local ancestral cults and shrines once again became and remained the focus of identity.

His lowly origins made Te Ua a man who was very concerned with legitimacy. As I discussed in chapter 4, his claims to prophetic authority rested on his visions and miraculous powers, which were in turn rooted in both indigenous Maori beliefs and in foreign, particularly Biblical, writings. Te Ua himself was more a Judeo-Christian prophetic figure than a Maori war chief or religious expert. Although he claimed the owl, especially revered by the Maori, as his guardian spirit and resurrected some Maori rituals and chants, his style and cult ceremonies were strongly influenced by Christianity. His legitimacy was rooted in revelations from a Judeo-Christian God; he preached sermons after the missionary fashion; and he led prayers taken from the Book of Common Prayer and hymns from the Church of England hymnal. Even his conscious alteration of certain Christian practices, such as his change of the Sabbath day and his substitution of the Maori words *hau* and *rire* for Amen, ironically reflected the deep impression that his missionary educators had made upon him in his youth.[19]

As leadership of the Pai Maire shifted from Te Ua to his more violence-prone subordinates, Christian symbols of legitimacy increasingly gave way to a renewal of customary Maori rituals and forms. In contrast to the Kingites, who had emphasized ancient Maori institutions designed for the peaceful resolution of disputes —such as the tribal assembly and the role of the chief as arbiter and counsellor—Pai Maire leaders stressed the role of the chief as war leader. Equally critically they restored the *tohungas* to their old place of preeminence as tribal soothsayers, head magicians, and the main military advisors of the chiefs. Deep-seated Maori war customs and beliefs—such as cannibalism and the drinking of the victim's blood—were revived. The heads of Captain Lloyd and other victims were smoked and used as oracles, as captured heads had been in pre-European times. Ancient war chants and dances were mixed with Christian hymns. Both chiefs and *tohungas* assumed their customary dress and ritual behavior and led their followers into battle in the manner sanctioned by the ancestors. The shift in legitimizing symbols that occurred as leadership passed from Te Ua to his early adherents is above all epitomized by the gradual but perceptible transition from reliance on Jehovah and guardian angels to invocations of Oraku, the Maori war god, and other Maori spirits.[20]

Of all those considered, the Birsite movement relied the most heavily on foreign institutions and thought systems, both Christian and Hindu, for its symbols of legitimacy. Birsa may have attempted to revive the idea of a Munda king, but his main emphasis was on religious and social innovations intended to raise the Mundas' self-esteem and status in relation to dominant lowland groups. Birsa attacked the animistic spirit worship of his people and laid stress on a single god who was conceived as a blend of Hindu and Christian concepts. He ordered his followers to refrain from sacrifices, which had been central to customary Munda worship, and exhorted them to pray, fast, and meditate instead. Like so many Indian reformers who have sought to raise the status of low caste groups,[21] Birsa instructed his followers to wear the sacred thread of the Hindu upper or "twice-born" castes, and refrain from eating meat, fish, and other foods associated with low caste or pariah groups.

Because his people were poor and lacked a highly developed material culture, the physical symbols invoked by Birsa were few. His emphasis was on patterns of behavior, and his central symbols of legitimization were closely linked to the practice of "sympathetic magic," which will be discussed below in detail. Birsa and his followers turned away from spirits and rituals which had failed the Mundas in their struggle with the lowland invaders. The Birsites reasoned that their status and the strength of their bargaining position could be improved only by adopting the symbols and forms of their more powerful adversaries, both European and lowland Indian.[22]

Though symbols of legitimacy tended to instill a sense of righteousness and enhanced solidarity among those who joined a particular movement, they could also engender hostility towards the prophet's followers among other colonized groups. Appeals based on the symbols and beliefs of one group could limit the potential scope of the prophet's attempts to recruit support for his resistance efforts. In Burma, for example, the symbols invoked by Saya San scared away most Western-educated, urban-based nationalists and all of the Burmans who served in the colonial administration. Equally important, these symbols were primarily those of the Burman Buddhist majority and, to some extent, of the Shan peoples of the northeastern highlands. Thus they emphasized deep-seated divisions between the Burmans and minority peoples like the Chins and Karens. During the rebellion, bloody interethnic clashes occurred in a number of areas. Generally, the minority peoples stood aloof from the revolt and in many cases helped the British suppress the rebellion by serving as soldiers and policemen.

Rituals for Solidarity and Battle

Since each of the movements considered here ended in rebellion, those who had been convinced by the prophet's message and persuaded of the legitimacy of his cause had to be further prepared. They had to be willing to march together into battle against an enemy with decisive superiority in military training, organization, and technology. Recruiting and planning for revolt also had to be clandestine, for secrecy would reduce the heavy odds against the rebels by granting them the advantage of surprise. Two key devices were employed to maintain secrecy and sustain commitment: (1) oaths and initiation ceremonies and (2) cult rituals, which were often held just before the faithful marched into battle.

Although oaths were invoked in the transmission of the *maji* medicine and were almost certainly employed to some extent in all of the movements under consideration, their most extensive use was in the Saya San rebellion.[23] In accordance with a tradition followed by troops being recruited into armies of the Burman kings,[24] an oath was administered to all who joined Saya San's forces. The leader held a special pot of oath water during the ceremony, which was drunk by the initiates after the oath had been administered. The oaths began with a call for supernatural forces to "listen to the solemn oath" and to support those who were "desirous of promoting Buddhism, the sacred religion of Buddha, the King of Kings" and who sought to "do away with all heretics." Having established the seriousness of the step about to be taken, the oaths committed the initiates to the rebel cause by having them swear by the "Kings of Gods, Bramahs [Hindu deities?], Nagas [mythical serpent-like creatures], and four guardian spirits of the world" neither to betray or disobey members of the rebel armies. The initiates promised that they would "always abide by the rules and regulations framed by this great body and . . . defend the Buddhist religion at the risk of [their] life and wealth." The initiates then were told that their adherence to the oath would bring, among other things, immunity to their enemies' weapons, victory over their adversaries, and "wealth and prosperity" that would increase "day by day." If they should fail to keep the oath, however, they prayed that they might:

be a victim of all kinds of sudden death, namely death caused by stick, *dah* [knife], spear, gun, cannon, tiger, elephant, horse . . . by 96 varieties of disease and plagues . . . by evil spirits, ghosts, demons and ogres, and death caused by water creatures . . . and also by falling of trees, rock, mountain, building, struck by lightning and running over by a car or train.

Having been done away with in an appropriately horrible manner, the unfaithful initiates would then be condemned to the "lowest of eight hells" of the Buddhist underworld for eons. After again calling on the gods to witness their oath and drinking the oath water, the initiates were irrevocably committed to the rebel cause.[25]

In addition to oaths, other types of initiation ceremonies and rituals to prepare recruits for battle were also employed in the Saya San rebellion. In some of these the faithful prayed to be protected or even possessed by spirits of the *nat* spirit pantheon that coexists with and frequently rivals Buddhism in the Burman belief system. In many instances rebel recruits blended propitiation of protective spirits with Buddhist worship, as offerings to the *nats* were followed by circumambulations of pagodas or prayers to the Buddha for victory.[26] In the other movements considered, similar ceremonies appear to have been more important than oaths in preparing the faithful for battle. Birsa blessed his followers and sprinkled them with a magical water that, he promised, would keep them from all harm.[27] In German East Africa, acceptance of the Maji Maji medicine, which might be drunk or poured over initiates' heads, committed the recruit irrevocably to the coming resistance against the alien invaders. Special messengers or religious experts administered the medicine in secret ceremonies in which instructions were whispered to the initiates. Although no detailed descriptions of these ceremonies are available, there is evidence that in some animal sacrifices were regularly made and that sexual intercourse was forbidden between the time the medicine was distributed and when the recruits went to battle. These observances indicate that the Maji Maji rituals were a blend of the initiation ceremonies associated with rites of passage in the societies of the region and rituals designed to prepare the warrior for battle.[28] No accounts of Javanese initiation or preparatory ceremonies were contained in the sources I have consulted, but it is possible that fasting, meditation, and (again) sexual abstinence were stressed. The Javanese have customarily employed these practices to prepare the soldier for battle or the rebel for revolt. They have regarded them as critical for the accumulation of magical powers and physical strength.[29]

Of all the movements considered, the Maori Pai Maire had the most elaborate rituals. These included the initiation of new members, the preparation of warriors for battle, and periodic "prayer meetings." These ceremonies were designed to rekindle the enthusiasm of the faithful and to solidify their resolve to drive away the white invaders. After control of the movement passed from Te Ua to his chief disciples, special rituals, which have been labeled *niu* ceremonies after their central ritual object, became the only real link between the different tribal and *hapu* groups which embraced the movement.[30] The *niu* was a tall pole from which pennants and ropes were hung. The adherents of the Pai Maire believed that the flags had special powers and that the ropes were the means by which their prayers were transmitted to heaven and by which legions of angels sent by Jehovah to assist them would descend to the earth. The meaning of the *niu* pole has been interpreted in various ways, but it seems probable that it stood for a variety of Maori and European objects. It was clearly patterned after a ship's mast and flagstaff. It derived its name from short wooden sticks customarily used by Maori *tohungas* in divination rituals connected with warfare. It may also have been associated with the white man's telegraph in the same way as similar ceremonial objects in the cargo cult movements of Melanesia.[31]

The format of the *niu* ceremony varied somewhat, but its basic ingredients were chants, ecstatic dancing and marching about the *niu* pole, and demonstrations by the ritual leader of his ability to speak in many tongues. To contemporary observers, the latter seemed to be the incantation of nonsense syllables or gibberish from English or some other foreign language. Normally the participants sang and danced until they drove themselves into a frenzy. As some individuals fell into trances or had convulsions, they were thought to have been possessed by Maori guardian spirits and thus to have received great powers. Also, in accordance with long-established practices of the *tohungas*, the ritual leaders of the *niu* ceremonies appear to have resorted frequently to hypnotism to bring the faithful to the proper pitch of ecstasy. Of the movements which I have examined in detail, only in the Pai Maire is there clear evidence of mesmerism, trance, and convulsions, but these have frequently been observed in revitalization movements in other areas.[32]

Before marching into battle, *tohunga* leaders also blessed and purified the Pai Maire warriors after the ancient Maori fashion. On a number of occasions they prayed for legions of angels to descend and march with the faithful into battle. Similar prayers were important features of the battle preparations in other millenarian rebellions, such as the Madhist movement in the Anglo-Egyptian Sudan and the Boxer revolt in China.[33]

Talismans

To a considerable extent the great impression that European technological capacity made on the minds of all non-Western peoples was due to the inability of the latter to comprehend the origins or workings of the machines and weapons that so rudely smashed through their protective buffers and soon threatened to topple their ancient sociocultural systems. Until Africans and Asians began to travel to Europe in fairly substantial numbers or to be trained as mechanics, engineers, and soldiers, European warships and mobile field artillery appeared to them to have been bequeathed by the gods or conjured up by powerful magic possessed by the Europeans alone. Suddenly confronted by these awesome engines of death, they had no notion of how they were produced or what made them work. They could not, as they had done in earlier centuries with simpler devices like muskets or siege cannon, merely make their own in imitation of captured or imported European (or Chinese or Muslim) models. The technical knowledge and engineering skills involved in the construction of a steam engine or Maxim gun were simply beyond the means of non-Western peoples. The frustration and futility of attempts to duplicate Western achievements in technology are poignantly illustrated by the Vietnamese Emperor Min Mang's attempt to have a steamship constructed in his shipyards. Even though the final product of his shipwrights' and carpenters' labors looked very much like a French steamship, it did not work like one because it had no engine or any of the other mechanical devices that made one run.[34] Similar frustrations and bewilderment were experienced by all non-Western peoples from the highly sophisticated Chinese to the primitive peoples of the interior of New Guinea. In the period before these peoples came to the conclusion that the only way to bridge the technological gap that grew ever wider between them and the Europeans was to adopt European ideas and methods, they frequently sought to overcome European military superiority through the use of magical protective charms.

The use of talismans, of course, was based on beliefs and practices whose origins long antedated the era of European colonial domination. Charms, occult incantations, and magical rituals had long been employed in virtually all societies that came under European colonial control. They were used to ward off all sorts of evils from demons to the curses of rivals, and to gain wealth, potency, fertility, or general good fortune.[35] In fact, magic and protective talismans were extremely important in European cultures themselves in the preindustrial era. Their vestiges linger in notions about the effects of spilling salt, breaking mirrors, or carrying Saint Christopher medals.[36] Non-Western peoples like the Matumbi and Ngindo employed magical talismans for all sorts of dangerous endeavors from hunting to war.[37] The *karakia* or ritual prayers, which were central to Pai Maire talismanic usage, had long played a key role in Maori beliefs and ceremonies. The Maoris believed that if the *karakia* were properly recited, the gods addressed had no choice but to do the *tohunga*'s bidding.[38] In Burma and Java there were rich traditions of the use of magical charms of all sorts. In Burma tattoos, which were once essential symbols of the Burman's transition to manhood, were the most commonly employed. In Java magical inscriptions, often written in Arabic on pieces of paper, wood, or battle flags, were the favorite talismans. In both of these cultures the use of talismans to gain invulnerability was particularly pronounced among bandits and soldiers.[39] Although long associated with the animistic religions that predated the rise or extension of the so-called great religions in areas like Burma or Java, recent research has shown that talismanic beliefs represent complex mixtures of both animistic ideas and elements of the "Great Traditions."[40]

The talismans employed by the adherents of the movements under study were designed to neutralize the technological and organizational advantages of their European adversaries. Through these charms, prophetic leaders sought to transfer magical protective powers to their adherents and to assure them of invulnerability in the battles that lay ahead. There were many types of talismans, but several recurrent patterns can be distinguished for the purposes of comparative analysis.[41] Two basic categories relate to the nature of the talisman itself: (1) those consisting of material objects and (2) those involving magical incantations or ritual gestures or both. Each of these categories can in turn be subdivided, according to the ends that the talismans were designed to achieve, into two main types: (1) those intended to confer special, frequently protective, powers and (2) those aimed at handicapping or destroying the enemy. These two types contained both offensive and defensive varieties of talismans, and frequently charms were designed to serve both of these ends. Physical objects usually tended to be used for the protection of their bearers rather than for inflicting damage on the enemy. They were also more generally all-purpose than chants and rituals, which seemed specifically designed for battle itself and were frequently aimed at disabling the enemy's forces. Physical objects, such as water-based potions or magic seeds, usually had fertility or healing implications. Battle standards inscribed with cabalistic stanzas also proclaimed the legitimacy of the cause of their bearers. In view of the great variety of physical objects and chants employed, a mere listing would be less valuable than a discussion of some of the more dominant types and the different sorts of powers they were thought to confer.

Rebel recruits frequently made use of magical turbans or clothing, tattoos, and special chants to render themselves invisible and thus invulnerable to the enemy's weapons. The Ngoni in Tanzania, for example, believed that they possessed medicines that would turn them into anthills, which the enemy would pass by without noticing. The participants in one of the Saya San risings tattooed themselves with special designs that would make them invisible to the British. Pai Maire adherents had special chants to summon fog or mists to enshroud them or to enlist the aid of living creatures to conceal them from the enemy. They prayed:

> Spiders hide my face,
> Ants obscure me from the foe;
> O Moko, [the god of volcanos and the earth]
> Come forth from thy pit,
> And let me enter it.
> Search all around,
> Gaze up and down,
> See nothing but the empty land.[42]

A second major function of both categories of talismans, but particularly ones consisting of different sorts of material objects, was to prevent enemy bullets or other missiles from entering their bearer's body. Tattoos and potions like the *maji* medicine were used on occasion, but usually small amulets or bits of metal were employed. At times rebels swallowed these objects or held them in their teeth, and in the Saya San rebellion, needles were embedded in the recruits' skin. In most instances these talismans were designed to provide either internal or external armor for those who used them. When a bullet or sword thrust threatened, it was believed that internal protection was provided because the amulet or needle would move quickly to the part of the bearer's body in jeopardy and deflect the aggressor's missile before it could do any harm. External armor was associated mainly with charmed oils and magic potions that were rubbed on or poured over the body. As the body was covered, the recruit uttered special prayers like the following from the Saya San rebellion: "May this make my flesh as hard and resisting as iron. May *dahs* [knives] be deflected and their edges turned. May my flesh remain unscathed."[43]

A final type of protective or power-enhancing talisman was directly linked to the user's ability to make war more effectively. The Matumbi warriors mixed the *maji* medicine with gunpowder to make their antiquated muskets more accurate. Special spears and daggers, which were said to have magical powers that made them superior to the enemies' rifles and artillery, were employed in a number of movements. Maori leaders claimed that they could walk on water or draw European ships on to the land. Birsa told his followers that if they gathered special bamboo stalks, they could be fired like rifles. Burman monks told rebel recruits that they knew magical formulas that would cause airplanes to drop from the sky or turn twigs into war horses. In the Saya San movement rebel groups employed charms that were said to render their bearers capable of running at great speeds and of leaping into the air in hand-to-hand combat.

Talismans designed to reduce the military capacity of the enemy can, like power-enhancing talismans, be divided into those which were primarily defensive and those aimed at injuring or destroying the enemy. The most frequently employed protective devices were those intended to prevent the enemies' guns from firing or to turn their shells, bullets, and at times the guns themselves to harmless objects ranging from wooden sticks to dust. By far the most common belief of this type was connected with talismans that were said to have the power to turn the Europeans' bullets to water. Not only was this belief present in all of the major cases of rebellion considered here but a survey of other studies reveals that it has been found in hundreds of similar protest movements from Oceania to Brazil.

A second way in which protection was sought through talismans designed to impair the enemy's fighting capacity was through chants and charms designed to deflect bullets and shells from their intended targets. Sacred flags and musical instruments were sometimes used, but magical chants and ritual gestures were most frequently resorted to. The most elaborate of these missile-diverting rituals was a central feature of the Pai Maire movement. The rebels would march toward the colonial troops with their right hand raised in front of their face chanting orders for the bullets of the Europeans to pass harmlessly over their heads. On a number of occasions Maori women and children stood on the fringes of the battle area waving imaginary bullets over their shoulders while chanting "Pass over, pass over."

In a number of cases, the magical force of certain talismans was aimed at disabling the colonial troops rather than their weapons. Javanese rebels carried slips of paper with Arabic inscriptions calling on supernatural agents to disable the Dutch in various ways.[44] Birsa prophesied that fire would come and destroy the hated lowland invaders of Munda country. One of the rebel leaders in the Saya San rebellion told his recruits that he would carry a sacred gong into battle that would stupify the colonial armies and render them incapable of resistance. In the Maji Maji revolt a Zaramo prophet-leader told his followers that he possessed powerful magic that would cause the earth to open and swallow the foreign invaders. He also promised to summon seven great lions that would devour all of the rebels' enemies.

How far the leaders who distributed these talismans or the followers who employed them in battle believed in their efficacy cannot be precisely determined. Contemporary European observers, and to some extent postrebellion testimony, indicate that such charms and incantations were an important ingredient in the fierce attacks of rebel forces, particularly in the early stages of resistance before European fire power began to take its toll. Massed charges by rebel forces, often over open ground, occurred in the early stages of all the rebellions except the Munda. In Java and New Zealand the rebels faced European artillery; in Burma and German East Africa they fearlessly charged into the deadly fire of machine guns and repeating rifles. In some cases the rebels' firm belief in their charms was shared by the indigenous mercenary troops whom the Europeans had recruited into their armies. The Hehe warriors who fought for the Germans, for example, were at first so apprehensive of the power of the *maji* medicine that their German officers reported that they were useless in battle. After several encounters with the rebels in which their German-supplied fire-arms wreaked havoc in the enemy ranks, however, the Hehe soon concluded that the *maji* medicine was weak and German rifles and their own medicines were far more potent.

In some rebellions, like the Pai Maire and the Maji Maji, rebel groups continued to employ the same talismans, even though costly defeats had clearly demonstrated that they were ineffective. In other movements like the Saya San, when early talismans were discredited, they were discarded and new charms and tattoos were adopted. Rather than simply demonstrating a lack of critical faculty among the groups who persisted in using these talismans,[45] their continuing faith can be attributed to the nature of their belief systems as a whole. Like most prescientific peoples, they tended to overlook or explain away failures in the practice of divination, healing, or magic.[46] They did so not because they lacked the ability to criticize but because their explanations for the failure of magic or prophecies did not involve the scrutiny of nor challenges to the more fundamental assumptions on which magical charms and millenarian visions were based, as it *might* have in scientifically oriented cultures. The failure of talismans was always explained in terms of the *specific* shortcomings of a *particular* leader or religious expert or a *particular* talisman, rather than by the deficiencies of general beliefs in miracles and magic. If a charm or cure failed, its users would blame its lack of power on the improper techniques of the individual who supplied it, or on the lack of faith or the disobedience of those who employed it, or perhaps on the caprice of the gods who were called upon to give the talisman potency. These explanations have frequently allowed prophetic figures to retain the loyalty of at least some of their adherents and to revive their flagging movements. Repeated failures, however, have almost always been fatal to these movements. The success that different prophetic figures have had in holding their followers despite setbacks has depended largely on the persuasiveness of individual leaders. This persuasiveness has been determined by the leader's personal courage, sense of conviction, and his ability to remain outwardly confident despite setbacks. However successful a leader might be in rallying his followers, the ultimate end of his efforts was invariably defeat. Eventually his adherents rejected specific talismans, but never their belief in magic.

The stress placed on talismans in the mobilization of rebel forces and the generation of fighting spirit in the face of European firepower should be tempered somewhat by calling attention to other factors at work. Prophetic revelations and personal persuasiveness; the influence and appeal of secondary leaders; group pressures; promised rewards for the faithful who fell in battle; and the desire of warriors to assert once again their manly worth were all important factors in the successful launching of violent assaults against the colonial overlords. It is impossible (in the absence of reliable sources) to determine the relative importance of each of these factors for different groups on specific occasions, but it is necessary to realize that the talismans did not function in a vacuum. Their successful employment depended on adherence to this complex of related beliefs and motives, a long tradition of their use, and world views that were receptive to magico-religious explanations of causality.

In the movements under study talismans played a critical role in promoting open rebellion by allaying the colonized peoples' fears of the technological capacity of the European overlords. Magical charms and cabalistic chants diminished—in terms of the rebels perception, though not in fact—the capacity of those in power for effective repression that has been regarded as a decisive factor in the prevention or eruption of violent protest.[47] The use of talismans also represented an effort by colonized peoples to reassert through their customary vehicle, war, their courage and manly stature after decades of submitting meekly to the orders of the man with the gun.

Sympathetic Magic

Paralleling the widespread use of talismans, which were rooted in the indigenous cultures of the colonized peoples, were attempts by some rebel groups to imitate the behavior or organizational patterns of their European conquerors. These efforts, which can be grouped under the heading of sympathetic magic, were largely products of a global "Great Tradition" spawned by the commercial-industrial revolutions in western Europe and disseminated by expansionistic European peoples. The basic idea underlying the practice of sympathetic magic was that by following European patterns the colonized peoples could gain the organizational capacity and technological prowess that they generally perceived to be essential to European dominance. This imitation also expressed the claims of the colonized to a status equal to that of their European overlords.[48] In some cases the behavior of European missionaries was copied, as in the Pai Maire and Birsite movements, but more frequently activities associated with the bureaucratic and military roles of the colonizers were stressed. The importance of these latter roles can be attributed both to the great power associated with them in colonial societies and to the fact that all of the movements considered involved violent attempts to overthrow existing political regimes.

Not surprisingly, sympathetic magic was the strongest in those movements, the Pai Maire and Birsite, that were mounted by peoples long exposed to foreign influences and whose cultures had been greatly weakened by these contacts. Alien institutions and activities took on a special importance for groups who had begun to lose faith in the efficacy of their own. In movements like Dipanagara's rising and the Maji Maji resistance, the continued strength of indigenous cultural forms meant that expressions of sympathetic magic were marginal. In the Maji Maji movement, ex-soldiers from the colonial armies drilled rebel recruits in the manner of Western-trained armies. In the Java War, the only recorded instance of sympathetic magic involved imitation of Islamic, not European, models. Dipanagara named the different regiments of his personal bodyguard after Ottoman equivalents and gave their commanders Ottoman titles.[49] Both of these acts were indicative of the high regard that early nineteenth-century Muslims in Indonesia had for the Ottoman Caliph, and their apparent ignorance of the defeats his empire was absorbing at the hands of European rivals. Some examples of sympathetic magic can also be discerned in the risings that made up the Saya San rebellion. However, the rich millenarian and talismanic beliefs of the Burmans and the fact that indigenous symbols of legitimacy were still very much alive made imitation less important than it was in the other areas of extensive sociocultural breakdown, New Zealand and Chota Nagpur.

Imitation of the Europeans took a number of forms. Often physical objects were employed which were patterned after those that seemed sources of European power, such as the *niu* pole which, as I have noted, was modeled after a number of European creations ranging from a telegraph pole to a ship's flagstaff. The Maoris also believed that Bibles could deflect bullets, and they wore protective patches which consisted of pieces of European uniforms.[50] In the Saya San rebellion, leaders issued enlistment tickets to recruits, who were dressed in makeshift uniforms.[51] In many instances use of physical objects was combined with attempts to imitate European behavior. In the Saya San rebellion, rubber stamps were used in imitation of colonial bureaucrats, and Maori rebels attempted to copy European bugle calls. The followers of the Pai Maire also regularly employed gestures that have been described as a mix of the sign of the cross and a military salute.[52] Most prominent in the movements under consideration was the imitation of European military drill patterns. In all of these rebellions, ex-policemen or former soldiers in colonial armies would bark orders to bewildered recruits. They would also count cadence with chants, many of which expressed the strong anti-European sentiments felt by the groups in protest.[53] Through drills, timetables, and imitation of European bureaucratic behavior, protest leaders hoped to create in their followers some of the discipline and precision that seemed major sources of European success.

Of the five leaders examined in some detail in this study, only Birsa and Te Ua associated themselves closely with European behavioral patterns or symbols. As noted earlier, both prophets adopted aspects of missionary behavior. Birsa may have consciously cultivated a physical likeness to Jesus as the latter was portrayed in prints that were popular in mission stations at the time. Birsa also clearly patterned aspects of his behavior after Hindu holy men, thus blending two traditions of his peoples' adversaries.[54] Te Ua's prophecies were also strongly derivative. When the millennium arrived, angels would descend to teach his followers Western sciences and the English language, which they would be able to learn in a single lesson.[55]

In movements like those led by Birsa and Te Ua there was considerable tension between the attraction of foreign ideas and modes of behavior and the proclaimed goal of ridding their homelands of alien invaders. To peoples like the Mundas and Maoris, this tension was inevitable. Long contact had established the desirability of many European imports, particularly material goods, and correspondingly shaken the colonized peoples' faith in indigenous belief and institutional systems. To abandon their own systems, however, or to acquiesce in the continued presence of the foreign invaders was to admit defeat and accept permanently the status of conquered, inferior, and exploitable peoples. Their own systems must be revived and the foreigners must be subdued or driven away, but the secrets of the invaders' material achievement must be obtained and access to their powerful god retained. Te Ua's millennial vision and Birsa's syncretic faith were both attempts to reconcile these contradictory ends. This reconciliation was in turn aimed at alleviating the deep tensions produced by the dilemmas known to all non-Western peoples who have been caught between a battered precolonial cultural system and the uncertainties of the patchwork systems that have resulted from accelerated foreign contacts in the age of European colonial dominance.

Forcible Recruitment

If all of the appeals discussed above failed to win certain groups or individuals to the prophets' cause, his followers were compelled to resort to threats and in some instances actual physical violence. The degree to which rebels were forcibly won to the movements under consideration is impossible to determine, but the importance of fear in the mobilization of resistance groups is certainly overstated in the reports and descriptions of contemporary missionaries and colonial officials. Captured rebels' accounts of having been bullied by displaced leaders or fanatic prophets into joining their movements were all too readily accepted by government functionaries. These officials found fear and superstition much more palatable explanations for outbursts of violent protest than failings on the part of the colonial regime. Nonetheless, it is probable that peer pressure and fear of ostracism, if not bodily injury, played some role in the mobilization of most rebel recruits. It is also reasonable to assume that the importance of these factors increased as the movement extended beyond the prophets' inner circle of hard-core adherents.

The use of force usually involved threats rather than actual physical violence, which in part reflected the limited organizational capacity of the groups in rebellion. Most frequently prophetic leaders would predict that those who refused to join their movement would be destroyed along with the foreign invaders when the day of judgment arrived. They also told recalcitrant villagers that nonbelievers would be assaulted by the powerful supernatural allies of the rebels, or that they would be turned to dust or stone.[56] The antisorcery themes associated with Kinjikitile's millennial vision in German East Africa gave rise to fears that those who refused to join the Maji Maji resistance would be reviled and persecuted as witches. These fears were reinforced by the Maji Maji messengers' orders that all who refused the medicine were to be put to death.[57]

In a striking illustration of a common technique of political control employed in preindustrial kingdoms with poor communications, Prince Dipanagara issued proclamations which notified the populations of certain areas that their failure to support him would force his followers to capture their wives and children and, if the men should actively resist his cause, their families would be put to death.[58]

Although there is no direct evidence in a number of cases, it is probable that actual killings followed the failure of recruiting efforts in all of the movements considered. Those who refused to join or support the rebels were often regarded as informers and sometimes were blamed for the failure of the prophets' magic.[59] At times threats or the actual murder of headmen or indigenous officials who had remained loyal to the colonial overlords made reluctant and understandably unreliable supporters of others. Perhaps as often, however, such intimidation generated hostility toward the prophet and his cause, thus fragmenting rather than uniting the colonized peoples. Threatened individuals or groups sought to avoid rebel bands and in some cases they were driven to side with the colonial overlords in the suppression of the protest movement.

The Rationality of Millennial Solutions and Magical Techniques

In the study of revitalization movements a good deal of attention has necessarily been given to the prophetic figures, millennial visions, elaborate rituals, and magical elements that have played such critical roles in their emergence, spread, and outcome. Unfortunately, these aspects of the revitalization process were generally regarded by colonial administrators and European missionaries as clear evidence that these movements were dominated by atavistic, superstitious, and irrational forces. In official reports and missionary accounts there was a strong tendency to treat millennial expectations and talismanic beliefs as symptoms of psychopathological behavior. This attitude strongly influenced the treatment of revitalization phenomena in the early published works on these movements. In these accounts messianic claims and the use of magical charms were treated as little more than bizarre tidbits for the able raconteur or isolated illustrations of the fantastic and irrational nature of the movement as a whole. This approach resulted both from the failure of contemporary European observers to attempt to understand millennial and magical beliefs in terms of the non-Western cultures and thought systems that produced them, and from the colonizers' insistence on judging these ideas according to Western, scientific criteria or the Judeo-Christian tradition as it was interpreted in the West.

In recent decades most scholars working on revitalization movements in the non-Western world have sought to overcome the narrow ethnocentrism and blatant bias that constricted earlier writers' understanding of this important form of collective behavior. Some writers, however, have continued to apply the criteria of nineteenth- and twentieth-century Western scientific thought in their attempts to assess the rationality or sanity of these movements. As a result, although they have been more sympathetic than earlier writers to the goals and grievances of the participants in revitalization movements and vastly more knowledgeable about the cultures which produced them, these writers have continued to stress the fundamental irrationality and neurotic tendencies exhibited by prophetic figures and the movements they generated.[60] These judgments, however, have been challenged by other social scientists, who have proposed a number of alternative approaches for evaluating the rationality of non-Western belief systems in general.[61] Although a detailed discussion of what has grown into a substantial debate over how alien belief systems are to be studied and interpreted is beyond the scope of this study,[62] the movements considered clearly have bearing on questions concerning the rationality or logic of millenarian and magical beliefs.

On the basis of the evidence provided by the case examples that I have selected and the broader literature on revitalization movements that I have used to test and supplement my own findings, I conclude that although Western scientific criteria alone are not sufficient to judge the rationality of these movements, these standards cannot be entirely disregarded. In this, I differ with some scholars who argue that Western scientific criteria are inappropriate for gauging the rationality or logic of the beliefs of non-Western, prescientific peoples. They contend that the beliefs associated with the movements under study can be judged only by the standards of the specific cultures that produced them.[63] Once this cultural context is understood, they argue, these beliefs can be seen to be rational because they are logical and coherent, and also because they are purposeful and goal-directed.[64]

This extreme position is in several respects as unconvincing as the Euro-centric or scientifically-oriented interpretations it opposes. To begin with, purposefulness or goal-orientation does not necessarily demonstrate rationality. A madman can have very definite goals, which he can elaborately justify, but these goals may be irrational by the standards of his society. More fundamentally, the refusal to admit that criteria for determining rationality exist independently of a particular culture leads ultimately to the conclusion that crosscultural communication on this issue and thought systems more generally is impossible.[65] In addition, since the movements under study involved confrontation between scientifically and technologically oriented European peoples and prescientific non-Western societies, judgments of their rationality by the standards of the alien, but dominant, Europeans are both appropriate and necessary. Thus, three sets of criteria must be employed in any judgment concerning the rationality of the beliefs of the participants in these movements: those of the culture that produced each movement, those of the scientifically-oriented West, and those that are crosscultural and can be applied to most known societies.

By the standards of the prescientific cultures that produced these movements, their millenarian and magical content was clearly rational. It was not only consistent with the basic premises of their broader belief systems but it formed a vital part of the process by which the grievances of the colonized were transformed into what many perceived to be a viable mode of collective protest. However unstable particular individuals or specific leaders might have been,[66] it was both sane and logical for peoples who lived their daily lives on the basis of magico-religious belief systems to seek magico-religious solutions to their problems. If supernatural forces were ever-present and constantly intervening in earthly affairs, it was perfectly rational for those who believed in these forces to expect that they could seek to achieve their purposes in the world through prophetic agents or miraculous occurences. This does not mean, of course, that those who shared the participants' prescientific world view and yet refused to join these movements were irrational. In some cases ethnic and religious differences, such as those found in Burma and German East Africa, meant that some groups among the colonized held beliefs about both the physical and metaphysical world that, though prescientific, varied significantly from those of the peoples in rebellion. In other cases groups or individuals who shared the culture and belief systems of the dissidents rejected *this* prophet, *these* teachings, or *these* talismans, while still adhering to the basic premises which made belief in these leaders and charms possible. Whether the decision to reject a prophet's teachings or to scorn his claims to magical powers arose from the conviction that he was a false messiah or from longstanding hostility to the groups committed to his cause, the effect was the same. The rebels lost potential support, and the European colonizers gained opportunities to form alliances with colonized groups or to divert men and materials from areas at peace to those in rebellion.

An understanding of the ways in which these beliefs were rational in terms of culture-bound criteria is essential to an evaluation of their rationality by general, crosscultural standards.[67] Only through an understanding of the participants' broader thought systems and evaluative standards is it possible to see that their magical and millenarian beliefs were internally consistent, coherent as ideologies, and based on premises that were both relevant and sufficient. Most critically, those who supported these movements not only believed that the means they employed to resist the European colonizers were effective but that they were the most potent modes of protest available to them. Although the procedures followed and the underlying criteria used to evaluate the efficacy of these means were quite different from those demanded by science, the beliefs and activities of dissident groups had been tested and to some extent systematized through generations of application and adjustment.[68]

If one insists on scientific techniques of testing and verification, it is obvious that the beliefs espoused by the participants in these movements were in many respects irrational.[69] From a scientific standpoint the basic premises of millennial and magical beliefs concerning cause and effect, the relationship between the mundane and the metaphysical, and the nature of what is real and what is imaginary are erroneous. Most critically for the outcome of these movements, they were irrational by scientific standards in terms of the glaring discrepancy between the exalted goals set by their participants and the means used to achieve these ends. When confronted by vastly superior European organization and technology (both products of the scientific-industrial revolution in the West), the rebels' faith in their leaders and talismans proved tragically insufficient. From this perspective, it is difficult to argue with Bryan Wilson's succinct conclusion that "magic does not wash; the millennium will not come."[70] But this judgment (as Wilson acknowledges) could not have been made by the participants in these movements. It can only be made in retrospect, and by those who know and accept scientific criteria. Thus, the gap between means and ends is not so much evidence of the irrationality of groups or individuals who embrace magical or millennial solutions, as an indication of their adherence to pre-scientific thinking and the limitations of a lower level of technological mastery than that attained by industrialized societies.[71] The groups in rebellion showed both good sense and considerable insight in calling to their assistance the most powerful allies they knew of—supernatural ones—to bridge the gap they knew to exist between their material means and the might and technological mastery of their European opponents.

SEVEN

Rebellion, Suppression, and Impact

The disgruntled and oppressed turned to prophetic leaders for deliverance and soon found themselves engaged in bloody struggles to drive off their alien European overlords. In all cases the struggles were unequal—the final outcomes rarely in doubt. Nonetheless, the scale of the rebellions mounted, the duration of resistance efforts, and the degree of success attained by groups in revolt varied widely.[1] Of the five cases examined in depth, the rebellion led by Dipanagara and the Birsite movement provide the greatest contrasts. Dipanagara's revolt involved most of the heavily populated core regions of central Java and affected the lives of millions of people of whom hundreds of thousands lost their lives in a struggle lasting nearly five years. The Birsite disturbances were confined to a minority of just one of many hill-dwelling peoples in east-central India. The violent phase of the Birsite movement lasted only several weeks and the number of lives lost, even according to the most inflated nationalist estimates, was not more than two hundred.

These variations are linked, of course, to fundamental differences between the societies and peoples who mounted each of the rebellions. The sheer size of the colonized population to which Dipanagara or Kinjikitile addressed their calls for protest and the resources that these rebel leaders could bring to bear were critical determinants of the magnitude of the movements they led. Te Ua and Birsa were operating in much smaller arenas, and the scale of their risings was consequently more limited. The ideology and personal appeal of prophetic leaders and the organizing capacity of their inner circle of followers also helped to determine the size of movements and their staying power. As noted in the discussions of mobilization, indigenous patterns of sociopolitical organization and ethnic divisions that long antedated the coming of colonial rule very often set limits on the prophet's appeal and the extent to which rebel leaders could coordinate protest efforts.

Beyond the factors outlined above, the scale and duration of a particular movement depended largely on the interplay between the capacity of insurgent leaders to organize and direct their supporters and the effectiveness of the European colonizers in employing the repressive means at their disposal. This interplay not only determined differences between movements but contributed to variations within individual movements in which risings in particular areas were far more serious than in others. Analysis of the factors responsible for these differences has bearing on broader questions relating to patterns of resistance by colonized and other dominated peoples, the structure of colonial societies, and the techniques employed by European colonial administrators to maintain control over subject populations that vastly outnumbered them.

Rebellion

The length and intensity of European contact and control had important effects on both the rebels' capacity for employing force and the colonizers' ability to curb violence. Generally, effective violent protest was much more difficult in areas where European penetration had been extensive. Peoples like the Javanese and the Matumbi or Ngindo, whose sociocultural systems remained largely intact, had distinct advantages in leadership and weaponry over the Burmans or Mundas, whose capacity for war had declined along with the general erosion of their indigenous institutions. Javanese, Matumbi, and Ngindo leaders still retained positions of considerable influence, and their respective military systems had not been completely dismantled. In Burma and Chota Nagpur, on the other hand, martial traditions were little more than vague memories, and indigenous military leaders had fallen in earlier invasions or resistance to European conquest. In New Zealand war leaders were present at the time of the Pai Maire disturbances, but the movement did not have the support of many of the most experienced war chiefs and *hapu* heads. Old rivalries and personal advantage caused many chiefs, like those of the powerful Arawa and Ngatiporou, to lead their kinsmen into war against tribes which had joined the Pai Maire movement. The Kingite tribes, especially those in the Waikato region, accepted the new faith only belatedly, in 1864, and never attempted to combine effectively with adherents in other areas.[2] Many of the chiefs who did join the movement were hampered by the refusal of subordinate *hapu* heads or rival leaders to support them and the inexperience of their peoples, who had not engaged in prolonged warfare for decades.

Groups in areas of more limited European penetration were also better armed than those where foreign control was more firmly established. Javanese troops, like the bodyguard of the Sultan of Yogyakarta that defected to Dipanagara, brought along their weapons. During the early stages of the rebellion, Dipanagara's supporters manufactured their own gunpowder, and later powder and firearms were smuggled into rebel-held areas from the north coast and other regions.[3] Rebel troops also obtained firearms from defeated Dutch columns. Thus, even though most of Dipanagara's followers were armed with slings or pikes, firearms were used on a considerable scale, especially in the major engagements that marked the early stages of the rebellion. The Matumbi were also well supplied with firearms at the time of the Maji Maji rebellion, largely as a result of their long struggle to resist Swahili slavers from the coast and other invaders. Their weapons were mainly antiquated muzzleloaders, but they were used with considerable effect in the ambushes that came to dominate the Matumbi struggle against colonial armies.[4]

Of all the groups in rebellion, the Maoris were perhaps the best supplied with European firearms. Decades of trading with the Europeans had given most *hapu* units a large number of firearms and substantial supplies of ammunition, despite intermittent efforts by colonial officials to check the flow of guns to the Maori.[5] Most Maori firearms, however, were outmoded flintlock muskets or doublebarreled shotguns. These firearms often proved less effective than indigenous spears and war clubs and were no match for the Enfield rifles and howitzers of the Europeans. Rebel groups in Burma and Chota Nagpur had virtually no firearms at the outset of their rebellions and raids on the houses of village headmen won only a handful of guns for Saya San's followers. The supporters of both rebellions relied heavily on indigenous weapons like knives, spears, and bows and arrows.

Although the availability of military leaders and living martial traditions contributed substantially to more effective mobilization and organization in Java, German East Africa, and (to a lesser extent) in New Zealand, such prebattle advantages sometimes proved to be impediments in conflict. The mere existence of military leaders and codes of war was not sufficient. Rebel success depended on the ability of military leaders to adapt customary patterns of warfare to offset European technological and organizational advantages. Given the overwhelmingly superior firepower of colonial armies, conventional battles and massed assaults on fortified positions were best avoided. Where deeply ingrained battle tactics and unwritten codes of martial honor led to precisely this sort of confrontation, crushing defeats for rebel forces invariably resulted. Thus, rebel success in all of the cases examined was closely linked to the use of guerilla-style tactics, which in several cases were rooted in precolonial traditions of warfare. Rebel resistance could be sustained only when large-scale encounters on open ground were avoided and resistance forces concentrated on surprise attacks on enemy columns or isolated outposts. Effective use of terrain favorable to such tactics and widespread support from the village populace were also critical to prolonged rebellion.

The supporters of Dipanagara fought a number of conventional battles in the early stages of the Java War, but the prince's commanders came to rely almost wholly on guerilla warfare. Deception and surprise as war tactics had long been valued by the Javanese, and the rugged, heavily wooded, riverine terrain where much of the rebellion was concentrated was well suited to ambushes and avoidance of pursuing enemy columns. From the earliest days of the rebellion, rebel groups had destroyed bridges and launched sudden attacks from heavily concealed positions along the often rudimentary roads that linked the major towns and court centers of the princely states. Devastating hit-and-run assaults were the hallmark of Dipanagara's more able commanders, especially the youthful Sentot and his special corps. The victories gained through these tactics were often impressive, and they repeatedly revived rebel spirits in the later stages of the rebellion when resistance weakened following Dutch successes in conventional encounters.

Javanese rebels were able to rely on the village populace for provisions, information about enemy movements, shelter, and new recruits because of the poor communications system and the inaccessibility of the villages in many areas of central Java. When the Dutch did appear, the bamboo-hedged, nucleated villages found over much of the area in revolt could quickly be transformed into makeshift fortresses, which the Dutch found costly to capture in frontal assaults. Because most of Dipanagara's supporters did not wear special uniforms, it was difficult for the Dutch to identify rebels who were not actually in action. Rebel groups could disband at the approach of Dutch columns and appear to be engaged in the everyday tasks of peasants. Once the government forces had moved on, the villagers could again take up arms and, in some cases, ambush the very troops who had just passed by. On occasion, the rebels would entice the Dutch to advance on strategic positions through forced marches and then destroy the target village or camp just as the Dutch came within reach. Widespread

support from the peasant population made it possible for Dipanagara and other rebel leaders repeatedly to evade elaborate Dutch
campaigns to capture them. In addition, the impossibility of major
military operations during the monsoon season gave hard-pressed
rebel forces periods of respite. The decision of Dipanagara and his
commanders to rely increasingly on guerilla warfare contributed
both to the length of the rebellion and its heavy cost to their Dutch
adversaries.[6]

In the short run, decentralized societies like those of the Matumbi and Ngindo enjoyed many of the advantages of rebel groups
in Java. After sustaining heavy casualties in several pitched battles
with the Germans in the early months of the Maji Maji rebellion,
these peoples reverted to their customary guerilla-style warfare.
The Matumbi, whose heavily wooded and hilly homeland was well
suited to guerilla tactics, proved perhaps the most difficult rebel
group for the Germans to bring under control. The elaborate sentry
system, hilltop fortresses, and cave hideouts that had served the
Matumbi so well in their resistance to earlier invaders were now
employed against the Germans. The Matumbi concentrated their
offensive efforts on ambushes and night attacks on unsuspecting
German outposts. They abandoned their village settlements and
carried off or destroyed their crops to deny the Germans provisions
and fixed targets.[7]

The Ngindo also went over to guerilla warfare after mounting
several massed assaults in the early days of the revolt. Because of
the unsuitability of their plateau heartland, however, Ngindo war
bands were forced to take refuge in the forest zone to the south. The
decisive advantage of guerilla warfare is clearly demonstrated by
the prolonged resistance maintained by the Matumbi, Ngindo, and
other peoples who emphasized guerilla tactics in contrast to the
fate of peoples who attempted mass assaults. For the latter, like the
Ngoni, conventional battles proved disastrous as poorly armed
rebel columns were ravaged by German machine guns and rifles.[8]

Although small-scale guerilla warfare was more effective than
pitched battles in the short run, its exclusive adoption foreclosed
any chance for ultimate victory by the rebels. Historically guerilla
warfare alone has not been enough to bring groups in rebellion to
power. It has succeeded only as one aspect of a broader strategy of
resistance. Ultimate victory has been achieved only by rebel groups
who have also been able to develop effective conventional military
forces or those who have faced incumbent regimes unable or unwilling to employ fully all the resources available to suppress dissi-

dent groups.[9] Neither condition was present in Java or German East Africa. Resistance in both cases became increasingly decentralized and defensive. Time worked against the rebels as the Dutch and Germans, both determined to reassert their control, grew stronger through reinforcements and ever-increasing familiarity with the tactics and terrain of their adversaries.

Given a strong reliance in pre-European Maori warfare on surprise, ambush, and the avoidance of frontal assaults,[10] the repeated, costly, and futile pitched battles fought by the adherents of the Pai Maire movement are somewhat puzzling. This is especially true since the initial Pai Maire successes came in ambushes of European troops. The self-defeating tactics adopted by many Pai Maire war parties can in part be explained by the inexperience of many of the leaders who embraced the new faith. It can also be attributed to the strong belief of those recruited to the movement in the protective rituals and talismans spread by Te Ua's disciples. Beyond these influences, however, there was a general shift among the Maoris toward increasing reliance on pitched battles after the early decades of the nineteenth century. This shift has not yet been fully explained, but it was clearly linked to the introduction of European firearms on a large scale in this period.[11] The repeated attempts of Pai Maire adherents to fight pitched battles and their costly efforts to defend elaborate fortresses, constructed according to ancient Maori designs, rendered them vulnerable to European firepower and allowed British commanders to concentrate the superior forces at their disposal. Guerilla warfare on the model of that in Java and German East Africa would have posed more serious problems for the government's forces, but it was never effectively applied. As a result, the Pai Maire disturbances were more easily suppressed than either Dipanagara's rebellion or the Maji Maji risings.

In Burma and Chota Nagpur, rebel groups attempted to fight pitched battles with far fewer firearms and much less experience than the Maoris. In both places these efforts resulted in costly defeats. The main risings of the Saya San rebellion were, with the exception of the initial assaults, which took the British by surprise, brief and easily suppressed. Effective resistance was largely confined to rebel bands that went over to guerilla tactics or to bandit gangs whose activities increased greatly during the period of unrest. In Chota Nagpur, Birsa and his followers failed to make use of the vast forests that might have permitted prolonged resistance.

After their decisive defeat by colonial troops, Birsa's followers used the forest to evade capture for a time. They were unable, however, to recover from their early reverses or from their loss of faith in their prophet-leader who deserted them during the one major engagement of the rebellion.

Suppression

Just as rebel leadership and tactical ability varied widely in quality, different colonial regimes showed varying degrees of skill in suppressing movements of protest. As a general rule, the later the rebellion was in time, the more effective was the European response. This improvement resulted mainly from advances in weaponry, organization, communications, logistics, and medicine, which were linked to the ongoing process of industrialization in Europe itself. The machine guns and rapid-firing rifles employed against the Maji Maji and Saya San rebels were far more devastating than the heavy and slow-firing artillery pieces hauled about by the Dutch during the Java War. The British use of airplanes for reconnaissance and bombing raids during the 1930 disturbances in Burma brought a whole new dimension to antiinsurgency warfare. Telegraph lines and improved roads also proved increasingly useful to the colonizers in suppressing rebellion. During the Java War in the early nineteenth century, Dutch troops in the field were often isolated from other units for weeks, and Dutch commanders found it difficult to coordinate campaigns against rebel forces. By the time of the Maori wars of the 1860s, and even more strikingly during the Maji Maji disturbances of the early twentieth century, colonial officials could rely on the telegraph for calling up reinforcements, directing troops movements, and obtaining information about rebel activities. In Burma the railroad came into play as a means of moving troops, weapons, and supplies into areas in revolt or those where outbreaks seemed imminent. As time passed, medicine also became an increasingly effective ally of the colonial incumbents. In the Java War malaria, dysentery, cholera, and other diseases decimated Dutch relief forces, ravaging some garrisons so heavily that their ability to defend themselves was seriously jeopardized.[12] The importance of disease varied by area, but in all tropical or subtropical regions it was a key factor in colonial military planning until well into the twentieth century. If government reports are an accurate gauge, it proved little impediment to British military operations in the 1930s in the Delta of Burma, where disease had taken a heavy toll of British and Indian troops during the first Anglo-Burman war of 1824–1826.[13]

As German difficulties in suppressing the Maji Maji disturbances indicate, advanced weapons and the support of a highly industrialized state were not all that was needed to put down rebellions. The degree of European penetration into a particular area, the extent of European administrative control, and European knowledge of subject lands and peoples were also critical. German ignorance of the peoples and geography of the areas involved in the Maji Maji movement greatly hindered their efforts to anticipate or suppress the early risings, and, perhaps more critically, made it impossible for them to determine where the rebellion would spread and how to confine it. In addition, the shortage of colonial administrators and troops in the affected areas and poor communications between the coast and the interior delayed repressive measures. This delay encouraged neighboring peoples to support those who had initially rebelled and thus greatly prolonged the disturbances.

In Java the Dutch soon became acutely aware of how little control they or their allies among the Javanese nobility exercised over the village population of the princely states once they had lost the support of regional and local elite groups. They were also suddenly confronted with the realization that, despite centuries of involvement in the princely states, they knew little about great stretches of terrain in Java's heartland away from the main roads and court centers. This ignorance made possible the success of rebel guerilla efforts. A similar situation existed over much of the North Island in New Zealand but, as noted above, the Máoris exploited this potential advantage much less effectively than did the Javanese.

In both Chota Nagpur and Lower Burma, communications were better than those in the other areas studied, and settled areas were extensively surveyed and mapped. In some instances, particularly in Burma, once rebel groups moved away from their home villages, government commanders possessed better knowledge of the terrain than their indigenous adversaries. Only in the depths of the forest could rebel groups find refuge. In settled areas, dissent was quickly crushed.

A combination of rebel guerilla tactics and European ill-preparedness rendered the Dipanagara and Maji Maji rebellions the most difficult to suppress. Both the Dutch and the Germans were forced to develop new tactics and mount costly and drawn-out campaigns, which in the Javanese case extended over a period of nearly five years. The Dutch commander, De Kock, increasingly relied on a network of small fortresses called *bentengs*. These fortified points were used both individually to pacify the villages within a certain radius and in combination to demarcate an ever-shrinking zone in which rebel forces were still able to operate. Equally effective were mobile columns deployed to reinforce threatened *bentengs*, patrol the areas between the forts, and relentlessly pursue enemy bands. At times the Dutch resorted in frustration to a modified scorched earth policy to deprive rebel forces of supplies and village support. A similar policy became the chief weapon of the Germans in areas like the Matumbi hills where guerilla resistance was the most effective. After dividing the areas in revolt into zones, the Germans systematically destroyed villages, burned crops, and smoked out rebels or suspected rebel supporters from caves and other hiding places. German officers frankly conceded that these measures were indiscriminate and costly in human lives, but famine seemed their most potent ally.[14] In conjunction with scorched-earth tactics and the deployment of available troops in mobile, small-scale units, the Germans secured their control over the interior by reinforcing and heavily fortifying a series of strategic positions that later provided the basis for lasting administrative control.

Beyond weapons and organizational capacity, European efforts to put down the rebellions examined here were vitally affected by their ability to exploit longstanding divisions among the colonized peoples and to forge alliances with indigenous groups and non-European immigrants. At times ethnic groups who were hostile to the group or groups in rebellion and who had no attachment to the symbols of legitimacy displayed by rebel prophet-leaders actively supported colonial campaigns to suppress violent resistance. This pattern was exemplified by Karen and Shan support for the British in Burma and the critical assistance that the Germans received from the Swahili-speaking coastal peoples in east Africa. In Chota Nagpur and New Zealand, religious conversion split the ranks of ethnically homogenous peoples as some Christianized Maoris and many Mundas remained loyal to their missionary-educators and new faiths. Some of the Christian Maori tribes actually fought against the adherents of the Pai Maire. Many Maoris, however, and most of the steadfast converts among the Mundas merely stood aloof from the rebellions, thus permitting the Europeans to concentrate their forces on the groups in revolt. In every colony except New Zealand, colonial armies were mainly made up of indigenous recruits. Some recruits were mercenaries under the direct command of European officers like the *askaris* in German East Africa, the Hindu or Muslim police in Chota Nagpur, and the Karen and Shan troops employed by the British in Burma. In New Zealand and Java, and to some extent in German East Africa, additional military support was provided by the troops of quasi-autonomous chiefs or lords who decided to support the European colonizers rather than the groups in rebellion. In the Java War, many of these reinforcements were drawn from the "outer islands," especially the Celebes and Madura.

In addition to military support, indigenous groups provided important assistance to the Europeans as spies and informers, sources of provisions (obtained both voluntarily and forcibly), carters and bearers, and workmen on road and bridge construction and repair. In some cases nonrebellious religious figures were drawn into European efforts to restore order. In Burma a number of Buddhist monks toured disturbed districts preaching peace and urging rebel groups to lay down their arms.[15] The Dutch employed Muslim religious teachers to prevent Javanese troops who were fighting against Dipanagara, from defecting to the enemy and, where possible, to persuade rebel soldiers to lay down their arms.[16] The important roles played by colonized groups in the suppression of all of the rebellions under study strikingly illustrates the complexity of the power structure and intergroup relationships in colonial societies. Although troops drawn from Europe itself and the potential force at the disposal of colonial administrators were essential to the maintainance of European dominance, these were less apparent sources of control than those derived from the colonized peoples themselves. The co-option of indigenous elite groups, the skillful manipulation of cultural differences and longstanding rivalries, and the extensive recruitment of colonized peoples into colonial armies and police forces provided the most immediate and most frequently employed props supporting the European colonial order. The leaders of the nationalist movements that were eventually to win independence for the colonized peoples were also confronted with these complexities and apparent contradictions. Consequently their strategies and responses were far more complicated and ambivalent than the straightforward, anti-European and antiimperialist reactions often pictured in works on decolonization.

Impact

The initial effects of each of the movements under consideration depended on the responses of European colonial officials. The lasting legacies of these movements, however, were determined by the differing socioeconomic contexts in which each movement occurred, and the nature and timing of other forms of political responses among colonized peoples in each area. In some cases prophetic rebellions were transformed into peaceful sects; in other instances they influenced the emergence of new movements of protest and resistance. In every instance the rebellions had some impact on the Western-educated, nationalist elites that emerged to lead the colonized in the struggle for independence, or in the case of the Maori, the search for a worthy place within the settler-dominated society of New Zealand. That impact, however, varied widely, ranging from mere tokenism to extensive influence on the ideas, tactics, symbols, and leadership styles of nationalist agitators.

It is difficult to separate the impact of the Pai Maire movement on European colonial officials from that of the Maori wars of the 1860s more generally.[17] The most immediate government response was almost wholly punitive and detrimental to the Maoris. It involved extending the land confiscation scheme, which had been introduced in 1863, to the territories of groups which had supported the Pai Maire. The confiscation scheme cost the Maoris as a whole nearly three million acres of land, a loss that severely impaired the efforts of affected tribal and *hapu* units to survive in a colony increasingly dominated by European settlers. The loss of land from outright confiscation was paralleled by the sale of millions of additional acres to the government and European settlers. This transfer was openly promoted by the Native Department, which continued to grow weaker and was virtually defunct by the late 1880s. It was also encouraged by the settler-dominated legislature, which intermittently passed measures that opened up Maori lands to direct purchase by individuals.

Despite these prodigious setbacks many tribal groups showed a remarkable ability to recover from repeated military defeats and disadvantages brought on by the ineptness of government agencies. Many tribes again took up commercial agriculture, especially stock raising, and some groups eagerly sought Western education and chances for advancement in settler-dominated sectors of the colonial society. Other tribes sought to preserve what remained of

Maori beliefs and institutions by withdrawing into enclaves in the rugged interior of the North Island and limiting their contacts with Europeans. The efforts of both groups were frequently frustrated by broken government promises to protect their legal and political rights and to shield them from the demands of the ever more vocal settlers. The Maoris survived depite a colonial government which was unwilling to assist in the revitalization of their customary order and unable to provide them with the means for successful participation in the multiracial society that had come to stay.

Despite the impressive scale and widespread occurrence of the Saya San risings and related disturbances, the British colonial regime and Burmese urban nationalist groups continued to delay much-needed agrarian reforms. The legislative council of the Province of Burma did not enact tenancy and land alienation measures until the late 1930s, and these were little influenced by the widespread unrest expressed in the 1930–1932 rebellion. A keenly felt sense on the part of many British administrators that they had been betrayed by the peasant masses, whose interests they had long favored, was a key factor in the delay of reform measures. This attitude was reinforced by the British conviction, voiced in numerous special reports, that the disturbances arose from sheer superstition rather than economic distress. Bureaucratic inertia was reinforced by nationalist vacillation over reforms that might be harmful to the interests of many Burmese political leaders. Not until the Thakins emerged in the mid-1930s, intent on building a mass base for Burmese nationalism, did pressure mount for significant agrarian reform. The legislation that was belatedly passed in the late 1930s had little effect on the condition of the peasantry, however, because the Japanese invasion of Burma in 1941 brought a sudden end to the fragile socioeconomic system established by the British nearly a century before.[18]

In Java the response of the Dutch government to Dipanagara's revolt was far less vindictive than those of the settler-dominated regime in New Zealand or of British administrators in Burma. Despite some official demands for harsh reprisals, Dutch policy was shaped primarily by the concern to prevent further unrest and to find new sources of revenue to cover the great costs of the long war. In order to reduce the risk of further rebellions in the princely states, the Dutch imposed a series of agreements on the courts of both Yogyakarta and Surakarta that greatly diminished the size of both kingdoms and effectively ended the autonomy of their rulers. The Dutch annexed all but the inner core regions of both kingdoms, but agreed to compensate the princes through annual cash payments for the revenue that would be lost through the surrender of large portions of their remaining territory. Unfortunately, these compensations and the other payments the Dutch agreed to make not only failed to make up for income lost through the cession of appanage lands but also reduced the princes and nobility to *de facto* pensioners who were dependent on the Netherlands Indies government. The Dutch clearly delineated the boundaries between the two kingdoms for the first time, introduced a Resident's Council into Yogyakarta, and expanded the jurisdiction of European courts of justice in the kingdom. They also increased their already substantial influence over the appointment and administrative activities of court and regional officials. The Dutch did abolish the hated toll system, but they had reestablished the land rental system in 1827, and it survived in the princely states well into the twentieth century.[19]

Perhaps the most important long-term impact of the Java War was the great burden it placed on the finances of both the colony and Home Government. Decades before 1825 the debts of the colony had begun to mount, and by the end of the war the Dutch faced the prospect of total bankruptcy. This crisis played an important role in policy decisions of the early 1830s that would shape colonial administration in Java for much of the rest of the century. Most notably, financial considerations led to the Home Government's support for the controversial economic schemes of Johannes van den Bosch, which have come to be known collectively as the Culture or, more accurately, the Cultivation System. This system of economic extraction, based on the part-time cultivation by Javanese peasants of cash crops to be collected by the government and sold overseas, was accepted largely because it promised larger and more rapid returns of revenue than alternative proposals. Although the full impact of the Cultivation System on subsequent Javanese and Indonesian history has yet to be determined, the available evidence suggests that it was extremely detrimental to long-term economic growth. Given the ecological system into which it was introduced, the Cultivation System also greatly distorted Javanese social and demographic development.[20]

In two of the cases considered, significant reforms and constructive shifts in colonial policy resulted from violent protest. In German East Africa the colonial government introduced measures to put an end to minimal administration, to shift control from military to civilian officials, and to improve the training of and government control over non-European subordinates. Although indigenous notables, particularly those who had supported the Germans during the Maji Maji disturbances, continued to exercise considerable power at the local level, the Germans introduced changes to increase the centralization of the colonial administration as a whole. The Germans also abolished forced cultivation, strove to curb the arbitrary exactions of colonial officials and European settlers, and encouraged the indigenous peoples to introduce new crops and improve their cultivation techniques. The designs of well-intentioned home ministers and colonial officials were frequently frustrated by settler opposition and continuing lack of trained manpower, but the changes brought real improvements in the living conditions of many of the colonized peoples. Without the Maji Maji rebellion these changes might never have been made. The evidence suggests that German administrators pushed colonial reforms not because of pressure from politicians in Germany but in order to prevent another rebellion among subordinate peoples who had clearly indicated that their interests must be taken into account.[21]

In Chota Nagpur the Birsite disturbances also prodded colonial administrators into introducing long overdue reforms. In 1902, an extensive survey of cultivated lands in Munda areas was undertaken which was designed to formally determine and record Munda land rights and obligations to landlord groups. The control of Munda cultivators who were still in possession of lands cleared by their ancestors was confirmed, and the Chota Nagpur Tenancy Act of 1908 established detailed regulations concerning tenant rights and obligations. In this same period the Government of India also abolished longstanding landlord demands for labor services to be performed by their Munda tenants. To insure that these new regulations were followed, the British established new courts and administrative divisions, which gave the Mundas greater access to the professional bureaucrats of the Indian Civil Service.[22] Despite the assertions of some British observers that these government measures had given the Mundas land rights far superior to those of any other group of Indian cultivators, a second land settlement survey between 1927 and 1935 revealed that serious problems remained. Most Munda cultivators were still heavily in debt, the landlords in some areas continued to demand labor services, and relations between the Mundas and landlords and moneylenders of lowland origins remained tense. In the 1920s and 1930s new movements of protest arose among both the Munda and neighboring

Oraon peoples, and many of the grievances that have produced periodic outbursts of violence persist to the present day.[23]

The Birsite movement, which was the smallest and least violent of those considered, was also the only one to outlive the phase of unsuccessful revolt, government suppression, and the removal of its prophetic leader. A small minority of the Munda people continued to adhere to the new faith proclaimed by Birsa before his first imprisonment. This small sect, which stresses passive withdrawal and forbids its members to marry non-Birsites, had dwindled to a few hundred faithful by the 1960s, but these remaining adherents clung tenaciously to beliefs and practices that they attributed to their ill-fated prophet.[24] For the Munda community more generally, Birsa has become a folk hero—a symbol of Munda resistance to dominance by lowland groups. Munda boys are frequently named after the prophet and songs are sung celebrating his exploits. Somewhat ironically, Birsa was also acclaimed for a time by leaders of the lowland-based, pan-Indian Congress Party. His considerable popularity in some Indian nationalist circles in the late 1930s was demonstrated by the gate erected in his honor at the annual Congress session in 1940 at Ramgarh, where he was proclaimed a champion in the fight against the British.[25] Although some overly enthusiastic Indian writers have further argued that Birsa and his movement anticipated many aspects of the style and tactics of Gandhi,[26] he was neither nonviolent nor an Indian nationalist working for the establishment of a European-model state. Birsa adopted techniques that were increasingly oriented to violence in an attempt to revive a subnational ethnic consciousness that long predated contacts with European colonizers. His stance was equally hostile to Europeans, Hindus, and Muslims and ran counter to the all-India identity that Congress leaders like Gandhi and Nehru were trying to establish.

Although the Pai Maire movement itself died out in the 1860s, it influenced subsequent sectarian movements that flourished among the Maoris in the last decades of the nineteenth century. The legacy of the Pai Maire can be seen most clearly in the beliefs and ritual practices of the best known Maori sect, the Ringtau, founded by Te Kooti. As sectarian withdrawal gave way beginning in the 1890s to renewed interest in Western education and increased Maori participation within the context of New Zealand society as a whole, the example of the Pai Maire movement faded. The beliefs and tactics of Te Ua and his warlike disciples were ill-suited to the new generation of Maori leaders that emerged in this period to arouse their people to begin the long, difficult, and familiar struggle of a disadvantaged minority for its rights.[27]

The movements led by both Saya San and Dipanagara may have inspired many of the prophetic leaders who followed them in continuation of centuries-old millenarian traditions,[28] but neither movement survived the loss of their prophet-instigators. Both, however, had significant effects on the styles, appeals, and even the ideologies of many nationalist leaders in each colonial area. In the first decades of the twentieth century, Dipanagara was transformed into a major nationalist hero, whom some proclaimed the "father of *Indonesian* nationalism." The beliefs in the *Radu Adil* that were so important in mobilizing support for Dipanagara were later associated with the meteoric rise of the first Indonesian nationalist leader with widespread mass appeal, H. O. S. Tjokroaminoto. Many of these same themes were also critical in Sukarno's rise to prominence in the nationalist movement in the late 1920s and later enhanced his ability to remain in power in independent Indonesia despite his frail political base.[29] Although Dipanagara's metamorphosis paralleled that of numerous prophetic figures, it had little relation to the man or the causes for which he fought. He was a Javanese, not an Indonesian leader—in fact, the idea of Indonesia did not yet exist. He fought the Dutch only to check their influence in the central Java heartland of his people and was content to let them remain in west Java and on the north coast.[30] He had little concern for the peoples beyond the princely states and felt no sense of betrayal when troops from Madura or Bali fought against him in Dutch-led armies.

Before organizing his own movement, Saya San had been a nationalist agitator and in his rebellion he made extensive use of nationalist-organized, village *athin* associations. His rebellion, however, was not nationalistic in the Western sense of that term in either its methods or objectives. His followers were almost entirely Burmans. They rallied to Burman symbols and to the defense of Buddhist beliefs that were alien to many of the ethnic groups that have come to be included in the present-day Burmese nation. Saya San's adherents fought in the name of a narrower, precolonial ethnic and cultural identity that was in many ways antithetical to Burmese nationalism. Consequently, they were opposed by most of the English-educated Burmese elite that had spearheaded the nationalist movement. Before the rebellion, articles appeared in

Burmese vernacular papers warning against "quacks" who claimed magical powers. U So Thein, the leader of a radical nationalist faction initially blamed by the British for the rebellion, expressed his opposition to Saya San's activities nearly two months before the first outbreaks of violence.[31] After the rebellion was under way, nationalist groups, even though they might express admiration for the audacity of the rebels, denounced the risings or stood aloof.[32] Their response was predictable, for there would have been few prospects for Western-educated Burmese politicians under a restored and ultraconservative Burman monarchy.

The tactics adopted by the followers of Saya San had little influence on the Thakins and other nationalist leaders who eventually won independence from the British colonizers. In this regard, the Burmah Oil Company workers' strike of 1938 represented a far more significant development in mass organization and agitation than the more dramatic risings which made up the Saya San rebellions. Eventually, however, Saya San, like Birsa and Dipanagara, was transformed into a nationalist hero and remains so today. Many of the themes that were prominent in his movement, like the restoration of Buddhism and veneration for *nat* spirits, were echoed in the style and message of leaders like U Nu who dominated the early postindependence era in Burma.

Of all the movements considered here, none so strongly anticipated the supraethnic appeal of European-style nationalism as the Maji Maji rebellion. Although coordination of the efforts of diverse and often distant peoples proved impossible, for a time many previously hostile groups were linked by adherence to a common message of resistance and salvation. In addition, many of the millenarian beliefs and political symbols that dominated the Maji Maji movement would reappear in later attempts to arouse nationalist sentiments and anticolonial opposition.[33] The movement also had a strong impact on the strategy adopted by the mainstream nationalist leaders in the struggle for the independence of what would become the nation of Tanzania. Although they dated the beginning of the nationalist struggle from the Maji Maji resistance, many emerging nationalist leaders saw the great loss of human lives in that rebellion as proof that violence was far too costly a way to overcome the European colonizers. Thus the great majority of the Western-educated nationalist leaders who emerged in the decades after 1905–1906 turned from revolt to mass rallies, boycotts, and other forms of constitutional agitation. They also substituted a selective acceptance of European ideological and institutional imports for Kinjikitile's near-total reliance on indigenous precedents and rejection of outside influences.[34]

However much nationalist leaders might allude to the memory of prophetic resistance efforts or adopt the symbols and appeals of prophetic leaders, their campaigns for independence were based on very different forms of mobilization and agitation. Whether they involved strikes and boycotts, passive resistance, constitutional agitation, or guerilla warfare, these techniques displayed a far greater understanding of the European adversaries and a much greater willingness to explore and adopt European ideas, technology, and organizational models. These techniques would at times result in defeats and disappointments. By learning from the weaknesses of prophetic protest movements, however, and by borrowing their viable components, alternative modes of mobilizing protest could be developed that proved to be more adequate responses to European colonial domination. They would also provide more effective ways to lay the basis for postcolonial nations.

EIGHT

Prophetic Rebellion as a Type of Social Protest

Despite great variations in the sociocultural milieus in which they arise, revitalization movements share a common origin in situations of accelerated change. Whether they take the form of new religious sects, passive withdrawal from unsatisfactory social systems, or violent challenges to the existing order, these movements have generally been associated with times when the process of gradual change and social adjustment, common to all human societies, is compressed and speeded up. The pace of both the gradual flux and the more compressed change has varied widely in different societies and historical epochs as has the way in which different peoples have perceived and responded to these processes. Almost invariably, however, a quickening in the pace of change has proved disruptive. As new groups emerge or existing ones improve their position, the status of other established groups is diminished or threatened. Technological innovations or new ideas and modes of organization undermine customary beliefs, institutions, and patterns of human interaction so rapidly that viable replacements often cannot be developed quickly enough to cushion the perilous transition to a new order.[1] Whatever form they take, the central aim of revitalization movements is to provide meaningful ideologies, codes of behavior, and systems of social interaction that will allow their adherents to overcome the feelings of deprivation and sense of disorientation that are pervasive in periods of accelerated change.

In preindustrial societies times of dynastic decline, severe natural calamities, or intense intercultural exchange frequently gave rise to revitalization movements of varying types.[2] In Europe and Japan the far-reaching changes generated by the spread of commercialization and the rise of the industrial order have also proved conducive to different forms of revitalization expression.[3] The European overseas expansion, which the commercial-industrial revolutions stimulated and sustained, led in turn to centuries of intense intercultural contact and accelerated change on a global scale. This process resulted in a great proliferation of revitalization

183

movements among non-Western peoples who came to be dominated politically by European colonizers and whose sociocultural
systems were threatened by the profound transformations engendered by European colonial penetration.[4] The five movements
examined in this study represent one type of those revitalization
responses which have been generated by the process of European
expansion. Each movement involved sustained collective protest
that came to be focused on prophetic leaders whose teachings ultimately led to rebellions against the European colonizers and their
allies.

As in revitalization movements more generally, support for
each of these prophetic movements was drawn primarily from
groups that had lost political power and social status and had
experienced a worsening of their economic condition because of
the advance of the European colonial order. Unlike many forms of
social protest associated with developing nations in Africa and
Asia, these prophetic revolts did not emerge from situations where
rising expectations could not be fulfilled; nor were they caused by
poverty or oppression in and of themselves. The main grievances
that led to each of these rebellions—elite displacement, threats
to indigenous belief systems and institutions, and the increasing
demands of expanding colonial bureaucracies—all represented a
sense on the part of dissident groups that their spiritual and material condition had declined relative to a level (real or imagined) that
they had enjoyed in the precolonial past. This sense of relative
deprivation was also rooted in the contrast that they perceived
between their low or declining status and standard of living and
the power and wealth enjoyed by the dominant colonizers, both
the Europeans and their indigenous and immigrant allies. The dissatisfaction aroused by these discrepancies was greatly intensified
because the Europeans and their allies possessed none of the legitimacy or supernatural sanctions that subject groups accorded to
their sacral kings or ritually consecrated kinship leaders.

The patterns of causation outlined above indicate that a number of widely held assumptions about the causes of revitalization
movements, particularly those of a millenarian nature, need to be
reconsidered. To begin with, emphasis on or exclusive attention to
groups of low social standing[5] may obscure important sources of
this form of social protest. In four of the five movements examined
in this study, groups of high social standing played key roles as instigators, organizers, and commanders of rebellions. This involvement of elite groups cannot be seen merely as a function of the

peasants' proverbial inability to generate their own effective leadership and their need to find leaders among nonpeasant groups.[6] Indigenous elite groups initiated movements of social protest as much in response to their own grievances as out of concern for the sufferings of their peasant followers. Therefore, to categorize these movements as those of the lowly and oppressed seems to me to distort the causes which gave rise to them and the forces which sustained them in the face of determined opposition from the European colonizers and their allies.[7]

The grievances that led to these movements also call into question the universal applicability of the notion that revitalization movements arise among rootless and marginal social groups who have been cut adrift by the breakdown of village communities during periods of profound change.[8] This pattern may be valid for some epochs and societies, but it does not hold true for most of the movements examined in this study. Except for Lower Burma (where the precolonial peasant community had been dismembered by political adjustments and sweeping economic transformations), the peasants who supported these prophetic rebellions were recruited primarily from village communities that were still viable and intact and not from vagabond or peripheral elements of the population. In each case the extension of colonial administrative control threatened the high degree of autonomy and economic security once enjoyed by local communities. However, these communities, even in Lower Burma, were still strong enough to serve as the organizational base for the prophetic movements that arose.

The viability of local communities may also explain another notable feature of these movements: the absence of class consciousness. Horizontal identification rarely extended beyond a participant's kinship group or fellow villagers. Support for prophetic leaders was recruited by kinship and community leaders or regional lords and was organized hierarchically with these customary leaders in firm control. Therefore, in contrast to the great peasant risings in Mexico and Algeria or Communist-inspired revolutions like those in China or Cuba,[9] a class-based analysis is inappropriate for movements of the prophetic-revitalization type. Peasants rose in revolt, not as the comrades-in-arms of their fellow peasants against landlords, tax collectors, or moneylenders, but as the followers of regional lords or local chiefs, the devotees of religious leaders, or the kinsmen of renowned warriors. If a broad consciousness existed, it was anticolonial but not merely antiwhite or anti-European. The enemy were the agents of the new order whether they were European, co-opted indigenous leaders, or African and Asian immigrants who served the Europeans as soldiers, merchants, and administrators.

Like other forms of revitalization expression, these movements were initiated and supported by subordinate groups who had little influence on or access to the wielders of power in their respective societies. Neither the European colonizers nor emerging, Western-educated nationalist leaders (if the latter existed at all at the time of the revolts in question) were sensitive to the grievances felt by displaced indigenous leaders or politically powerless peasants. Courts, police officials, and constitutional agitation seemed to dissident groups to favor the rich and influential and thus to degrade further those who had little or no access to these avenues of redress.

Other forms of protest had been tried with little success in each of the cases considered. Social banditry, avoidance migration, sectarian movements, and violent resistance to colonial conquest preceded prophetic rebellions in one or more of the societies studied. However, none of these means of protest proved effective. Social banditry and guerilla resistance posed no serious threats to the colonial order,[10] and the Europeans' superior organization and weapons technology rendered conventional military encounters suicidal for the colonized. The relentless advance of European communications and bureaucratic control meant that flight, one of man's oldest responses to oppression, provided at best only a temporary solution. In areas like Lower Burma, Java, and Chota Nagpur, where most of the arable land had been settled, avoidance migration was scarcely an option at all. New religious beliefs brought some solace to subjugated and alienated groups, but they could do little to ameliorate deeply felt grievances linked to displacement, colonial exactions, or harsh treatment and disdain meted out by alien rulers.

The failure or absence of alternative means of protest greatly enhanced the appeal of prophetic leaders who emerged to champion the cause of dissident groups. Through their proclamation of millennial visions, their claims to magical powers, and their skillful use of meaningful symbols, these prophetic leaders decisively influenced the mode of protest adopted by the groups under consideration. The prophets' millenarian visions, which combined key elements of the belief systems and traditions of the cultures in which each leader arose, provided a means of dramatically articulating the grievances of those groups to whom the prophets hoped to appeal. These revelations also contained divinely sanctioned remedies by which to eradicate the sources of frustration and oppression identified by the prophets' adherents. These remedies, however, manifested to differing degrees a fundamental ambivalence toward the Europeans and the products of their civilization. Although each of the prophets sought to salvage some elements of the existing order that were European in origin, they repudiated the illegitimate colonial order as a whole and promised supernatural assistance for their followers' efforts to destroy it.

Counterbalancing these destructive elements in the millennial visions of each of the prophets were embryonic designs for a new and more satisfying sociocultural order. The prophets proclaimed that their followers' tribulations and struggles would usher in an age of bliss in which the faithful would preside over societies without injustice, illness, or conflict. In this way prophetic protest was genuinely revolutionary—that is, it was aimed at far-reaching transformations of total societies, and these changes involved the norms that govern human interaction and the values that shape men's lives.[11] Prophetic leaders and their millennial revelations provided the nexus for countersystems that rivaled those dominated by the European colonizers. The extent to which these countersystems were fashioned on indigenous precolonial models or based on patterns copied or adapted from the European colonizers depended both on the origins and personal experiences of each of the prophetic leaders and on how far European colonization had disrupted and undermined the sociocultural systems of each of the peoples who rose in rebellion.

Whatever their ideological and institutional basis, these movements promised to create new and larger communities that their adherents hoped would prove more effective than localized village units or kinship systems in providing security and solidarity in times of bewildering transformations. They also gave promise of a new epoch and a more just social order for the powerless and oppressed. Thus, each of the prophets was regarded as a powerful healer who offered supernaturally-endowed cures for a society weakened by the disease-like effects of accelerated change and intense exposure to technologically superior and politically dominant alien cultures.

Beyond its central role in shaping the ideology of the movements under consideration, the emergence of prophetic leaders deeply influenced the mobilization patterns and tactics of the protest adopted by dissident groups. Although kinship ties and the influence of local and regional leaders were essential to success in recruiting supporters for each of the prophets examined, the widespread belief that these men were divine or divinely inspired was essential to their ability to attract large numbers of adherents. The belief that these prophetic leaders could call upon supernatural agents assured their followers that they had the means to successfully confront and overcome their powerful European overlords. This confidence, which was reinforced by the use of magical rituals and protective talismans, clearly contributed to the dissident groups' willingness to employ violence to redress their grievances and fulfill their longing for a new and utopian order. In each movement, the prophet's followers were convinced that his powerful magic would serve as an antidote to the demonstrated superiority of the colonizers' weapons, communications systems, and modes of organization.

The prophet himself also played a critical role in the decision to resort to violent protest in each of the movements considered. Kinjikitile and Saya San plotted for rebellion from the outset of their campaigns to attract followers. Dipanagara and Birsa were initially more ambivalent toward the use of violence. Both were in a very real sense driven to open rebellion by the colonial authorities' abortive attempts to suppress their activities. Bungled repression together with Te Ua's weakness as a leader were crucial in transforming his essentially peaceful faith into an ideology for holy war. Although kinship heads and community leaders were the ones who actually led the prophets' supporters into battle, they did so in the prophets' names, for the purpose of fulfilling their millennial prophecies, and under the protective aura of their magical potency. Following defeats at the hands of the colonizers, the prophets' roles diminished and their adherents' beliefs in their magical powers declined. In those movements that survived these disheartening setbacks, secondary leaders took on increasing importance, and there was a pronounced shift to reliance on guerilla tactics rather than talismans to offset the advantages of the colonizers' armies.

However successful talismans and millennial visions may have been in attracting followers and mounting movements of social protest, when violent conflicts with the European colonizers and their allies resulted these appeals and devices failed those who relied on them. In the rare instances where they seemed to succeed, as in the initial Maji Maji risings or the early stages of Dipanagara's revolt, surprise, overwhelming numerical superiority, or the skillful use of terrain hostile to the colonizers' armies were actually the key factors. More frequently, however, faith in their prophets' predictions or their protective talismans led rebel groups to attempt suicidal, frontal assaults on well-armed government forces. The dead on the battlefields from Mahenge in east Africa to the Taranaki Reserve in New Zealand provide ample testimony to the illusionary nature of the prophets' claims to magical powers and to the uselessness of their talismans against the devastating firepower of the colonizers.

The grim toll of human lives lost in these unequal contests and their pronounced tendencies toward self-destruction[12] must be set against the widely touted claims by Frantz Fanon that violence has served as a source of renewal, uplift, and solidarity among colonized peoples.[13] Fanon's own evidence contradicts these assertions, and his propositions do not hold up under empirical testing.[14] Though oppressed groups may come to consider force essential to relieve their degradation and deprivation, the great cost in human lives of violent social protest should not be minimized or its physical or psychological ravages mistaken for agencies of moral regeneration. These cautions seem particularly relevant in situations like those examined in this study where the gaps between the force that incumbents and protesters can bring to bear on each other in conflict situations is so overwhelmingly unequal. Although these prophetic movements may have given their adherents new hope, a sense of worth and autonomy, and a means of self-assertion for a time, when they turned violent they brought defeat, destruction, and renewed despair.[15] However much they raised the self-esteem of contemporary Western-educated nationalists who stood aloof or later nationalist leaders who saw in them the beginnings of mass anticolonial agitation, they meant death to large numbers of people who rose in violent protest against the colonial order. For the rebels who were fortunate enough to survive, there were bitter memories of friends and relatives lost in unequal combat and of the sufferings and reprisals that invariably accompanied the suppression of the groups in revolt. For the colonizers, who were the nominal victors, there were personal losses and lingering memories of nightmarish and seemingly senseless slaughters of poorly armed rebels. For an introspective few among the colonial elite, there was also the disconcerting realization that these movements were symptomatic of the inherent inequities and injustices of the colonial order.

Notes

INTRODUCTION

1. Anthony Wallace, "Revitalization Movements," pp. 264–66.
2. For a list of the many labels that have been applied to these movements, see Vittorio Lanternari, "Nativistic and Socio-Religious Movements," pp. 486–87.
3. For examples see Wilhelm Mühlman, *Chiliasmus und Nativismus*, pp. 7–9; and Henri Ellenberger, "Les mouvements de libération mythique," pp. 248–49.
4. For examples see Weston La Barre, "Materials for the Study of Crisis Cults."
5. See especially Norman Cohn, *The Pursuit of the Millennium*; Eric Hobsbawm, *Primitive Rebels*, chaps. 4–6; Georges Balandier, *Sociologie actuelle de l'Afrique noire*, chap. 3; Peter Worsley, *The Trumpet Shall Sound*; and Kenelm Burridge, *Mambu*.
6. See especially Terence O. Ranger, "Connexions between 'Primary Resistance' Movements and Modern Mass Nationalism in East and Central Africa."
7. For a superb example, see Bernhard Dahm, *Sukarno and the Indonesian Struggle for Independence*.
8. Although the term "prophet" originated in the Judeo-Christian tradition, I use it in this study because it seems to be the broadest and least culture-bound term available for the general type of leaders considered here. In contrast to terms like "messiah," which have very specific theological connotations closely tied to Judeo-Christian beliefs (see, for example, Henri Desroche, "Les messianismes et la catégorie de l'échec," p. 64), the term prophet has come to be accepted as appropriate for salvationist leaders in diverse cultures. Like the term "millenarian," it seems well suited to comparative studies such as this, which focus on non-Western societies. For a more detailed discussion and somewhat different resolution of these terminological problems, see Guglielmo Guariglia, *Prophetismus und Heilserwartungs-Bewegungen*, especially pp. 33–46.
9. Max Weber, *The Sociology of Religion*, pp. 47–48; and Katesa Schlosser, "Der Prophetismus in niederen Kulturen," pp. 68–69.
10. Norman Cohn, "Medieval Millenarianism," pp. 31–43.
11. See Max Weber, *The Theory of Social and Economic Organization*, pp. 358–73.
12. Ibid., p. 358.
13. For the importance of a link to a divine being see Carl J. Friedrich, "Political Leadership and the Problem of Charismatic Power," esp. pp. 12–19.
14. Many writers have emphasized the importance of follower responses. See especially Mühlmann, *Chiliasmus*, p. 255; Claude Ake, "Charismatic Legitimation and Political Integration," pp. 4–6, 10; and Johannes Fabian, "Führer und Führung in den prophetisch-messianischen Bewegungen," pp. 782, 791–92.
15. For the best of these efforts see T. K. Oommen, "Charisma, Social Structure and Social Change," pp. 85–99; and Arthur Schweitzer, "Theory and Political Charisma," pp. 150–81. In his recent work, *The Noble Savages*, Bryan Wilson seeks to reestablish the supernatural and social dimensions of charisma. His development of the concept, however, does not resolve many of the problems discussed above, nor could it be applied to most of the leaders or societies dealt with in this study.
16. For more extended critiques see especially Ake, "Charismatic Legitimation," pp. 4–5; and K. T. Ratnam, "Charisma and Political Leadership," pp. 343–45.
17. Important exceptions include Sartono Kartodirdjo's *Peasant Protest in Rural Java* and *The Peasant's Revolt of Banten in 1888*; the writings of Peter Carey on the Java War and of John Iliffe and Gilbert Gwassa on the Maji Maji rebellion cited below; the

works of Georges Balandier on religious movements in the Congo; and Bryan Wilson's insightful thematic treatment in *Magic and the Millennium*, especially chapters 8 and 9. General coverage of some of the better known millenarian movements in the context of a broader study of religion and protest can be found in Guenther Lewy's *Religion and Revolution*.

18. Ralph Linton, "Nativistic Movements," pp. 230–40.

19. See, for examples, Fokke Sierksma, *Een nieuwe Hemel en een nieuwe Aarde*, pp. 260–63; Roger Bastide, "Messianisme et développement économique et social," pp. 8–9; Judy Inglis, "Cargo Cults: The Problem of Explanation"; and Ian C. Jarvie, "Theories of Cargo Cults," pt. 1, pp. 1–31, pt. 2, pp. 108–36.

20. Kenelm Burridge, *New Heaven New Earth*, p. 128.

21. For a detailed discussion of this problem see Sartono, *Banten Revolt*, pp. 16–20.

22. Bastide, "Messianisme et développement," p. 9.

23. For the purposes of this study, "peasants" may be defined as rural cultivators who produce primarily for their own needs rather than the market but who are compelled to yield a share of their produce and labor to supra-village elite groups in the form of taxes, tribute, or rents. If this definition is strictly applied, some of the peoples considered were not peasants in the precolonial period, but all of them conformed to the criteria during the time period when the movements studied occurred. For more detailed discussions of the problems involved in defining the term peasant see Eric Wolf, *Peasants*, pp. 2–17; and George M. Foster, "What Is a Peasant?" pp. 2–14.

24. Lloyd and Susanne Rudolph, *The Modernity of Tradition*; Milton Singer, "Beyond Tradition and Modernity in Madras," pp. 160–95; Reinhard Bendix, "Tradition and Modernity Reconsidered," esp. pp. 307–17; and especially Dean C. Tipps, "Modernization Theory and the Comparative Study of Society," pp. 199–226.

CHAPTER 1

1. For a more detailed and explicit discussion of these critical relationships see Neil Smelser, *The Theory of Collective Behavior*, pp. 18–20, 380.

2. The following account of the rise of Dutch power and Javanese responses is based primarily on the relevant sections of Hermanus J. de Graaf, *Geschiedenis van Indonesië*; G. P. Rouffaer, "Vorstenlanden," pp. 587–653; Marinus L. van Deventer, *Geschiedenis der Nederlanders op Java*; Eduard S. de Klerck, *History of the Netherlands East Indies*; Merle C. Ricklefs, *Jogjakarta under Sultan Mangkubumi, 1749–1792*, esp. chap. 1; Soemarsaid Moertono, *State and Statecraft in Old Java*; Marie A. P. Meilink-Roelofsz, *Asian Trade and European Influence in the Indonesian Archipelago*; and Hermann T. Colenbrander, *Koloniale Geschiedenis*, vol. 2. In this and the following discussions of general conditions, only specific references to other works and quoted passages will be individually cited.

3. This decline of trading outlets has not as yet been studied in detail. For brief discussions see de Graaf, *Geschiedenis*, p. 207; Moertono, *Statecraft*, pp. 134–35; Ricklefs, *Sultan Mangkubumi*, pp. 18–19.

4. See, for example, the detailed description of the rise and structure of the coffee tribute system in Priangan in Fonger de Haan, *Priangan*, vol. 1, chaps. 7–11.

5. The following brief account of the rebellion is based primarily on Pieter F. J. Louw and Eduard S. de Klerck, *De Java-Oorlog van 1825–1830*, vol. 1–5; August W. P. Weitzel, *De Oorlog op Java van 1825 tot 1830* (compiled from the posthumous papers of the Dutch commander, Merkus de Kock), 2 vols. ; and Huibert G. Nahuys van Burgst, *Verzameling van officiële Rapporten betreffende den Oorlog op Java in de Jaren 1825–1830*, 4 vols.

6. Dutch casualties are based on the estimates in de Graaf, *Geschiedenis*, p. 399. Estimates of Javanese population losses were taken from A. Bram Peper, "Population Growth in Java in the 19th Century," p. 82.

7. European explorers reached New Zealand as early as 1642, but initial European contacts were brief and apparently had little impact on Maori life.

8. The best accounts of pre-European Maori culture and history may be found in Peter Buck, *The Coming of the Maori*; Elsdon Best, *The Maori as He Was* and *Maori Religion and Mythology*; Joan Metge, *The Maoris of New Zealand*; Maharaia Winiata, *The Changing Role of the Leader in Maori Society*; Ernest Beaglehole, "The Polynesian Maori," pp. 49–74; Apirana T. Ngata, "Religious Influences," pp. 336–73; D. M. Stafford, *Te Arawa*; and Raymond Firth, *Economics of the New Zealand Maori*.

9. William Martin, *The Taranaki Question*, p. 8.

10. Numerous works have been devoted to the history of Maori-European interaction. The following analysis of key features is based on appropriate sections in John B. Condliffe and Willis T. Airey, *A Short History of New Zealand*; Harold Miller, "Maori and Paheka, 1814–1865," pp. 75–95, and *New Zealand*; Alan Ward, *A Show of Justice*, chaps. 1–8; Keith Sinclair, *A History of New Zealand*; Winiata, *Changing Role*; John Houston, *Maori Life in Old Taranaki*; the relevant chapters in James Hight, ed., *The Cambridge History of the British Empire*, vol. 7, pt. 2; E. J. Tapp, *Early New Zealand*; and especially Harrison M. Wright, *New Zealand 1769–1840: Early Years of Western Contact*; and Firth, *Maori Economics*, chap. 13.

11. Ward, ibid., p. 13. Ward cites the estimates of D. Pool. See also T. Wi Repa, "Depopulation in New Zealand," pp. 227–34.

12. Many of the factors emphasized in this treatment of Maori responses were suggested by Norman Chance's discussion of the somewhat similar case of the Alaskan Eskimo. See "Acculturation, Self-Identification, and Personality Adjustment," esp. pp. 372–73. The most useful sources on the determinants of Maori reactions are the superb chapter on "Maori and Pakeha," in Ward, ibid.; Wright, *New Zealand*; Apirana Ngata, "Maori Land Settlement," pp. 97–98, 102–103; and Firth, ibid., p. 450.

13. John Miller, *Early Victorian New Zealand*, pp. 101–103; and Firth, ibid., pp. 446–50.

14. The best discussions of the Christian missionaries and their early impact are found in Wright, *New Zealand*; Ann J. Gibson, "Religious Organization among the Maoris of New Zealand after 1860;" J. Anderson, "The Missionaries and the Maoris," pp. 47–59; and the exchange between J. M. R. Owens and Judith Binney, "Christianity and the Maoris," pp. 18–40, and pp. 143–65.

15. By John S. Galbraith in his "Myths of the 'Little England' Era," pp. 34–48.

16. James Hight, "The Maori Wars, 1843–1872," p. 30.

17. William Fox, *The War in New Zealand*, pp. 139–40.

18. James Cowan's *The New Zealand Wars*, vol. 2, remains the standard work from a Euro-centric viewpoint on the Pai Maire movement and the Maori wars as a whole. Also useful is Stuart B. Babbage's *Hauhauism*. For detailed accounts of the Maori wars from the British viewpoint see Brian J. Dalton, *War and Politics in New Zealand, 1855–1870*; and Angus J. Harrop, *England and the Maori Wars*. For the best account of the Pai Maire from the Maori perspective see Paul Clark's *'Hauhau': The Pai Maire Search for Maori Identity*.

19. This seems to be a reference to the more commonly called *kerta* (or *satya*) *yuga*, which is the first and longest of the four main divisions of the Brahmanic cosmic time cycle. This is traditionally viewed as a period when men are good and existence blissful.

20. The fourth and shortest of the cosmological *yugas*, or eras, when evil and suffering reign supreme before the great cataclysms that will set the stage for the beginning of a new cycle.

21. Quoted in Sarat Chundra Roy, *The Mundas and Their Country*, p. 30. I have slightly rephrased Roy's late-Victorian translations.

22. The basic source for my discussion of the general outlines of Munda history and culture is Roy, ibid., which is supplemented by Surendra P. Sinha, *Life and*

Times of Birsa Bhagwan; Stephen Fuchs, *Rebellious Prophets,* pp. 21–34; Lewis S. S. O'Malley, *Bengal District Gazetteers: Singbhum, Saraikela, and Kharsawan;* John Reid, *Report on the Survey and Settlement Operations in the Ranchi District, 1902–1910;* and Suresh Singh, *The Dust-Storm and the Hanging Mist,* chap. 1.

23. Roy, ibid., chap. 2.

24. Over most of the South Asian cultural zone the owl is considered a foolish creature and an object of derision rather than a symbol of wisdom and learning as in the West.

25. Roy, *Mundas,* pp. 93–94. Again I have slightly altered Roy's translation.

26. The best accounts of the Birsa rebellion may be found in Singh, *Dust-Storm and Mist,* chaps. 4–6; and Sinha, *Birsa Bhagwan,* pp. 89–105.

27. These estimates are taken from Gilbert C. K. Gwassa, "African Methods of Warfare during the Maji Maji War, 1905–1907," p. 123.

28. This necessary emphasis on the Ngindo and Matumbi is problematical because these peoples have as yet been very little studied and very little has been written on their history in the precolonial period. This account of Matumbi and Ngindo culture and history is based primarily on the fragmentary information available in the Provincial and District Books in the Tanzanian National Archives in Dar es Salaam. Most of the information that I have used from this invaluable source was taken from microfilm copies of sections of the *Mtwara Provincial Book* and the *Kilwa* and *Rufiji District Books.*

29. My discussion of precolonial transformations is based primarily on ibid.; Gwassa, "Methods of Warfare," and "The German Intervention and African Resistance in Tanzania," pp. 85–123; Ernst Nigmann, *Die Wahehe;* Terence O. Ranger, "The Movement of Ideas, 1850–1939," pp. 161–88; Basil Davidson, *The Growth of African Civilization in East and Central Africa to the Late Nineteenth Century;* Allison Smith, "The Southern Section of the Interior, 1840–1884," pp. 251–96; and especially Andrew Roberts, "Political Change in the Nineteenth Century," pp. 57–84. Since a great deal of new work is currently being done on Tanzanian history, future research may well require revision of some of the assertions made in this introductory discussion of prior conditions and general trends.

30. R. M. Bell, "The Maji Maji Rebellion in the Liwale District," pp. 44–45.

31. Tanzania Provincial and District Record Books, *Mtwara Province,* sheets on the Ngindo and Ndonde and census abstracts, and the map on population density in German East Africa in Heinrich Schnee, ed., *Deutsches Kolonial-Lexikon,* vol. 2, pp. 368–69.

32. The sources on German colonization in east Africa are extremely uneven. This account of the origins and early effects of the German advance is based primarily on Hans-Ulrich Wehler, *Bismarck und der Imperialismus,* esp. pp. 334–67; Henri Brunschwig, *L'expansion allemande outre-mer du XVᵉ siècle à nos jours,* esp. pp. 111–22; Gwassa, "Resistance in Tanzania"; John P. Moffett, *Handbook of Tanganyika;* William O. Henderson, "German East Africa, 1884–1918," pp. 122–62; and, for contemporary German views, Gustav A. von Götzen, *Deutsch-Ostafrika im Aufstand 1905–1906,* esp. chap. 1.

33. Wehler, *Imperialismus,* p. 338.

34. Ibid.

35. John Iliffe, "The Organization of the Maji Maji Rebellion," p. 497.

36. For a detailed account of German involvement in the northwest see Ralph A. Austen, *Northwest Tanzania under German and British Rule.* A number of German writers argued that the lack of extensive German penetration in the areas affected by the rebellion proved that "native" superstitions and sorcerer plots and not German colonization were responsible for the outbreaks. See Albert Prüsse, *Swanzig Jahre Ansiedler in Deutsch-Ostafrika,* pp. 99–100.

37. Wilhelm Methner, *Unter Drei Gouverneuren,* pp. 76–77.

38. The best narratives of the Maji Maji rebellion to date are those written by

contemporary German officials. This summary account is based mainly upon von Götzen, *Ostafrika im Aufstand*; and Moritz Merker, "Ueber die Aufstandsbewegung in Deutsch-Ostafrika."

39. Gerald F. Sayers, *The Handbook of Tanganyika*, p. 74; and Iliffe, "Maji Organization," p. 495.

40. This outline of the historical context of the Saya San rebellion is based on John S. Furnivall, *An Introduction to the Political Economy of Burma* and *Colonial Policy and Practice*; Michael Adas, *The Burma Delta*; Cheng Siok-Hwa, *The Rice Industry of Burma, 1852–1940*; and John Cady, *A History of Modern Burma*.

41. In current usage, the people who speak Burmese and whose early homeland was the Dry Zone of Upper Burma are referred to as Burmans, whereas Burmese is used to denote all of the ethnic groups who presently make up the nation of Burma, including Burmans, Mons, Shans, Karens, and Chins. Since the Saya San rising was primarily a Burman movement and was in part directed against other *indigenous* ethnic groups, this distinction is critical for the purposes of this study.

42. For different approaches to this phenomenon, see Stanley J. Tambiah, *Buddhism and the Spirit Cults in North-East Thailand*; and Melford Spiro, *Burmese Supernaturalism*.

43. See John Gallagher and Ronald Robinson, "The Imperialism of Free Trade," pp. 1–15.

44. For a discussion of these concepts see Philip Curtin, "Nationalism in Africa, 1945–1965," p. 144.

45. This brief account of the course of the Saya San rebellion is based primarily on the following reports issued by the Government of Burma: "Report on the Rebellion in Burma up to the 3rd May, 1931"; *The Origin and Causes of the Burma Rebellion (1930–1932)*; and "(Confidential) Report on the Rebellion in Burma, April 1931–March 1932."

46. Letter from R. A. Butler to George Hall, 29 May 1934, no. 2160 in Government of India, *Political and Judicial Correspondence* (hereafter cited as *PJC*), File 7347.

47. Godfrey E. Harvey, *British Rule in Burma, 1824–1942*, p. 75.

48. Robert Redfield has aptly labeled this complex of custom, the "moral order." See *The Primitive World and Its Transformation*, pp. 48, 73.

49. As Emile Durkheim has defined the term in his work on *The Division of Labor in Society*, pp. 364–73.

CHAPTER 2

1. Both because of the nature of the available sources and my own concern with collective behavior, this study focuses on group rather than individual responses. As Weston La Barre has observed, however, these group responses represent "conflicts in personality and cultural alternatives in an individual mind, socially multiplied." See "Materials for Crisis Cults," p. 20.

2. The studies which have most influenced my application of the theory of relative deprivation are those by David Aberle, including his articles on "The Prophet Dance and Reactions to White Contact," pp. 77–83, and "A Note on Relative Deprivation Theory," pp. 209–14; Aberle's book on *The Peyote Religion Among the Navahos*; and Ted Gurr's volume on *Why Men Rebel*.

3. For a more detailed discussion of these aspects of deprivation see Gurr, ibid., pp. 13, 24–29.

4. Aberle, *Peyote Religion*, p. 210.

5. The insistence that these complex interconnections be recognized and analyzed was one of the most important challenges posed by Karl Marx's writings for the social scientist over a century ago. Unfortunately, his arguments generally have been debased by scholars and polemicists alike and have appeared in the guise of simplistic "theories" of economic determinism.

6. See Roland Mousnier, *Peasant Uprisings in Seventeenth-Century France, Russia and China,* esp. pp. 306–12, 329–32, 348.

7. See Charles Crosthwaite, *The Pacification of Burma;* and H. R. Alexander, ed., "The Pacification of Upper Burma: A Vernacular History." Some Burmese leaders collaborated with the British and thus retained their positions or were promoted. In certain cases, rebel leaders who surrendered to the British were given places in the new administration.

8. The best accounts of British administrative changes at the local level may be found in Daw Mya Sein, *Administration of Burma,* pp. 81–115, 157, 161, 165–75; John S. Furnivall, *Colonial Policy and Practice,* pp. 74–76; and John Cady, *A History of Modern Burma,* pp. 141–44.

9. Albert Moscotti, "British Policy in Burma, 1917–1937," pp. 38–41; and David Pfanner, "Rice and Religion in a Burmese Village," pp. 72–76.

10. The Government of Burma reported in 1931 that at least 38 headmen had been killed and 256 assaulted during the revolt, which still had several months to run in some areas (*Report on the Administration of the Province of Burma 1931–1932,* p. 72). See also Government of Burma, *The Origin and Causes of the Burma Rebellion,* pp. 3–6, 15.

11. Leslie Palmier, "The Javanese Nobility under the Dutch," pp. 197–227; and Bertram J. O. Schrieke, "The Native Rulers," pp. 167–201 and "The Position of the Regents from the Days of the Dutch East India Company to the Constitutional Regulation of 1854," pp. 202–21.

12. John Kaye and George B. Malleson, *History of the Indian Mutiny,* vol. 1, chaps. 2 and 3.

13. Pieter F. J. Louw and Eduard S. de Klerck, *De Java-Oorlog van 1825–1830,* vol. 1, pp. 10, 75–76, 108; P. H. van der Kemp, "De economische Oorzaken van den Java-oorlog van 1825–1830," pp. 38–42, 45–47; Hermann Colenbrander, *Koloniale Geschiedenis,* vol. 3, p. 165; and François de Stuers, *Mémoires sur la guerre de l'île de Java de 1825 à 1830,* pp. 17, 23.

14. Kemp, ibid., pp. 23–24; and Hendrik G. van Hogendorp, *Willem van Hogendorp in Nederlandsch-Indië, 1825–1830,* p. 148.

15. J. F. Walraven van Nes, "Verhandeling over de waarschijnlijke Oorzaken die Aanleiding tot de Onlusten van 1825," pp. 137–43; Louw and Klerck, *Java-Oorlog,* vol. 1, pp. 9–11; Soemarsaid Moertono, *State and Statecraft in Old Java,* pp. 7, 99, 117–18, 134; de Stuers, *Mémoires,* pp. 28–49; and G. P. Rouffaer, "Vorstenlanden," p. 593.

16. Peter B. R. Carey, "The Origins of the Java War (1825–1830)," pp. 59, 75–76; August W. P. Weitzel, *De Oorlog op Java van 1825 tot 1830,* vol. 1, pp. 30, 35–37, 40; F. Roorda, "Verhaal van de Oorsprong en het Begin van de Opstand van Dipå-něgårå," pp. 140, 182, 193, 196; van Nes, ibid., p. 161; and de Stuers, ibid., pp. 27, 41.

17. Louw and Klerck, *Java-Oorlog,* vol. 1, pp. 32–44, 85–87, 93–96, 111–12, 123, 131–32, 149; P. H. van der Kemp, "Dipanegara, eene geschiedkundige Hamlettype," pp. 358–65, 395–99; van Nes, ibid., pp. 153–55, 159; and Jan J. van Sevenhoven, "De Oorzaken van de Oorlog op Java van 1825 tot 1830," pp. 106–107.

18. Moertono, *Statecraft,* pp. 9, 67ff, 93–100; Louw and Klerck, ibid., vol. 1, pp. 32–33, 44, 93; van Nes, ibid., pp. 126–28, 143–44; and van Hogendorp, *Hogendorp in Nederlandsch-Indië,* esp. p. 146.

19. On the question of succession, see Louw and Klerck, ibid., vol. 1, pp. 108–17, 125–30, 143–44; and Kemp, "Eene Hamlettype," pp. 302–304, 321–26, 335ff. On the 1922 regulation, see Kemp, "Economische Oorzaken," p. 9; and on Dipanagara's opposition, Louw and Klerck, pp. 47ff, 111–12, and Kemp, supra fn. 20.

20. Louw and Klerck, ibid., vol. 1, pp. 10–12, 22–24; Hermanus de Graaf, *Geschiedenis van Indonesië,* p. 390; and Carey, "Java War Origins," pp. 70–71, 75.

21. For an excellent comparative discussion of the patron-client breakdown and

its consequences, see James C. Scott, "The Erosion of Patron-Client Bonds and Social Change in Southeast Asia," pp. 5–38; and on the *desa* tradition of avoidance see Clifford Geertz, "The Javanese Kijaji," p. 242; and Moertono, *Statecraft*, pp. 85–92, 118.

22. Louw and Klerck, *Java-Oorlog*, vol. 1, pp. 123, 140, 205–207; Weitzel, *De Java Oorlog*, vol. 1, pp. 14–15, 30–31; Carey, "Java War Origins," pp. 75–76; Peter Carey's translation of the *Surakarta Kraton Babad* in his study "Dipanagara and the Making of the Java War," pt. 2, pp. 396–97; and Roorda, "Oorsprong van de Opstand," pp. 101–102, 190–91.

23. Sarat C. Roy, *The Mundas and Their Country*, pp. 108–109.

24. The best accounts of this revolt may be found in M. G. Hallett, *Ranchi District Gazetteer*, pp. 33–40; and Roy, ibid., pp. 113–22.

25. John Reid, *Report on the Survey and Settlement Operations in the Ranchi District, 1902–1910*, p. 46.

26. Gustav A. von Götzen, *Deutsch-Ostafrika im Aufstand 1905–1906*, pp. 34–35, 43–44, 49, 52–53, 64; Gilbert C. K. Gwassa, "African Methods of Warfare during the Maji Maji," pp. 126, 128, 133; and Gwassa and John Iliffe, *Records of the Maji Maji Rising*, pt. 1, pp. 7–8; and Per Hassing, "German Missionaries and the Maji Maji Rising," p. 382.

27. The following description of the *jumbe*'s position is based upon R. M. Bell, "The Maji Maji Rebellion in the Liwale District," pp. 54–56; von Götzen, *Ostafrika im Aufstand*, pp. 236–39; and Gwassa, "Methods of Warfare," p. 128.

28. On this point see Gilbert C. K. Gwassa, "The German Intervention and African Resistance in Tanzania," p. 121.

29. The headman-sorcerer plot interpretation was first proposed by Moritz Merker in his article "Ueber die Aufstandsbewegung in Deutsch-Ostafrika," no. 45, pp. 1023–26. On the role of village and clan leaders in the rebellion see von Götzen, *Ostafrika im Aufstand*, pp. 145, 153, 156–57, 163, 240; Gwassa, "Methods of Warfare," pp. 128, 130, 137–38; and Bell, "Maji in Liwale," pp. 48–50. For a discussion of quite different patterns of displacement and leadership among the Ngoni see O. B. Mapunda and G. P. Mpangara, *The Maji Maji War in Ungoni*, pp. 13–15; and Patrick M. Redmond, "Maji Maji in Ngoni: A Reappraisal of Existing Historiography," pp. 410–13.

30. Maharaia Winiata, *The Changing Role of the Leader in Maori Society*, p. 46. See also Ann J. Gibson, "Religious Organization among the Maoris of New Zealand after 1860," p. 26.

31. Gibson, ibid., pp. 26–29; and J. Anderson, "The Missionaries and the Maoris," p. 57.

32. Harrison Wright, *New Zealand, 1769–1840: Early Years of Western Contact*, pp. 142–56, 181, 189–90; Keith Sinclair, *The Origins of the Maori Wars*, pp. 13–14; Winiata, *Changing Role*, pp. 50–52; Harold Miller, *New Zealand*, pp. 47, 56–57; James Hight, "The Maori Wars, 1843–1872," pp. 126, 130–31; and Alan Ward, *A Show of Justice*, pp. 32, 84–85.

33. Sinclair, ibid., pp. 126, 138–39; and Winiata, ibid., pp. 48–49.

34. Von Götzen, *Ostafrika im Aufstand*, pp. 28–29, 43–44, 236–37; and Merker, "Aufstandsbewegung," no. 45, pp. 1023–26.

35. Von Götzen, ibid., pp. 70–72, 90–92; and Bell, "Maji in Liwale," pp. 48–49.

36. For missionary activity in Tanzania in this period see Per Hassing, "German Missionaries"; Marcia Wright, *German Missions in Tanganyika*; or Sigvard van Sicard, *Christian Missions on the Coast of Tanzania*. The best discussion of Maji Maji ideology is contained in Gilbert Gwassa's essay on "Kinjikitile and the Ideology of Maji Maji," pp. 202–17.

37. For a fine analysis of comparable rituals associated with the installation of African leaders see Victor Turner, *The Ritual Process*, esp. pp. 82–88. On the involvement of local leaders in the Maji Maji see von Götzen, *Ostafrika im Aufstand*, pp. 236–37, 240; and Gwassa, "Methods of Warfare," pp. 128, 138–39, 146.

38. For detailed discussions of the reciprocal relationships between Buddhism and the precolonial Burman state, see Donald E. Smith, *Religion and Politics in Burma*, pp. 12–19, 23–31, 43–44; Melford Spiro, *Buddhism and Society*, pp. 379–82; U Aung Than, "Relation between the Saṃgha and State and Laity," pp. 4–5; and especially E. Michael Mendelson, *Sangha and State in Burma*, chaps. 1 and 2.

39. The best general accounts of the decline of Buddhism in colonial Burma are found in Smith, ibid. pp. 43–57; Furnivall, *Colonial Practice*, pp. 123–30; and Emanuel Sarkisyanz, *Buddhist Backgrounds of the Burmese Revolution*, pp. 110, 98–99, 136–37.

40. Spiro, *Buddhism*, pp. 383–85.

41. For discussions of the importance of monastic education in Burman society and its problems in the colonial period see John F. Brohm, "Burmese Religion and the Burmese Religious Revival," pp. 43–53, 303–308; David Pfanner, "Rice and Religion in a Burmese Village," pp. 104–107, 286, 328, 394–95; Smith, *Religion and Politics*, pp. 75–86; B. S. Cary, "Hints for the Guidance of Civil Officers," p. 4; and Mendleson, *Sangha and State*, pp. 150–61. On the link between the decline of monastic education and increasing crime rates see Government of Burma, *Report(s) on the Police Administration of Burma*, 1912, p. 19, and 1913, pp. 3–4.

42. For examples, see Government of Burma, *Settlement Reports—Myaungmya (1903–1904)*, p. 6; *Myaungmya-Bassein (1901–1902)*, p. 7; *Maubin (1925–1928)*, p. 8; *Tharrawaddy Gazetteer*, p. 3; *Insein Gazetteer*, pp. 56–57; and Charles W. Dunn, *Studies in the History of Tharrawaddy*, pp. 41–42. Regional fairs and other pastimes were prohibited in some areas by the colonial government, whose officials regarded them as potential occasions for brawls or demonstrations by unruly crowds (*Police Administration*, ibid., 1915, p. 12).

43. Spiro, *Buddhism and Society*, p. 20.

44. Sarkisyanz, *Buddhist Backgrounds*, 82–86, 101–107; and Robert Heine-Geldern, "Conceptions of the State and Kingship in Southeast Asia," pp. 17–24.

45. For examples of Buddhist monastic involvement see Government of Burma, *Origins and Causes Report*, pp. 4, 16–19, 24–26, 32–36, 42–43.

46. For examples see *PJC-File 7349*, no. 1622, p. 2; no. 5084, p. 10; no. 5515, p. 4; no. 5832, p. 549; *7350*, no. 898, p. 145; and R. C. Morris, "Causes of the Tharrawaddy Rebellion (1931)," Appendixes I and H.

47. Moertono, *Statecraft*, pp. 2–4, 26–28, 33–37, 83–84; and Justus M. van der Kroef, "Javanese Messianic Expectations," pp. 304–307.

48. Gustav E. von Grünenbaum, *Essays in the Nature and Growth of a Cultural Tradition*, pp. 131–32.

49. For examples see Sartono Kartodirdjo, *The Peasants Revolt of Banten in 1888*, pp. 169–73; Harry Benda, *The Crescent and the Rising Sun*, pp. 13, 18–19; and Marinus Deventer, *Geschiedenis van Nederlanders op Java*, vol. 2, pp. 15–18, 283–84.

50. On Dipanagara's religious concerns in general and his desire to be a *pantagama* specifically see Kemp, "Eene Hamlettype," pp. 307–14; Peter B. R. Carey, *The Cultural Ecology of Early Nineteenth Century Java*, pp. 16–22, 33–37; Louw and Klerck, *Java-Oorlog*, vol. 1, pp. 44–47, 81, 91–93, 121–24; vol. 3, pp. 249, 262, 265–66; Sevenhoven, "Oorzaken," pp. 107–108; Weitzel, *De Java Oorlog*, vol. 1, pp. 76–78; vol. 2, p. 324; and Roorda, "Oorsprong van de Opstand," pp. 143–48.

51. Carey, ibid., pp. 19–21, 29, 33–37, 50–51; Weitzel, ibid., vol. 1, pp. 177, 211, 219, esp. 304, 325; vol. 2, pp. 323–24, 257–62; Louw and Klerck, ibid., vol. 1, pp. 138, 153–54, 263, esp. Appendixes 45 and 58; vol. 2, pp. 212–13, 244, 261; and vol. 3, pp. 249, 260–68; and Huibert G. Nahuys van Burgst, *Verzameling van officiële Rapporten betreffende den Oorlog op Java in de Jaren 1825–1830*, vol. 2, pp. 322–33; vol. 3, pp. 260, 273, 363–66.

52. Suresh Singh, *Dust-Storm and Hanging Mist*, pp. 6–7, 10–13, 19–26; Surendra Sinha, *The Life and Times of Birsa Bhagwan*, pp. 22–23, 36–42 et passim; and Roy, *Mundas*, pp. 144–53, 167–87.

53. Sinha, ibid., pp. 48–49, 56, 73ff.; and Roy, ibid., pp. 189–90.

54. Roy, ibid., p. 192; and Singh, *Dust-Storm and Mist*, pp. 53, 77–81.

55. Winiata, *Changing Role*, pp. 46, 51–52; James Cowan, *The Maoris of New Zealand*, pp. 107–108, 114–15; Wright, *New Zealand*, pp. 152–59; Ward, *Show of Justice*, pp. 20–21; and Judith Binney, "Christianity and the Maoris," pp. 150–56.

56. Stuart Babbage, *Hauhauism*, pp. 38–39; James Cowan, *The New Zealand Wars*, vol. 2, pp. 3–6, 77, 179, 191 et passim; and Gibson, "Religious Organization," pp. 99–100.

57. Sinclair, *Origins*, pp. 67–69, 79–80; Babbage, ibid., pp. 14–15; and Cowan, ibid., p. 4.

58. Aberle, "Deprivation Theory," p. 211. For a theoretical discussion of this form of deprivation, termed by Ted Gurr "decremental deprivation," see *Why Men Rebel*, pp. 46–50. For parallel patterns in other areas see, for examples, Peter Worsley, *The Trumpet Shall Sound*, pp. 41, 51, 164, 175, 248; Carl Brown, "The Sudanese Mahdiya," p. 158; Audrey Whipper, "The Gusii Rebels," pp. 385–86, 411–12; and Udo Oberen, "Die Aufstandsbewegung der Pende," p. 77.

59. For examples of these arguments see Henri Brunschwig (quoting Jules Ferry), *Mythes et réalités de l'impéralisme colonial française*, pp. 71–77; Hans-Ulrich Wehler, *Bismarck und der Imperialismus*, pp. 112–54 et passim; and Arthur Girault, *Principes de colonisation et de législation coloniale*, pp. 29–31.

60. This discussion of the forced cultivation scheme and its mismanagement is based largely on John Iliffe, "The Organization of the Maji Maji Rebellion," pp. 497–98; Gwassa, "Methods of Warfare," pp. 129–30; Wilhelm Methner, *Unter Drei Gouverneuren*, pp. 75–76; and Hermann Paasche, *Deutsch-Ostafrika*, pp. 133–34, 345. It is revealing to note that von Götzen, the administrator responsible for the introduction of the scheme in German East Africa, scarcely mentions it in his detailed account of the Maji Maji rising.

61. Methner, ibid., p. 76. See also Paasche, ibid., pp. 134, 345; John Iliffe, "The Effects of the Maji Maji Rebellion on German Policy in East Africa," p. 560; and Gwassa and Iliffe, *Records*, pp. 4–6, 10.

62. Gwassa, "Resistance in Tanzania," p. 121, "Methods of Warfare," p. 125; and Gwassa and Iliffe, *Records*, pp. 4–5.

63. Gwassa and Iliffe, ibid., pp. 4–5, 7; and Bell, "Maji in Liwale," p. 56.

64. Iliffe, "Organization of the Maji Maji," pp. 497–500; and "Effects of Maji Maji," pp. 560–61.

65. Bell, "Maji in Liwale," p. 44; Iliffe, "Organization," p. 499; and Margaret Bates, "Introduction" to Abdul Karim bin Jamaliddini's *Utenzi wa vita vya Maji Maji*, pp. 8–9.

66. Karim bin Jamaliddini, ibid., p. 35; Iliffe, ibid., p. 499; Bell, ibid., p. 49; Gwassa and Iliffe, *Records*, pp. 4–7, 10; Gwassa, "Methods of Warfare," pp. 140–41; and von Götzen, *Ostafrika im Aufstand*, pp. 52–53.

67. Carey, "Java War Origins," pp. 63–65; Louw and Klerck, *Java-Oorlog*, vol. 1, pp. 10–12; de Graaf, *Geschiedenis*, p. 390; and Moertono, *Statecraft*, pp. 144–51. For a detailed list of tax burdens born by the peasantry, see Louw and Klerck, vol. 1, pp. 86–87.

68. This discussion of the land rental system is based upon Louw and Klerck, ibid., pp. 48–51, 59–67, 78–79; Kemp, "Economische Oorzaaken," pp. 16–24; de Graaf, ibid., pp. 390–91; J. Hageman, *Geschiedenis van den Oorlog op Java van 1825 tot 1830*, pp. 42–52; and C. T. Elout, "Staatkundig-ekonomische Beschouwingen omtrent de Landverhuringen in Soerakarta en Djokjokarta tot op den Javaschen Oorlog van 1825 tot 1830," pp. 1–36. For the most detailed defense of the rental system see, J. S. Parvé, "Landverhuur in de vorstenlanden en Javasche oorlog," pp. 22–37, 52–57. In the coastal areas that fell under Dutch control beginning in the seventeenth century, the V. O. C. granted leases to Chinese renters much earlier. See Marinus L. van Deventer, *Geschiedenis der Nederlanders op Java*, vol. 2, pp. 77–78.

69. The following discussion of the abolition and its effects is based upon van Nes, "Waarschijnlijke Oorzaken," pp. 147–53; Louw and Klerck, ibid., pp. 51–56, 69–77, 80–82; Kemp, ibid., pp. 24–38; de Graaf, ibid., pp. 390–91; de Stuers, *Mémoires*, pp. 33, 215–16; and Elout, ibid., pp. 17–31. Some Dutch writers have argued that the abolition and not the rental system itself was responsible for Dipanagara's revolt. See van Hogendorp, *Hogendorp in Nederlandsch-Indië*, pp. 142–43, 147–49.

70. The best treatments of the toll system and its relationship to the rebellion may be found in Louw and Klerck, ibid., pp. 9, 12–18; Kemp, ibid., pp. 42–46; de Graaf, ibid., p. 390; Colenbrander, *Koloniale Geschiedenis*, vol. 3, pp. 164–65; Carey, "Java War Origins," pp. 65–71; and S. van Praag, *Onrust op Java*, pp. 77–83.

71. Louw and Klerck, ibid., p. 309, Appendix 57.

72. Ibid., pp. 267, 269, 273 et passim; and Weitzel, *De Java Oorlog*, vol. 1, p. 41.

73. This analysis of landlord-Munda relations before the Birsa rising is based mainly upon Sinha, *Birsa Bhagwan*, 23–25, 30–36, 68–70; Reid, *Ranchi Settlement Report*, pp. 33–36, 78–90, 97–105; Roy, *Mundas*, pp. 121–22, 154–60, 173–78; Hallett, *Ranchi Gazetteer*, pp. 46–47; and John Hoffman et al., *Encylcopedia Mundarica*, vol. 2, p. 565.

74. The best information on this rather poorly covered aspect of the Munda situation is available in Reid, ibid., p. 79; Hallett, ibid., p. 162; and Sinha, ibid., pp. 25, 30. On the closing of the forest see esp. Reid, ibid., p. 125; Sinha, ibid., p. 53; and Singh, *Dust-Storm and Mist*, p. 190.

75. Sinha, ibid., pp. 49–50, 55–56, 82–83 et passim; Reid, ibid., pp. 46–47, 78, 142; Singh, ibid., pp. 53, 57, 59–60, 72, 75, 87–89 and Appendixes, pp. 104, 110–11.

76. Keith Sinclair, *History of New Zealand*, p. 97. See also John Houston, *Maori Life in Old Taranaki*, pp. 92–93; and Raymond Firth, *Economics of the New Zealand Maori*, chap. 11, and p. 454.

77. Quoted in Sinclair, ibid., p. 96. See also Sinclair, *Origins*, pp. 45–47.

78. This survey of the land tenure crisis is based primarily on the superb studies of Keith Sinclair cited above, which have been supplemented by Miller, *New Zealand*, pp. 59–62; William Martin, *The Taranaki Question*, passim; Apirana Ngata, "Maori Land Settlement," pp. 96–136; John Condliffe and William Airey, *A Short History of New Zealand*, pp. 69–70, 77, 93; and Ward, *Show of Justice*, pp. 88, 108, 151 ff.

79. Sinclair, *Origins*, pp. 41, 83–84, 128; Miller, ibid., pp. 59–60; and Condliffe and Airey, ibid., pp. 95–96.

80. Martin, *Taranaki Question*, passim; Babbage, *Hauhauism*, pp. 10–15; and Sinclair, ibid., pp. 110 ff.

81. Cowan, *New Zealand*, vol. 2, pp. 1–3, 143–44, 153; Babbage, ibid., pp. 16–21; and A. J. Harrop, *England and the Maori Wars*, chap. 7.

82. Babbage, ibid., pp. 19–21, 54, 59, 69–71; and Cowan, ibid., pp. 1–4.

83. See, for examples, Government of Burma, "Report on the Rebellion in Burma up to the 3rd May 1931," pp. 11–12; R. C. Morris, "Causes of the Tharrawaddy Rebellion," p. 17; and Government of Burma, *Origin and Causes Report*, pp. 1, 43.

84. The most detailed analysis of this crisis may be found in Michael Adas, *The Burma Delta*, chaps. 6, 7.

85. I have calculated these percentages from the statistics in Government of Burma, *Report of the Provincial Banking Enquiry Committee 1929–1930*, vol. 1, p. 53, and vol. 3, pp. 264–68.

86. I have calculated these and all other percentages cited from the statistics on the ownership of agricultural land in the Government of Burma, *Report on the Land Revenue Administration of Burma for 1929–30*, pp. 54–55. The few Upper Burma districts where major disturbances occurred are not included in these averages because Upper Burma was annexed later than the Delta and was far less exposed to market

influences. Averages for these areas are therefore much lower than those for Lower Burma. In addition, all of the major risings in Upper Burma were instigated by leaders from the Delta or touched off by prior disturbances in Lower Burma districts.

87. Thomas Couper, *Report of Inquiry into the Condition of Agricultural Tenants and Labourers*, pp. 29–32, 41–42.

88. Government of Burma, *Report of the Land and Agriculture Committee*, pt. 2, pp. 52–53.

89. T. Couper, *Agricultural Inquiry*, p. 53.

90. On the anticapitation tax campaigns see Government of Burma, "3rd May Report," p. 2; Moscotti, "British Policy," pp. 40–41; and Cady, *Modern Burma*, pp. 191, 252–53, 258.

91. Ma Mai Lei, "The Real Origins and Causes of the Burman Rebellion, 1930–32," pp. 377–78. This suggestion is supported by the chronology presented by Morris, "Tharrawaddy Rebellion," pp. 8–9.

92. U Saw, *The Burmese Situation*, pp. 1–2, 7, 11.

93. See the Secret Tribunal Judgements in *PJC—File 7349*, no. 3555, pp. 331–32, and *File 7350*, no. 1869, p. 158.

94. For examples, see the Secret Tribunal Judgements in *PJC—File 7347*, 16 February 1932, pp. 164, 167; *File 7349*, no. 3555, p. 2, no. 4768, p. 331, no. 5084, p. 10, no. 5515, pp. 1–2, no. 5895, pp. 3, 8; *File 7350*, no. 898, p. 145, no. 2901, p. 1, no. 4759, p. 27. In his recent and stimulating analysis of *The Moral Economy of the Peasant*, James C. Scott has especially stressed the rigidity of the colonial regimes' revenue demands as a cause of anticolonial rebellions in general and the Saya San rebellion in particular (esp. pp. 52–55 and 91–105). He argues that refusal by colonial governments to demand less revenue in times of crop failures or market slumps pushed many cultivators below the subsistence level and thereby gave rise to violent protest. He asserts that this pattern occurred in Burma during the Depression crisis of the early 1930s and was a major cause of the Saya San rebellion. These assertions are not supported by the manuscript and published sources that I have examined.

The assumption that the colonial regime's taxation policies were uniform, rigid, and blind to the peasants' needs bears little relation to the actual system used in assessing land revenue. Resisting heavy pressure at various times from the Government of India, revenue officials in Burma refused to introduce fixed assessments, despite the great savings in time and money that would have resulted for the provincial government. In both Upper and Lower Burma, the government took a percentage of the *net* output of the cultivator's lands that was adjusted for variations in soil types, water conditions, crops produced, etc. In Lower Burma, where rainfall and crop returns were more dependable, the assessment was based on the number of acres cultivated. In Upper Burma, which was prone to drought and repeated crop losses, the revenue was assessed on the amount of the *mature* crop. After years in the field many district officers became quite sensitive to variations in local conditions and adjusted revenue demands accordingly (see Government of Burma, *Report of the Committee to Examine the Land Revenue System*, vol. 1, pp. 18–25, 60–65; 67–68, 110–11 et passim).

The contention that the government extracted the full assessed demand regardless of the condition of the peasantry is also flatly contradicted by the hundreds of thousands of rupees in land revenue remissions granted by the Government of Burma all through the years of the Depression—remissions that were given *despite* falling revenue returns. In fact, the policy of remissions for cultivators in areas hit by drought, floods, or market slumps had been followed for nearly a century before the 1930s crisis. In addition to remissions, which were often rendered unnecessary by the flexibility of the revenue system, the government provided public relief works to buffer the impact of severe natural or market setbacks on the agrarian population (see for examples and statistical details the sections on land revenue returns and the "condition of the people" in Government of Burma, *Reports on the Administration of Burma* for the 1920s and 1930s).

There is little evidence that land taxes, as opposed to the capitation, or head tax (which many British officials criticized sharply as extremely regressive), were a major factor in driving the supporters of Saya San to rebellion. In the secret judgments from the tribunals conducted after the rebellion, the participants stressed indebtedness, land alienation, high tenancy rates, and the competition of Indian laborers as the economic causes of their discontent. Although there are general references to abolishing all taxes (which are commonly associated with millennial risings), only capitation taxes are specifically mentioned. In this respect it should be pointed out that landless tenants and laborers, the groups whose subsistence might have been the most threatened by the market slump, were little affected by the government's policies regarding taxes on land. Small landholders and big landlords were not faced with starvation. On the contrary, they had all too much rice to eat because they could not sell it at a decent price or at all. The vast majority of peasants in Lower Burma, where the Saya San rebellion was centered, were market, not subsistence, oriented. For the landowners the Depression meant a loss of income and consumer amenities to which they had grown accustomed and not the threat of starvation. For the laborers and tenants, rent enhancements, declining wages, and job shortages and not land revenue payments were the major threats to their survival.

95. For a fine statement of this position, see Eric Hobsbawm, *Primitive Rebels*, p. 79. For other examples of this view see Gurr, *Why Men Rebel*; Aberle, "Deprivation Theory," p. 201; Harry Eckstein, "On the Etiology of Internal Wars," pp. 125–26; and James C. Davies, "Toward a Theory of Revolution," p. 7.

96. On these patterns of vertical mobility, see Adas, *Burma Delta*, pp. 69–82.

97. See Mehmet Beqiraj, *Peasantry in Revolution*, esp. pp. 1–21. For further discussions of tensions within the "little community" see Robin Horton, "African Traditional Thought and Western Science," pp. 55–56; or George Foster, "Peasant Society and the Image of the Limited Good," pp. 300–323.

98. Writing of a later period, Sartono Kartodirdjo has noted significant erosion of the communal solidarity of Javanese villages located in privately-owned estate areas. See *Protest Movements in Rural Java*, p. 26.

99. For a fine discussion of similar patterns related to a different type of rebellion see Eric Wolf, *Peasant Wars of the Twentieth Century*, pp. 276–83.

100. As Fokke Sierksma has argued (*Een nieuwe Hemel en een nieuwe Aarde*, p. 244), studies of acculturation have too often focused on European/non-European confrontations and ignored important exchanges between different non-European groups.

101. On communal competition in Burma and the communal aspects of the Saya San risings, see Adas, *Burma Delta*, chaps. 7 and 8.

102. Sinclair, *Origins*, pp. 74, 78, 207; Condliffe and Airey, *Short History*, p. 94; Miller, *New Zealand*, p. 62; Alan Ward, "The Origins of the Anglo-Maori Wars," pp. 163ff.

103. For examples see Georges Balandier, *Sociologie actuelle de l'Afrique noire*, pp. 417, 424–25, 436, 441; Vittorio Lanternari, *Religions of the Oppressed*, pp. 21, 24–25, 26–29, 33–34, 40; and Worsley, *Trumpet*, pp. 21, 29, 47, 52–57, 74, 81, 96.

104. As Wilhelm Mühlmann has pointed out, the Europeans (and this should be extended to their non-European allies) also controlled the economic links to the outside and often monopolized marketing and banking skills that had great influence on the living conditions of the colonized peoples. See *Chiliasmus*, pp. 357–58.

CHAPTER 3

1. For critiques of the deprivation approach to causation in social protest movements focusing on this argument see Kenelm Burridge, *New Heaven New Earth*, pp. 56–57; Peter Lupsha, "Explanation of Political Violence," pp. 91–98; and H. L. Nieburg, *Political Violence*, pp. 39–40.

2. Eric Wolf, *Pveasant Wars of the Twentieth Century*, p. 289.

3. One of the most striking examples of this pattern in connection with a millenarian rebellion is described in Nelson Reed's *Caste War of Yucatan*, pp. 98–100. Maya insurgent leaders saw their forces dwindle on the eve of victory as peasant recruits deserted in order to honor their more fundamental allegiance to the cropping cycle.

4. For a fine discussion of these weaknesses of colonial bureaucracies see Wolf, *Peasant Wars*, pp. 283–86.

5. Margaret Bates, "Introduction" to *Utenzi wa vita vya Maji Maji*, p. 16; Gilbert C. K. Gwassa, "African Methods of Warfare during the Maji Maji," pp. 128–29; O. F. Raum, "German East Africa," p. 176; and for a German defense, Gustav A. von Götzen, *Deutsch-Ostafrika im Aufstand 1905–1906*, pp. 32–35, 236–39.

6. See for examples P. H. van der Kemp, "Dipanegara, eene geschiedkundige Hamlettype," esp. pp. 376–85; Pieter F. J. Louw and Eduard S. de Klerck, *De Java-Oorlog van 1825–1830*, vol. 1, pp. 9, 46, 81 ff, 123, 131–32; J. F. Walraven van Nes, "Verhandeling over de waarschijnlijke Oorzaken die Aanleiding tot Onlusten van 1825," pp. 153–55, 158; and Egbert O. Kielstra, "Eenige Personen uit den Java-oorlog," pp. 291–94.

7. Louw and Klerck, ibid., pp. 82–88, 131–32; Kemp, "Economische Oorzaaken," pp. 10, 24–25: and Peter B. R. Carey, "The Origins of the Java War (1825–1830)," p. 67.

8. The following discussion of British administrative impotence is based on John Reid, *Ranchi Settlement Report, 1902–1910*, pp. 6–20, 26–32, 34–36, 41–46; Sarat C. Roy, *The Mundas and Their Country*, pp. 106, 119, 121–29, 154–60; and Surendra Sinha, *The Life and Time of Birsal Bhagwan*, pp. 16–24.

9. Reid, ibid., p. 26.

10. For the most detailed discussion of these patterns, see Alan Ward, *A Show of Justice*, esp. chaps. 3–7 passim. See also Harold Miller, *New Zealand*, pp. 60–62; John Condliffe and Willis Airey, *A Short History of New Zealand*, pp. 67–70, 93; Keith Sinclair, *The Origins of the Maori Wars*, pp. 29–30, 38–39; and Angus J. Harrop, *England and the Maori Wars*, p. 207.

11. Miller, ibid., pp. 60–61; and Sinclair, ibid., pp. 91–92; *History of New Zealand*, p. 60.

12. Miller, ibid., pp. 63–64.

13. Ward, *Show of Justice*, pp. 44–54, 61–68, 74–82, 85–86, 90–93, and chap. 9; Condliffe and Airey, *Short History*, pp. 90–95; Sinclair, *Origins*, pp. 85–95, 242–45; and Miller, ibid., pp. 48–49, 53, 61.

14. On the legislative struggles see John Cady, *A History of Modern Burma*, pp. 163–68, 278; or Cheng Siok-Hwa, *The Rice Industry of Burma, 1852–1940*, pp. 147–56, 166–70.

15. For more detailed discussions of these patterns in nineteenth-century India see Anil Seal, *The Emergence of Indian Nationalism*.

16. John Hoffman, *Encyclopedia Mundarica*, vol. 2, pp. 566–67; Sinha, *Birsa Bhagwan*, pp. 2–24; M. Hallett, *Ranchi Gazetteer*, pp. 46–49; and Suresh Singh, *Dust-Storm and Mist*, 26–30.

17. The fullest account of the King Movement remains John Gorst's *The Maori King*. For good, brief discussions see also Miller, *New Zealand*, pp. 62–65; Sinclair, *Origins*, pp. 66–81; and Maharaia Winiata, *The Changing Role of the Leader in Maori Society*, pp. 61–66.

18. Gorst, ibid., p. 150.

19. Cady, *Modern Burma*, pp. 231–34, 250–58.

20. Personal communication from Robert Taylor. See also the relevant portions of his recent dissertation on "The Relationship between Burmese Social Classes and British-Indian policy on the Behavior of the Burmese Political Elite, 1937–1942."

21. Sinha, *Birsa Bhagwan*, pp. 22–23, 38–43, 89–90: Hoffman, *Encyclopedia Mundarica*, vol. 2, pp. 566–67; and Stephen Fuchs, *Rebellious Prophets*, pp. 26–27, 31–32.

22. Peter Worsley, *The Trumpet Shall Sound*, pp. 212, 240–41 et passim.

23. Stuart Babbage, *Hauhauism*, pp. 28–29, 33; and Ann Gibson, "Religious Organization among the Maoris of New Zealand after 1860," p. 54.

24. Sinclair, *Origins*, pp. 222–24; and Apirana Ngata, "Religious Influences," p. 346.

25. Gibson, "Religious Organization," pp. 33–35, 44–46; Babbage, *Episode*, pp. 20, 38, 49, 70; and Ngata, ibid , p. 348.

CHAPTER 4

1. On the problem of nonoccurrence see Kenelm Burridge, *New Heaven New Earth*, pp. 74, 273–274; Henning Silvert, "Book Review: The Religions of the Oppressed," p. 456; and Sylvia Thrupp, ed., *Millennial Dreams in Action*, p. 27.

2. For discussions of these themes in different cultural settings, see Robin Horton, "African Traditional Thought and Western Science," pt. 2, pp. 156–87; Stephen Fuchs, *Rebellious Prophets*, pp. 1–20; Heinrich Zimmer, *Myths and Symbols in Indian Art and Civilization*, pp. 3–53; and Gerardus W. J. Drewes, *Drie Javaansche Goeroe's*, esp. pp. 29–68. For interesting variations see F. Errington, "Indigenous Ideas of Order, Time and Transition in a New Guinea Cargo Movement," pp. 255–57.

3. For the role of secret societies in millenarian risings see Susan Naquin, *Millennial Rebellion in China*; and Victor Purcell, *The Boxer Uprising*, esp. chap. 7.

4. For prophets without millennial visions see Bernt Sundkler, *Bantu Prophets in South Africa*, passim; and Bryan Wilson, *Magic and the Millennium*, pp. 133 ff. For an interpretation that explicitly deemphasizes the importance of prophetic leadership, see Peter Worsley, *The Trumpet Shall Sound*, esp. pp. ix–xx. The very lively debate over this issue is surveyed in Johannes Fabian, "Führer und Führung in den prophetisch-messianischen Bewegungen," pp. 777–78, 791–92.

5. This brief sketch of Dipanagara's life is based primarily on his personal history or *Babad*. Ann Kumar has translated portions of this account in *Indonesia* 13 (1972): 69–118. For this study I have relied more heavily on the fuller translation and detailed commentary in Pieter F. J. Louw and Eduard S. de Klerck, *De Java-Oorlog van 1825–1830*, chaps. 6 and 7, as well as the detailed accounts of his life contained in P. H. van der Kemp, "Dipanagara, eene geschiedkundige Hamlettype," and S. van Praag's *Onrust op Java: De Jeudg van Dipanĕgara*.

6. J. F. Walraven van Nes, "Verhandeling over de waarschijinlijke Oorzaken, die Aanleiding tot de Onlusten van 1825," p. 136.

7. Katesa Schlosser, "Der Prophetismus in niederen Kulturen," p. 64.

8. On Dipanagara's role as an astute estate manager and reform-conscious leader see Peter B. R. Carey, "The Origins of the Java War (1825–1830)," pp. 60–61.

9. Merle C. Ricklefs, "Dipanagara's Early Inspirational Experience," pp. 230–31.

10. The standard study of Javanese chiliastic beliefs is Gerardus W. J. Drewes, *Drie Javaansche Goeroe's*. The best studies of the links between Dipanagara and this tradition are Peter B. R. Carey, *The Cultural Ecology of Early Nineteenth Century Java*; and Ricklefs, ibid., pp. 227–58. These works have been supplemented in the following discussion by Hermanus J. de Graaf, *Geschiedenis van Indonesië*, esp. pp. 17–18, 25–26, 52–53; Soermarsaid Moertono, *State and Statecraft in Old Java*, pp. 2–3, 35–37, 54, 81–83 et passim; Bertram Schrieke, *Indonesian Sociological Studies*, vol. 2, pp. 77–86; and Justus van der Kroef, "Javanese Messianic Expectations," pp. 299–323.

11. For a discussion of these attitudes and their historical importance see Kroef, ibid., esp. pp. 299–305; Drewes, ibid., pp. 188–89; or Moertono, ibid., pp. 3, 37–38, 83, 87 ff. As Justus van der Kroef has pointed out, these changes—such as the demolition of old buildings or the construction of a new road—may seem minor to an outside observer, but the latter occurrence in fact precipitated Dipanagara's revolt. See Louw and Klerck, *Java-Oorlog*, vol. 1, pp. 138–39.

12. Th. G. Th. Pigeaud, "Erucakra-Vairocana," pp. 270 ff.; Jakob A. B. Wiselius, "Djåjå Båjå, zijn Leven en Profetieën," pp. 172–207; and Drewes, ibid., pp. 143–47.

13. On Prophetic-millennial aspects of resistance to Dutch dominance on Java, both before and after Dipanagara, see Bernhard Dahm, *Sukarno and the Struggle for Indonesian Independence.* chap. 1 et passim; Carey. "Java War Origins," p. 55; Emanuel Sarkisyanz, *Russland und der Messianismus des Orients,* pp. 297–305; and Sartono Kartodirdjo, *Peasant Protest in Rural Java,* "Agrarian Radicalism in Java," pp. 71–126, and *The Peasants' Revolt of Banten in 1888.*

14. This brief account of the millenarian themes manifested in Dipanagara's revolt represents an attempt to reconcile and summarize the interpretations and information contained in the fine studies by Carey, *Cultural Ecology,* esp. pp. 18–19, 25–37, 42, 53–55; and Ricklefs, "Inspirational Experience," pp. 235–47; and the earlier accounts published in Louw and Klerck, *Java-Oorlog,* vol. 1, pp. 91–93, 130–31, 136–37; Kemp, "Eene Hamlettype," esp. pp. 366–74; Drewes, *Drie Goeroe's,* pp. 132, 135; and Abraham B. Cohen Stuart, "Eroe Tjakra," pp. 285–88.

15. Biographical information about Saya San can be found in R. C. Morris, "Causes of the Tharrawaddy Rebellion," p. 8; the Government of Burma, *Police Proceedings,* no. 326c31, 20 August 1931 in *PJC—File 7347,* no. 4895; the *Rangoon Gazette,* 10 August 1931, p. 5; and Ba U, *My Burma,* pp. 104–10.

16. For excellent discussions of these sects see E. Michael Mendelson, "A Messianic Buddhist Association in Upper Burma," pp. 560–80; and Melford Spiro, *Buddhism and Society,* chap. 7.

17. Quoted portions from Emanuel Sarkisyanz, *Buddhist Backgrounds of the Burmese Revolution,* pp. 64, 153–54. This discussion of Burman *Sektya-Min* prophecies is based largely on Sarkisyanz (149–61 et passim); Spiro, ibid., pp. 162–74, 180–86; and E. Michael Mendelson, "The King of the Central Weaving Mountain," pp. 231–36.

18. Spiro, ibid., pp. 164–71.

19. Ibid., pp. 171–74; and for sample revolts see Sarkisyanz, *Buddhist Backgrounds,* pp. 155–58; and Herbert T. White, *A Civil Servant in Burma,* pp. 266–70.

20. Government of Burma, *Origin and Causes of the Burma Rebellion,* p. 19; Maurice Collis, *Trials in Burma,* pp. 213–14; Sarkisyanz, *Buddhist Backgrounds,* p. 104; Mendelson, "Weaving Mountain," pp. 235–36, and "Messianic Association," p. 576n.; and Government of Burma, "Report on the Rebellion in Burma up to 3rd May 1931," p. 6.

21. A translation of his diary was published in the *Rangoon Gazette Weekly Budget,* 5 October 1931, p. 18.

22. Gustav A. von Götzen, *Deutsch-Ostafrika im Aufstand 1905–1906,* pp. 64–65.

23. See especially "Kinjikitile and the Ideology of Maji Maji," pp. 209, 211, 214–15; and "African Methods of Warfare during the Maji Maji," pp. 131–35.

24. The most detailed account of their beliefs is contained in Gwassa's article, "Ideology of Maji Maji," ibid., which provides the basis for much of the following discussion.

25. "African Traditional Thought," pt. 2, pp. 173–75. See also Max Gluckman, *Order and Rebellion in Tribal Africa,* pp. 142–43 et passim.

26. My attention was first drawn to this connection by J. Iliffe's article, "The Organization of Maji Maji Rebellion," p. 508. For detailed discussions see Mary Douglas, "Techniques of Sorcery Control in Central Africa," pp. 123–41; and *The Lele of Kasai,* esp. pp. 244–58. See also Jan Vansina, "Les mouvements religieux Kuba (Kasai) à l'époque coloniale," pp. 157, 161, 182–183; Terence Ranger, "The Movement of Ideas, 1850–1939," pp. 169–72, 181; and R. G. Willis, "Instant Millennium: The Sociology of African Witch-Cleansing Cults," pp. 129–39.

27. Horton, "African Thought," pt. 2, pp. 176–80.

28. Quoted portions in John Iliffe, *Tanzania under German Rule, 1905–1912,* p. 296; Götzen, *Ostafrika im Aufstand,* pp. 45–46, 90; Iliffe, "Maji Organization," pp. 502–503; Gilbert Gwassa and Iliffe, *Records of the Maji Maji Rising,* pp. 10, 17; and Moritz Merker, "Ueber die Aufstandsbewegung in Deutsch-Ostafrika," no. 45, p. 1025.

29. Gwassa, "Ideology of Maji Maji," pp. 204 ff, 210; and "Methods of Warfare," p. 127. See also Terence O. Ranger, "Connexions between 'Primary Resistance' Movements and Modern Mass Nationalism in East and Central Africa," pp. 450-51.

30. Gwassa, "Ideology," pp. 204-208; Martin Klamroth, "Beitrage zum Verständnis der religiösen Vorstellungen der Saramo im Bezirk Daressalam," pp. 139-53; A. R. W. Cross-Upcott, "The Origin of the Maji Maji Revolt," pp. 71-73; and Gwassa and Iliffe, Records, pp. 16-17. As J. H. Driberg contends in his article on the "Yakan" cult movement in Uganda (pp. 415, 419), there are striking parallels between the Maji Maji and movements in the Sudan and Uganda. Nubian mercenaries may well have carried elements of the northern cults to Tanganyika when they went there to serve under German officers. However, I have found no direct evidence of this link.

31. Gwassa, ibid., pp. 207-209; Gwassa and Iliffe, ibid., pp. 9, 10, 16; R. M. Bell, "Maji Maji in the Liwale District," p. 44; O. Mapunda and G. Mpangara, The Maji Maji War in Ungoni, pp. 20-21; and Gwassa, "The German Intervention and African Resistance in Tanzania," pp. 117-18.

32. The only recorded pre-Birsite movement among the Mundas with millenarian overtones was the Sons of Mael cult in 1881. The leader of the cult claimed to be John the Baptist and promised to establish a new Munda kingdom. His arrest by the colonial authorities put a quick end to the movement. See Surat C. Roy, The Mundas and their Country, pp. 163-64; or M. G. Hallett, Ranchi District Gazetteer, p. 47.

33. The fullest accounts of Birsa's life are contained in Suresh Singh's The Dust-Storm and Hanging Mist, chaps. 2, 3; and Surendra Sinha's The Life and Times of Birsa Bhagwan, esp. pp. 44-53, 62-63, 70-79. I have supplemented these accounts with the information found in Fuchs, Prophets, pp. 29-34; Roy, Mundas, pp. 188-90; and Sachchidananda, Culture Change in Tribal Bihar, Munda and Oraon, pp. 91-92 and "Birsa—An Adivasi Fighter for Freedom," pp. 103-108.

34. Roy, ibid., pp. 189-90, 327-31, 338ff.; Fuchs, ibid., pp. 28-31; Sinha, ibid., pp. 51, 55-56, 73-77; and Singh, ibid., pp. 196-200.

35. The most detailed studies of Maori thought and mythology remain Elsdon Best's voluminous Tuhoe: Children of the Mist and Some Aspects of Maori Myth and Religion.

36. This account of Te Ua's life is based on rather meager biographical information gleaned from a number of sources, including James Cowan, The New Zealand Wars, vol. 2, pp. 4-5; Stuart B. Babbage, Hauhauism, pp. 22-23, 73-74; Ann Gibson, "Religious Organization among the Maoris of New Zealand after 1860," pp. 49-52; and especially the sympathetic and carefully researched account in Paul Clark's 'Hauhau', chap. 1.

37. The date of Te Ua's birth is not recorded in any of the sources that I have consulted. Kimble Bent, a renegade halfbreed who joined the Pai Maire movement, said that Te Ua was between forty and fifty years old in the mid-1860s (John Houston, Maori Life in Old Taranaki, p. 158), an impression supported by a surviving photograph taken of the prophet at the time of his capture in 1865.

38. Apirana Ngata, "Religious Influences," p. 351.

39. Clark, 'Hauhau', chap. 4 and pp. 113-31; Gibson, "Religious Organization," p. 53; Robin W. Winks, "The Doctrine of Hauhauism," p. 232; Cowan, New Zealand Wars, vol. 2, pp. 5-6, 14, 17; and Babbage, Episode, p. 36. Clark's uncertainty concerning the extent to which the Pai Maire was millennial (pp. 87-88) appears unwarranted both because of the evidence he himself provides and in light of all other published accounts of the movement. As I argue below, the prophecy of immediate transformations by prophetic leaders, which Clark sees as absent from the Pai Maire, is not a key feature of all millenarian visions.

40. Gibson, ibid., pp. 35-36, 41-42, 46-47; Harrison M. Wright, New Zealand 1769-1840: Early Years of Western Contact, pp. 178ff.; Clark, ibid., pp. 104-105; and O. Wilson, "Papahurihia, First Maori Prophet," pp. 473-83.

41. William Fox, *The War in New Zealand*, pp. 139–40; or T. W. Gudgeon, "Maori Superstition," p. 171.

42. P. 187. For similar conclusions set forth by other scholars of revolution see Jeffry Race, *The War Comes to Long An*, pp. 14–16; and Eric Hobsbawm, *Primitive Rebels*, pp. 60–61.

43. Hobsbawm, ibid., pp. 57–58. Given the limited evidence available, it is difficult to know how much the participants in these movements comprehended the different aspects of their leaders' teachings or how far they were committed to them. The millenarian ideologies that I have attempted to reconstruct were rarely, if ever, transmitted from prophet to adherents as complete or wholly coherent systems. Different groups and individuals seized upon different ideas and promises in accordance with what they were told by the prophet or his disciples, their understanding of what was being communicated, and their own needs.

44. For examples see Francis Hill, "Millenarian Machines in South Vietnam," pp. 325–50; Georges Balandier, *Sociologie actuelle de l'Afrique Noire*, pp. 419–21, 437, 452–53 & 478; and for particular attention to this theme his article on "Messianismes et nationalismes en Afrique noire," pp. 41–64. See also M. I. Perira de Queiroz, "Messiahs in Brazil," pp. 78, 83–84.

45. For more detailed discussions of these patterns see Fokke Sierksma, *Een nieuwe Hemel en een nieuwe Aarde*, pp. 262, 273–74; and Kenelm Burridge, *New Heaven New Earth*, pp. 9–13, 25–27, 140 et passim.

46. For similar conclusions based on other case examples see Sierksma, ibid., esp. pp. 248–54.

47. For a superb discussion of this pattern in another cultural context see Keith Thomas, *Witchcraft and the Decline of Magic*, pp. 423–25.

48. For more detailed discussions of these qualities see Robert Kaufman, *Millénarisme et acculturation*, pp. 9, 23; and Yonina Talmon, "Pursuit of the Millennium," pp. 130–32.

49. This and the following references are to Cohn's article on "Medieval Millenarianism," pp. 32–43.

50. Worsley, *Trumpet*, 44, 47, 96, 115, 135 et passim; Audrey Whipper, "Gusii Rebels," pp. 398–99; and Roger Bastide, "Messianismes et développement," p. 255.

51. Fuchs, *Prophets*, pp. 28–29.

52. For parallel examples of "new morality" emphasis in other movements see Sierksma, *Nieuwe Hemel*, pp. 259–60; Balandier, "Messianismes et nationalismes," p. 58; Hobsbawm, *Primitive Rebels*, pp. 61–62, 82–84; and Lucy Mair, "Independent Religious Movements on Three Continents," pp. 128ff. In only one of the cases considered here did the prophet encourage his followers to flaunt established social practices (a pattern which has often been observed in this type of movement). The Maori leader Te Ua encouraged promiscuous mating of his followers so that his people would multiply rapidly and thus be able to withstand the whites. See Gibson, "Religious Organization," p. 54.

53. These differences from the "soon and sudden" transformation pictured by Cohn underscore the importance of the distinction between pre- and post-millenarianism developed by a number of scholars of these movements. See H. Desroche, "Les messianismes et la catégorie de l'échec," pp. 76–77. The movements considered in this study were clearly of the latter type, while Cohn's description fits the premillenarian.

54. For examples, see Henri Ellenberger, "Les mouvements de libération mythique," pp. 263–64; Mair, "Movements," p. 131; Worsley, *Trumpet*, pp. 52–53, 103, 111, 115, 119; and Sierksma, *Nieuwe Hemel*, pp. 276–77.

55. See P. H. van der Kemp, "De economische Oorzaaken van den Java-oorlog," pp. 1–2, 10–11, 14–15.

56. Supplementary examples have been taken primarily from the following works: Balandier, *Sociologie* (Simon Kimbangou); Franz Michael, *The Taiping Rebellion* (Hung Hsui-ch'üan); Sartono, *Peasant Protest* and *Banten Revolt* (various Javanese

prophets); Euclides da Cunha, *Rebellion in the Backlands* (Antonio Conselheiro); James Mooney, *The Ghost Dance Religion* (Wovoka); Glenn Tucker, *Tecumseh, Vision of Glory*, chap. 7 (Tenskwatawa); A. Wallace, "Handsome Lake and the Great Revival in the West," pp. 149–65; George Shepperson and Thomas Price, *Independent African* (Chilembwe); Carl Brown, "The Sudanese Madhiya," and R. H. Dekmejian and M. J. Wyszomirski, "Charismatic Leadership in Islam," (Muhammad Achmad); David Sturtevant, "Philippine Social Structure," (Apolinaro de la Cruz); Nguyen Tran Huan, "Histoire d'une secte religieuse au Vietnam, le Caodaisme," (Ngo Van Chieu); and Worsley, *Trumpet* (Ndugumai). Only references to sources other than these will be footnoted individually.

57. As the prophet Tenskwatawa of the Shawnee Indians illustrates vividly, prophets of this type could also preach far-reaching social reforms and even considerable accommodation to the ways of outside groups.

58. For the original formulation of this useful concept see Eric Wolf, "Aspects of Group Relations in a Complex Society," pp. 1065–78.

59. For one of the most striking examples of this quality see Wilhelm Mühlmann's discussion of the elevation of Jomo Kenyatta to prophetic status by adherents to the Kenya African Union. The faithful sang hymns extolling Kenyatta as one who had been to Europe and had learned there how to rule. See "Zwischen Erweckung und Terror: Der Mau-Mau-Aufstand in Kenya," pp. 129–31.

60. For a sample case study see Schlosser, "Prophetismus," pp. 64–65.

61. Schlosser (ibid., p. 64); Guglielmo Guarliglia (*Prophetismus und Heilserwartungs-Bewegungen*, pp. 271–72); and Fuchs (*Prophets*, p. 5), after examining large samples of prophets in Africa, India, and Oceania, all conclude that substantial education is frequently associated with leaders of this type. For Christian examples see Worsley, *Trumpet*, passim; and for Muslim examples see Sartono, *Peasant Protest*, passim.

62. See Jack Goody, *Literacy in Traditional Societies*, pp. 11–20.

63. For special emphasis on this theme, see Wilson, *Magic and Millennium*, chaps. 4, 6, 11; H. W. Lindig and A. M. Dauer, "Prophetismus und Geistertanz-Bewegung," p. 48; Traian Stoianovich, "Les structures millenaristes sud-Slaves aux XVIIe et XVIII ss," p. 815; and Balandier, *Sociologie*, p. 427.

64. On the close links between the role of community healer or medicine man and the emergence of prophetic personalities see Guariglia, *Prophetismus*, pp. 43–44 and Katesa Schlosser, *Propheten in Afrika*, p. 404.

65. Louw and Klerck, *Java-Oorlog*, vol. 1, pp. 151–52.

66. *Bandits*, pp. 28ff.

CHAPTER 5

1. Peter Lupsha, "Explanation of Political Violence," pp. 91–98.

2. See especially Harry Eckstein, "On the Etiology of Internal Wars," p. 124.

3. J. F. Walraven van Nes, "Verhandeling over de waarschijnlijke Oorzaken, die Aanleiding tot de Onlusten van 1825," pp. 156–58; J. Hageman, *Geschiedenis van den Oorlog op Java van 1825 tot 1830*, p. 61; and especially Peter B. R. Carey, "Dipanagara and the Making of the Java War," pt. 2, fn. 34, and pp. 11, 26–29, 31–32; and *Cultural Ecology of Early Nineteenth Century Java*, pp. 29, 33, 51–53.

4. P. H. van der Kemp, "Eene geschiedkundige Hamlettype," especially pp. 327–37.

5. Carey, "Dipanagara and the Java War," pt. 2, pp. 415, 447–55, 460–62; Kemp, ibid., pp. 305, 331–33, 391–407; and Pieter F. J. Louw and Eduard S. de Klerck, *De Java-Oorlog*, vol. 1, pp. 131–47.

6. Paul Clark, '*Hauhau*', esp. pp. 10–12, 16–19, 23–26, 98–101; Robin W. Winks, "The Doctrine of Hauhauism," passim; and Ann Gibson, "Religious Organization among the Maoris of New Zealand, pp. 52ff. In his well-argued and researched study Clark has stressed the peaceful nature of Te Ua's teachings and of the follow-

ers who remained loyal to the prophet. I think this has caused him to understate the impact of the Pai Maire on those leaders who wished to continue warfare against the Europeans and their Maori allies. I can understand his wish to counter the standard view expressed in accounts contemporary with the movement, which linked *all* Maori resistance to the "bloodthirsty" new faith, but unfortunately this treatment obscures the important role (indicated in various places in Clark's own discussion) played by elements of the Pai Maire in sustaining or renewing violent resistance among different Maori groups.

7. The standard account is in James Cowan, *The New Zealand Wars*, vol. 2, pp. 15–19. For an alternative interpretation see Clark, ibid., pp. 12–14.

8. The following discussion of the precipitants of the Birsa outbreak is based on Surendra Sinha, *The Life and Times of Birsa Bhagwan*, pp. 53–59, 70 ff.; Surat C. Roy, *The Mundas and Their Country*, pp. 88–92; Stephen Fuchs, *Rebellious Prophets*, pp. 28–31; and Suresh Singh, *The Dust-Storm and the Hanging Mist*, pp. 60–70, 75 ff.

9. For case examples see Georges Balandier, *Sociologie actuelle de l'Afrique noire*, chap. 3; Berndt Sundkler, *Bantu Prophets in South Africa*; and esp. Katesa Schlosser, *Propheten in Afrika*.

10. Moritz Merker, "Ueber die Aufstandsbewegung in Deutsch-Ostafrika," no. 46, pp. 1024–25.

11. Gustav A. von Götzen, *Deutsch-Ostafrika im Aufstand*, pp. 52–53, 63–64.

12. R. C. Morris, "Causes of the Tharrawaddy Rebellion," pp. 8–14.

13. U Saw, *The Burmese Situation*, pp. 1–2; and Ba U, *My Burma*, p. 103.

14. Government of Burma, "Report on the Rebellion in Burma up to the 3rd of May, 1931," pp. 2–15; and *Origin and Causes of the Burma Rebellion*, passim.

15. On the *weikza* pattern see Melford Spiro, *Buddhism and Society*, chap. 7; and E. Michael Mendelson, "A Messianic Buddhist Association in Upper Burma." On the riots and earthquake see Michael Adas, *The Burma Delta*, pp. 196–99; and Maurice Collis, *Trials in Burma*. pp. 142–43.

16. Crane Brinton, *The Anatomy of Revolution*, see esp. pp. 90–95.

17. Carey, "Dipanagara and the Java War," pt. 2, fn. 168.

18. See Soemarsaid Moertono, *State and Statecraft in Old Java*, pp. 96, 108; and Merle Ricklefs, *Jogjakarta under Sultan Mangkubumi*, passim. For Dutch attitudes toward the considerable fighting abilities of the Javanese at the time of the Java War, see the comments of the Dutch commander, Merkus de Kock, in August W. P. Weitzel, *De Oorlog op Java van 1825 tot 1830*, vol. 1, pp. 29–31 et passim.

19. Keith Sinclair, *A History of New Zealand*, p. 128. For the most detailed account of the Maori struggles see Cowan, *New Zealand Wars*, 2 vols.; and for the best study of Maori martial traditions see Andrew P. Vayda, *Maori Warfare*.

20. On German conflicts with the Hehe see especially Ernst Nigmann, *Die Wahehe*, pp. 14–19.

21. Roy, *Mundas*, pp. 106, 112 ff., 144, 162 ff., 177.

22. Perhaps literally traumatic, for Htin Aung has suggested that at least one Burman ruler went mad as a result of defeats at the hands of the British: see *The Stricken Peacock*, p. 40.

23. For illustrations of resistance patterns before the Saya San rebellion see the Government of Burma, district gazetteers for *Tharrawaddy*, pp. 24–37, *Henzada*, pp. 23–26, *Bassein*, pp. 16–18; and Emanuel Sarkisyanz, *Buddhist Backgrounds of the Burmese Revolution*, pp. 155–58.

24. Perhaps the best discussion of these patterns can be found in Geoffrey Fairbairn's *Revolutionary Guerilla Warfare*.

25. The following account of secondary leadership in the Java War is based primarily upon Peter B. R. Carey, "The Origins of the Java War (1825–1830)," pp. 75–76 and *Cultural Ecology*, pp. 19–20; Louw and Klerck, *Java-Oorlog*, vol. 1, pp. 27, 30–31, 72 ff., 150–54, 203–208 and vol. 3, pp. 60–63, 272–76; and vol. 4, pp. 309–14, 606–607, 676–77, appendixes 18, 19; François de Stuers, *Mémoires sur la guerre de*

l'île de Java, pp. 14–15, 32, 95; Huibert G. Nahuys van Burgst, *Verzameling van officiële Rapporten*, vol. 1, pp. 143–44; Weitzel, *De Oorlog*, vol. 1, pp. 54–55, 338–39 and vol. 2n pp. 322–23; and Egbert B. Kiel tra, "Eenige Personen uit den Java-oorlog," pp. 296–98.

26. "Java War Origins," pp. 75–76.

27. Franz Michael, *The Taiping Rebellion*, pp. 28–37 ff.; and Peter M. Holt, *The Mahdist State in the Sudan 1881–1898*, pp. 4–5, 51–53, 122–25, 135–46 et passim. The longevity of these movements calls into question Bryan Wilson's assertion that millennial movements in the Third World are short-lived, as well as his conclusion that the mixture of millenarianism and military action has always been disastrous (see *Magic and the Millennium*, pp. 34, 196, 348, 386, 492).

28. This analysis of secondary leadership in the Saya San rebellion is based on my calculations from the trial extracts in *PJC*, Files 7347–50 (1930).

29. The best discussions of leadership in the Maji Maji movement may be found in von Götzen, *Ostafrika im Aufstand*, pp. 43–44, 145–46, 241; R. M. Bell, "Maji Maji in the Liwale District," pp. 40–41, 49–50, 55–56; and especially Gilbert C. K. Gwassa, "African Methods of Warfare during the Maji Maji," pp. 128–31, 137–39.

30. On the diffusion of power in the Pai Maire see Clark, *'Hauhau'*, pp. 12–16, 19–26, and chap. 3; Cowan, *New Zealand Wars*, vol. 2, pp. 4, 9, 18, 72, 87; Gibson, "Religious Organization," pp. 52, 55, 100, 106; William Greenwood, "The Upraised Hand," pp. 9–10; Apirana Ngata, "Religious Experience," pp. 348, 350; and Maharaia Winiata, *The Changing Role of the Leader in Maori Society*, pp. 67–70.

31. The best discussion of Sardar involvement in the Birsite rising may be found in Singh, *Dust-Storm and Mist*, esp. chap. 4. See also John Hoffman, *Encyclopedia Mundarica*, vol. 2, p. 568.

32. For the fullest discussion of this pattern see Gil Carl Alroy, *The Involvement of Peasants in Internal Wars*, pp. 12, 16, 18 et passim.

33. For a fine statement of the factors leading to the assumption of leadership roles among peasants see Mehmet Beqiraj, *Peasantry in Revolution*, pp. 10–14 et passim. The standard statement of the political implications of the "limited good" thesis is contained in George Foster, "Image of the Limited Good," especially pp. 303–304.

34. For a superb discussion of the nature of patron-client relationships and the threats to them in the colonial era see James C. Scott. "Patron-Client Politics and Political Change in Southeast Asia," pp. 91–113.

CHAPTER 6

1. Carlo Cipolla's *Guns, Sails and Empires* remains the best introduction to the comparative study of the relationship between European technological development and overseas expansion. Frederic Mauro's *L'expansion européenne, 1600–1870*, esp. pp. 101–24 and 269–88, contains detailed discussions of advances in communications and naval technology through the early stages of the industrial revolution. For the critical developments of the nineteenth century see John F. C. Fuller, *The Conduct of War, 1789–1961*, esp. pp. 86–138; or the more detailed discussion in Andre Reussner and Louis Nicolas, *La puissance navale dans l'histoire*, vol. 2, esp. pp. 35–89, 117–225.

2. *African Nationalism*, p. 157. For examples of these reactions in comparable contact situations see H. Alan C. Cairns, *Prelude to Imperialism*, pp. 46–47; Octave Mannoni, *Prospero and Caliban*, esp. pp. 80–82, 162–63; and Gustav Jahoda, *Whiteman*, pp. 24–34, 78, 103.

3. For a superb discussion of early Chinese efforts to cope with these dilemmas see Frederick Wakeman, Jr., *Strangers at the Gate*; and for a detailed and perceptive analysis of efforts to come to grips with the profound problems raised by Western technological superiority generally see Benjamin Schwartz, *In Search of Wealth and Power: Yen Fu and the West*.

4. Trung Buu Lam, *Patterns of Vietnamese Response to Foreign Intervention: 1858–1900*, pp. 86–87.

5. The most extreme statement of this aspect of colonial rule is contained in Frantz Fanon's essay "Concerning Violence," in *The Wretched of the Earth*, pp. 35–106.

6. For fine discussions of this pattern in medieval and early modern Europe, see Keith Thomas, *Religion and the Decline of Magic*, pp. 86, 89, 107; or Norman Cohn, "Medieval Millenarism," pp. 34, 43.

7. For examples in situations of colonial domination similar to the cases studied in depth see Peter Worsley, *The Trumpet Shall Sound*, pp. 101, 115, 118–20; Kitsiri Malagoda, "Millennialism in Relation to Buddhism," p. 437; and Sartono Kartodirdjo, *The Peasants' Revolt of Banten in 1888*, pp. 66–67, 168. The most detailed examination of the links between natural calamities and millenarianism may be found in Michael Barkun, *Disaster and the Millennium*.

8. See respectively Maurice Collis, *Trials in Burma*, pp. 142–43; Moritz Merker, "Ueber die Aufstandsbewegung in Deutsch-Ostafrika," no. 45, pp. 1024–25; Surendra Sinha, *The Life and Times of Birsa Bhagwan*, pp. 70, 83–84; and John Reid, *Ranchi Settlement Report*, p. 16.

9. On the association of natural calamities with millenarianism see Soemarsaid Moertono, *State and Statecraft in Old Java*, pp. 24, 74 ff., 85; and Jakob A. B. Wiselius, "Djâbâ Bâjâ, zijn Leven en Profetieën," pp. 185–86; and on Dipanagara's visions and disturbances before the rebellion see Peter B. R. Carey, *The Cultural Ecology of Early Nineteenth Century Java*, pp. 30–33, 52, 55, and "The Origins of the Java War (1825–1830)," p. 68; and Pieter F. J. Louw and Eduard S. de Klerck, *De Java-Oorlog*, vol. 1, pp. 25–26. Although the Maoris also placed great emphasis on oracles and interpretation of natural signs, I have not been able to find evidence of natural calamities in the period before the emergence of Te Ua.

10. For a general discussion of the use of rumors in this manner see Raymond Firth, "Rumor in Primitive Society," esp. pp. 131–32.

11. Wiselius, "Djâjâ Bâjâ," pp. 183–89; Carey, *Cultural Ecology*, pp. 51–56; Maurice Collis, *Into Hidden Burma*, pp. 88–89; Government of Burma, *The Origin and Causes of the Burma Rebellion (1930–1932)*, pp. 25–26; and B. S. Cary, "Hints for the Guidance of Civil Officers," p. 2.

12. Worsley, *Trumpet*, pp. 24, 124, 154–56; Katesa Schlosser, "Der Prophetismus in niederen Kulturen," p. 66; Audrey Whipper, "Gusii Rebels," p. 391; and Sitaram, *From Sepoy to Soobadar*, pp. 64, 144–45.

13. See respectively, Gilbert C. K. Gwassa, "Kinjikitile and the Ideology of Maji Maji," pp. 212–13; R. M. Bell, "Maji Maji in the Liwale District," p. 44; Sinha, *Birsa Bhagwan*, pp. 82–86ff.; and James Cowan, *The New Zealand Wars*, pp. 9–10, 13–14, 17.

14. This description is based on Saya San's diary in *The Rangoon Gazette Weekly Budget*, 5 October 1931, p. 18; Collis, *Trials in Burma*, pp. 213–14; Robert Heine-Geldern, "Conceptions of State and Kingship in Southeast Asia," pp. 17, 19–26; Emanuel Sarkisyanz, *Buddhist Backgrounds of the Burmese Revolution*, pp. 86, 101–106, 156, 161–62; and Yi Yi, "Life at the Burmese Court under the Konbaung Kings," pp. 85–129.

15. Bertram J. O. Schrieke, *Indonesian Sociological Studies*, pt. 2, p. 79; Moertono, *Statecraft*, pp. 18–22, 40, 62–64, 79–80, 92; August W. P. Weitzel, *De Oorlog op Java van 1825 tot 1830*, vol. 1, pp. 32–33; Hermanus J. de Graaf, *Geschiedenis van Indonesië*, pp. 88–89, 113; and especially Carey, *Cultural Ecology*, pp. 22ff. and Merle Ricklefs, "Dipanagara's Early Inspirational Experience," pp. 232–49.

16. Moertono, ibid., pp. 65–67, 78–79; Louw and Klerck, *Java-Oorlog*, vol. 1, pp. 207–208, 434–35, 443–46, 498–99; de Graaf, ibid., pp. 394, 397; Weitzel, ibid., vol. 1, pp. 53 ff.; and François de Stuers, *Mémoires sur la guerre de l'île de Java*, pp. 91–94.

17. Moertono, ibid., p. 53ff.; Louw and Klerck, ibid., p. 88; and Carey, *Cultural Ecology*, pp. 3–7.

18. The following interpretation of legitimizing symbols in the Maji Maji is based primarily on the information supplied by Gilbert Gwassa ("African Methods of Warfare during the Maji Maji," pp. 134–39, 145–46 and "Ideology of Maji Maji," pp. 206, 209–13).

19. Robin Winks, "The Doctrine of Hauhauism," pp. 208, 214–15, 218–21, 226–28, 233; Ann Gibson, "Religious Organization among the Maoris of New Zealand after 1860," pp. 58–59, 62–63, 100–101, 106; and Herbert Meade, *A Ride Through the Disturbed Districts of New Zealand*, pp. 127–28.

20. Winks, ibid., pp. 210, 223, 234 et passim; Gibson, ibid., pp. 53–54, 97–100; Maharaia Winiata, *The Changing Role of the Leader in Maori Society*, pp. 35–36, 67–70; Cowan, *New Zealand Wars*, vol. 2. pp. 3–4, 7, 179, 191, and vol. 1, pp. 77, 396–97; Peter Buck, *The Coming of the Maori*, esp. pp. 489–500; and Elsdon Best, *The Maori as He Was*, pp. 168–73.

21. For numerous examples of this pattern see Stephen Fuchs, *Rebellious Prophets*; Lloyd and Susanne Rudolph, *The Modernity of Tradition*, pt. 1; and for a detailed case study, Robert Hardgraves, *The Nadars of Tamilnad*.

22. Sinha, *Birsa Bhagwan*, pp. 73–77; and Fuchs, ibid., p. 28.

23. The following discussion of the multifaceted functions of oaths is based upon an analysis of rebel oaths from risings in Tharrawaddy and Prome Districts. See *PJC—File 7347*, no. 4060, letter from the Secretary of the Government of Burma to the Secretary of the Government of India, 25 July 1931. For a published rebel oath see C. V. Warren, *Burmese Interlude*, p. 92.

24. R. R. Langham-Carter, "The Burmese Army," pp. 257, 369.

25. For parallel themes and further examples see Eric Hobsbawm, *Primitive Rebels*, pp. 151–52, 192; and Sartono, *Banten Revolt*, pp. 199, 202, and *Peasant Protest in Rural Java*, pp. 73, 193.

26. For a detailed discussion of the complex relationship between animistic *nat* beliefs and Buddhism in Burma see Melford Spiro, *Burmese Supernaturalism*, esp. chap. 14; and on "apotropaic Buddhism" see Spiro, *Buddhism and Society*, chaps. 6, 7. On protective rituals in the Saya San, see, for examples, *PJC—File 7349*, no. 3555, 9 May 1931, pp. 2–3; *File 7350*, no. 898, 29 Nov. 1931, p. 157; and Government of Burma, "(Confidential) Report on the Rebellion in Burma April 1931–March 1932," pp. 6, 15.

27. Sinha, *Birsa Bhagwan*, pp. 87–88.

28. Abdul Karim bin Jamaliddini, *Utenzi wa Vita vya Maji Maji*, p. 61; Bell, "Maji in Liwale," pp. 41, 45–46; Gustav A. von Götzen, *Deutsch-Ostafrika im Aufstand*, p. 120; Gwassa, "Ideology of Maji Maji," pp. 209–10 and "Methods of Warfare," p. 133; and John Iliffe, "The Organization of the Maji Maji Rebellion," p. 507. For descriptions of prebattle rituals and rites of passage similar to those of the peoples who supported the rebellion, see Ernst Nigmann, *Die Wahehe*, esp. 25–34, 119–20; and Victor Turner, *The Ritual Process*, esp. chap. 3.

29. Moertono, *Statecraft*, pp. 18–19, 79–80; Bernhard Dahm, *Sukarno and the Indonesian Struggle for Independence*, p. 2; and P. M. Van Wulfften-Palte, *Psychological Aspects of the Indonesian Problem*, p. 28.

30. For descriptions of Pai Maire ceremonies see Meade, *Disturbed Districts*, pp. 126–27; Gibson, "Religious Organization," pp. 52, 56–62; and Cowan, *New Zealand Wars*, vol. 2, pp. 6, 9–10, 12–14.

31. Henri Ellenberger, "Les mouvements de libération mythique," p. 261; Worsley, *Trumpet*, p. 113; and Mircea Eliade, " 'Cargo Cults' and Cosmic Regeneration," p. 141.

32. On the importance of trance, convulsions, and hypnotism in customary Maori rituals see Buck, *Maori Coming*, esp. pp. 473–74; on these patterns in other movements see Schlosser, "Prophetismus," pp. 63–64; Whipper, "Gusii Rebels,"

pp. 405–406; and Fokke Sierksma, *Een nieuwe Hemel en een nieuwe Aarde,* pp. 263, 272–73 et passim.

33. Francis R. Wingate, *Mahdism and the Egyptian Sudan,* pp. 34–47; and Victor Purcell, *The Boxer Uprising,* pp. 286, 230, 236–38.

34. As related in Alexander Woodside's superb study, *Vietnam and the Chinese Model,* p. 396.

35. The most perceptive and detailed discussion of the principles behind these many uses of magic remains Bronislaw Malinowski's essay in *Magic, Science, and Religion and Other Essays,* esp. pp. 28–29, 70ff., 79–84. Although much of what Malinowski has to say about magic has come under heavy criticism in recent decades from scholars like A. R. Radcliffe-Brown, Dorothy Hammond, and George Holmans. his ideas on the functions of magic have continued to hold wide acceptance and have been confirmed by the studies of E. E. Evans-Pritchard, John Middleton, Peter Worsley, and most recently Keith Thomas.

36. On these belief see Thomas, *Religion and Magic,* esp. chap. 1 et passim; and Bryan Wilson, *Magic and the Millennium,* pp. 104–105.

37. Gwassa, "Methods of Warfare," pp. 126–27; and for a discussion of the use of talismans by a neighboring and comparable people see Nigmann, *Die Wahehe,* p. 28.

38. Buck, *Maori Coming,* pp. 489–90, 499–500; Gibson, "Religious Organization," pp. 19–20; and Elsdon Best, *Maori Religion and Mythology,* pp. 78–79, 86–87.

39. James G. Scott and John P. Hardiman, *Gazeteer of Upper Burma and the Shan States,* vol. 2, pp. 75–83; Hla Baw, "Superstitions of Burmese Criminals," pp. 379–80; Wulfnten-Palte, *Psychological Aspects,* pp. 27–29, 32. Although Birsa employed talismans in his rebellion, I have not been able to find references to the use of these in the literature on Munda society.

40. For discussions of these talismanic beliefs in different religious traditions see Spiro, *Buddhism and Society,* esp. chaps. 6 and 11; Gerardus W. J. Drewes, *Drie Javaansch Goeroe's,* esp. pp. 52–61 (Islam) and Thomas, *Religion and Magic,* esp. chap. 1 (Christianity).

41. The following classification of talismanic types has been to some extent influenced by the detailed study of Robert Texter, "An Inventory of Non-Buddhist Supernatural Objects in a Central Thai Village." Since individual citations in the discussion of talismans employed in the movements under consideration would require an inordinate number of footnotes, I will indicate at the outset the sources used in each case on this subject. Only direct quotes or references to examples from other movements will be specifically cited. The major sources by case example are:

(1) The Java War: Peter B. R. Carey, "Dipanagara and the Origins of the Java War," pt. 2, pp. 434–36, 576, 597–98; Louw and Klerck, *Java-Oorlog,* vol. 1, pp. 29–30, 154n., 208, 436, 549; de Stuers, *Mémoires,* p. 93; Weitzel, *De Java Oorlog,* vol. 2, pp. 146–47; Onghokham, "The Residency of Madiun Pryayi and Peasant in the Nineteenth Century," pp. 64, 90–91; J. Knebel, "Amulettes Javanaises," pp. 497–507; and Drewes, *Drie Goeroe's,* pp. 47, 51ff., et passim.

(2) The Pai Maire movement: Stuart Babbage, *Hauhauism,* pp. 27–28, 34–35, 42–43, 59–60; Cowan, *New Zealand Wars,* vol. 2, pp. 7–9, 12, 21–26, 33–34, 40, 81–85, 89, and *The Maoris of New Zealand,* pp. 223–27; and Winks, "Hauhauism," pp. 207–208, 212, 215–16, 228–29.

(3) The Birsa rising: Fuchs, *Prophets,* pp. 29–30, 32; and Sinha, *Birsa Bhagwan,* pp. 56, 78, 86–88, 91–92; and Suresh Singh, *The Dust-Storm and Hanging Mist,* pp. 56, 81, 87–90, and Appendixes, pp. 114–15, 118, 125.

(4) The Maji Maji rebellion: Bell, "Maji in Liwale," pp. 41, 45–46, von Götzen, *Ostafrika im Aufstand,* pp. 46–47, 107–108, 113, 149; Gwassa, "Ideology of Maji Maji," p. 210, and "Methods of Warfare," pp. 126–27; Gwassa and Iliffe, *Records,* pp. 9–10, 12, 17–21; Iliffe, "Maji Organization," pp. 502, 505–507; Karim bin Jamaliddini, *Utenzi wa Vita,* pp. 35–37, 43, 45, 49; Nigmann, *Die Wahehe,* pp. 28, 88, 120;

Martin Klamroth, "Beitrage zum Verständnis der religiösen Vorstellungen der Saramo," p. 140; and Merker, "Aufstandsbewegung," no. 65, p. 1531.

(5) The Saya San rebellion: John Brohm, "Burmese Religion and the Burmese Religious Revival," pp. 33–36, 187–89, 230–33; Collis, *Trials*, pp. 216–18; Anonymous, "Curiosities of the Burmese Rebellion," pp. 350–51; Government of Burma, *The Origin and Causes of the Burma Rebellion (1930–1932)*, pp. 1, 3–9 et passim; and *PJC—Files* 7349, 7350, 7351, passim.

42. Cowan, *The Maoris*, p. 227.

43. Anon., "Curiosities," p. 350. For a detailed discussion of this sort of talismanic belief see Textor, "Inventory," pp. 100–101. As Melford Spiro has pointed out (*Buddhism and Society*, p. 165), talismans involving the insertion on metal into the body may be traceable to the ancient connection in alchemic thought between metal as one on the five basic elements and the acquisition of the power to maintain life eternally.

44. I am indebted to Peter Carey for information on these prayers.

45. For such an interpretation see Schlosser, "Prophetismus," p. 63.

46. These arguments are based primarily upon insights found in Robin Horton's superb essay on "African Traditional Thought and Western Science," pt. 2, pp. 156–57, 167–68.

47. Harry Eckstein, "On the Etiology of Internal Wars," pp. 143–47.

48. This notion is developed by Lucy Mair in "Independent Religious Movements on Three Continents," pp. 120–21. At times a longing for equality gave rise to the anticipation that the faithful would acquire white skins like their European overlords. See Guglielmo Guariglia, *Prophetismus ind Heilserwartungs-Bewegungen*, p. 33.

49. Carey, *Cultural Ecology*, pp. 36–37.

50. Harrison Wright, *New Zealand*, p. 176; and Gibson, "Religious Organization," pp. 32, 56.

51. R. C. Morris, "Causes of the Tharrawaddy Rebellion (1931)," pp. 13, 17, and Appendix G; and Government of Burma, *Origins and Causes Report*, p. 8.

52. Anon., "Curiosities," p. 350; Cowan, *New Zealand Wars*, vol. 2, p. 40; Gibson, "Religious Organization," p. 56.

53. For sample drills see Gwassa and Iliffe, *Records*, pp. 11–12; Cowan, ibid., pp. 10–11; William Greenwood, "The Upraised Hand," pp. 6–7; Clark, '*Hauhau*', p. 97; and *PJC—File* 7349, no. 3555, 9 May 1931, p. 3.

54. Francis O. Bradley-Birt, *Chota Nagpur, A Little-Known Province of the Empire*, p. 76; Fuchs, *Prophets*, pp. 27–28; and Sinha, *Birsa Bhagwan*, pp. 49–51.

55. Babbage, *Hauhauism*, p. 36; and Gibson, "Religious Organization," p. 54.

56. For examples see Babbage, ibid., pp. 35–36, 46–47; Georges Balandier, *Sociologie actuelle de l'Afrique noire*, pp. 413, 441; Fuchs, *Prophets*, pp. 28–30; Government of Burma, "Confidential Report," p. 9; Sartono, *Peasant Protest*, p. 50; Wolfgang H. von Lindig and Alfons M. Dauer, "Prophetismus und Geistertanz-Bewegungen," p. 54; Schlosser, "Prophetismus," p. 68; Whipper, "Gusii Rebels," pp. 390–91, 402; and Worsley, *Trumpet*, pp. 102, 106, 111–12.

57. Bell, "Maji in Liwale," pp. 45–46; Gwassa and Iliffe, *Records*, pp. 18–20.

58. Huibert G. Nahuys van Burgst, *Verzameling van officiële Rapporten betreffende den Oorlog op Java in den Jaren 1825–1830*, vol. 2, pp. 332–33.

59. Fuchs, *Rebellious Prophets*, pp. 10–11; and Ellenberger, "Les Mouvements," p. 265.

60. The most persuasive statement of this position can be found in Sierksma's *Nieuwe Hemel*, esp. pp. 252–56, 261–63. Sierksma's discussion, however, goes far beyond the psychopathological dimensions of these phenomena and places them in the context of culture contacts and resulting social breakdown. For less reserved statements of the irrational and psychopathological nature of this type of movement see Norman Cohn, *The Pursuit of the Millennium*, passim; Weston La Barre, "Materials for the Study of Crisis Cults," pp. 9–10, 18, 20, 25–26; Ralph Linton, "Nativistic

Movements," pp. 232–33 and his typology; Lucy Mair, "The Pursuit of the Millennium in Melanesia," pp. 172–82; and Schlosser, "Prophetismus," pp. 63–64. For penetrating critiques of the views of many of these writers see Ian C. Jarvie, "Theories of Cargo Cults," pt. 1, pp. 17–19, 26–27, and pt. 2, pp. 128–29.

61. For a superb and concise discussion and critique of these often divergent positions see Stephen Lukes, "Some Problems about Rationality," pp. 247–64.

62. Some of the major positions in this lively debate are set forth in a volume on *Rationality*, edited by Bryan Wilson. Though the approaches of earlier writers are discussed in detail in these essays, the most relevant can be found in the writings of E. E. Evans-Prichard and Lucien Levi-Bruhl.

63. For a full defense of this position see the work of Peter Finch, especially "Understanding a Primitive Society," pp. 307–24; and *The Idea of a Social Science and Its Relation to Philosophy*.

64. Ian C. Jarvie has emphasized the goal-directedness and purposefulness of actions as criteria for rationality. See "Theories of Cargo Cults," passim; *The Revolution in Anthropology*, pp. 131–44; and Jarvie and Joseph Agassi, "The Problem of Rationality in Magic," pp. 55–74.

65. Discussions of this dilemma may be found in S. Lukes, "Problems about Rationality," pp. 255–58, 260–64; Alastair Macintyre, "Is Understanding Religion Compatible with Believing?" pp. 118–24; and Martin Hollis, "The Limits of Irrationality," pp. 265–71.

66. None of the five prophets considered at length in this study was believed to be insane by contemporary observers or appears to have been a psychopath on the basis of the (admittedly limited) evidence we have concerning him.

67. For a brief but useful summary of some of the possible criteria for rationality that may be employed across cultures see Lukes, "Problems about Rationality," pp. 259–60.

68. For a fine discussion of the relevant parallels and differences between Western scientific thinking and prescientific thinking with special reference to Africa see R. Horton, "African Thought," passim.

69. Lukes, "Problems about Rationality," passim.

70. *Magic and Millennium*, p. 500. Jean Baechler argues that this discrepancy is *the* most critical attribute for those attempting to categorize millenarian movements (see *Revolution*, pp. 83 ff.). I heartily disagree.

71. For an excellent discussion of the "rationality of ignorance" and the complex problems involved in the means-ends criteria see Jarvie, *Revolution in Anthropology*, pp. 137–44.

CHAPTER 7

1. This discussion of the patterns of violent protest in the movements under consideration is based mainly on the sources cited in chapter 1 in the sections devoted to general descriptions of each of the rebellions. Only additional sources and specific references of particular relevance will be cited in the following analyses.

2. Maharaia Winiata, *The Changing Role of the Leader in Maori Society*, pp. 67ff.; Apirana Ngata, "Religious Influences," pp. 352–53; Paul Clark, 'Hauhau', esp. 15–16, 32–33, 44–49; and Alan Ward, *A Show of Justice*, pp. 167–79.

3. Pieter F. J. Louw and Eduard S. de Klerck, *De Java-Oorlog*, vol. 1, pp. 142, 207, 259, and vol. 3, p. 61.

4. Moritz Merker, "Ueber die Aufstandsbewegung in Deutsch-Ostafrika," no. 46, pp. 1085–86; and Gustav A. von Götzen, *Deutsch-Ostafrika im Aufstand*, pp. 48–49.

5. In this connection Governor Gore Browne's relaxation of the prohibition of gun sales to the Maoris in the 1850s has been seen as one of the factors that contributed to the wars of the 1860s, including the Pai Maire movement. See James Hight, "The Maori Wars, 1843–1872," pp. 129, 133.

6. Detailed discussions of Javanese tactics in the rebellion can be found in August W. P. Weitzel, *De Oorlog op Java van 1825 tot 1830*, vol. 1, pp. 28–31; Louw and Klerck, *Java-Oorlog*, vol. 1, pp. 203–208; and François de Stuers, *Mémoires sur la guerre de l'île de Java*, pp. 3–8, 58, 71ff. The best descriptions of the war terrain published to date may be found in Weitzel, vol. 1, pp. 12–28; and Louw, vol. 1, pp. 230–50.

7. Merker, "Aufstandsbewegung," no. 46, pp. 1085–89.

8. For a poignant description of such an engagement see Gilbert C. K. Gwassa and John Iliffe, *Records of the Maji Maji Rising*, pp. 20–21.

9. For an extended consideration of these patterns see Arthur Campbell, *Guerillas*.

10. The best discussion of these aspects of Maori warfare may be found in Andrew P. Vayda, *Maori Warfare*, especially pp. 14–18, 30, 42–60.

11. For engagements illustrating this shift see ibid., pp. 16, 38, 42–43, 63, 76.

12. For sample discussions of the impact of disease on Dutch forces see Louw and Klerck, *Java-Oorlog*, vol. 3, pp. 2–3, 92, 110, 117; and vol. 4, pp. 170–71, 177–79, 364–65; and Weitzel, *De Java Oorlog*, vol. 1, pp. 52, 55, 73ff., 155, 167.

13. Arthur Phayre, *History of Burma*. pp. 240, 247–48.

14. Merker, "Aufstandsbewegung," no. 65, p. 1538; and von Götzen, *Ostafrika im Aufstand*, pp. 132–33, 149ff., 173, 178–79.

15. Government of Birma, "(Confidential) Report on the Rebellion in Burma, April 1931–March 1932," pp. 9–10.

16. Hendrik G. van Hogendorp, *Willem van Hogendorp in Nederlandsch-Indië 1825–1830*, pp. 160–61.

17. This discussion of the effects of the long Maori resistance is based on Keith Sinclair, *History of New Zealand*, pp. 127–31, 175; John B. Condliffe and Willis T. Airey, *A Short History of New Zealand*, pp. 108–113; and especially Alan Ward, *A Show of Justice*, part two.

18. Michael Adas, *The Burma Delta*, pp. 201–208; and John Cady, *A History of Modern Burma*, pp. 318–21, 404–407.

19. G. P. Rouffaer, "Vorstenlanden," pp. 595–98, 627–33, 643–44; Hermanus J. de Graaf, *Geschiedenis van Indonesië*, pp. 395, 399–401; and for detailed examinations of the different agreements resulting from the rebellion, Louw and Klerck, *Java-Oorlog*, vol. 6.

20. Clive Day, *The Dutch in Java*, pp. 244–48. See also Bertram J. O. Schrieke, "The Native Rulers," pp. 190, 219; and Friedrich Stapel, ed., *Geschiedenis van Nederlandsch Indië*, vol. 5, pp. 227ff. On the impact of the cultivation system see especially Clifford Geertz, *Agricultural Involution*, pp. 52–82.

21. The best discussion of German administrative responses may be found in John Iliffe, *Tanganyika under German Rule*, esp. pp. 7, 26–28, 49–55, 64–78, 147–56, 168–69, 180–82. See also von Götzen, *Ostafrika im Aufstand*, p. 36.

22. John Reid, *Ranchi Settlement Report*, pp. 47–50; Surat C. Roy, *The Mundas and their Country*, pp. 197–200; Suresh Singh, *The Dust-Storm and Hanging Mist*, pp. 181–86; and Surendra Sinha, *The Life and Times of Birsa Bhagwan*, pp. 117–20.

23. On later conditions and movements see especially F. E. A. Taylor, *Final Report on the Revisional Survey and Settlement Operations in the District of Ranchi, 1927–1935*, pp. 3, 51–56; and Singh, ibid.

24. Sachchidananda, *Culture Change in Tribal Bihar*, pp. 93–96, 135; and Stephen Fuchs, *Rebellious Prophets*, pp. 33–34.

25. Fuchs, ibid., p. 34; and Sinha, *Birsa Bhagwan*, pp. iv–v.

26. Sinha, ibid., pp. 1, 12 et passim.

27. On the sects which succeeded the Pai Maire see Paul Clark, *'Hauhau'*, pp. 105–108; Ann Gibson, "Religious Organization among the Maoris after 1860," pp. 64ff; Joan Metge, *The Maoris of New Zealand*, pp. 45–51; John A. Williams, *Politics of the New Zealand Maori*; and Bryan Wilson, *Magic and the Millennium*, pp. 397–403.

28. On the long succession of millennial movements after Dipanagara see Sartono Kartodirdjo, *Peasant Protest in Rural Java*, esp. chap. 3 and "Agrarian Radicalism in Java." For millenarian activity in Burma since 1930–1932 see the writings of E. Michael Mendelson or Melford Spiro, *Buddhism and Society*, chap. 7.

29. On the many links between Javanese chiliasm and kingship and Indonesian nationalism see Bernhard Dahm, *Sukarno and the Struggle for Indonesian Independence*; and the provocative essay by Benedict Anderson on "The Idea of Power in Javanese Culture." On nationalist eulogies to Dipanagara see R. M. van der Kroef, "Prince Diponegoro: Progenitor of Indonesian Nationalism," pp. 424–25, 449–50.

30. On this point see especially Peter B. R. Carey, "Javanese Histories of Dipanagara," pp. 285–88.

31. Translations of a "Special Notice to Wunthanus" from the *Mawrawaddy News*, 29 November 1930, and a letter from U So Thein to Ko Tha Ya, dated 11 November 1930, in R. Morris, "Causes of the Tharrawaddy Rebellion," Appendixes K, J.

32. For examples of varying contemporary nationalist responses see Mi Mi Khaing, *The Burmese Family*, p. 97; Emanuel Sarkisyanz, *Buddhist Backgrounds of the Burmese Revolution*, pp. 164–65; Godfrey Harvey, *British Rule in Burma*, pp. 75–76; and Ba U, *My Burma*, pp. 105–108.

33. The best discussions of these links may be found in Terence O. Ranger, "Connexions between 'Primary Resistance' Movements and Modern Mass Nationalism in East and Central Africa," pt. 2, pp. 634–36.

34. Julius K. Nyerere, *Freedom and Unity*, pp. 2, 40–41; and Ebrahim N. Hussein's drama, *Kinjeketile* (Dar es Salaam, 1970) in which the great cost of human lives of rebellion against the colonizers is repeatedly stressed.

CHAPTER 8

1. For a sensitive analysis of the effects of accelerated change, see Mancur Olson, "Rapid Growth, A Destabilizing Force."

2. For studies of these patterns in different areas see Stephen Fuchs, *Rebellious Prophets*; Emanuel Sarkisyanz, *Russland und der Messianismus des Orients*; Emil Abegg, *Der Messiasglauben in Indien und Iran*; and Armand Abel et al., *Religions du Salut*.

3. For Europe see especially Howard Kaminsky, *A History of the Hussite Revolution*; Christopher Hill, *The World Turned Upside Down*; and Norman Cohn, *The Pursuit of the Millennium*. For Japan see Irwin Scheiner, "The Mindful Peasant: Sketches for a Study of Rebellion."

4. For numerous case examples of movements arising under these conditions see Guglielmo Guariglia, *Prophetismus und Heilserwartungs-Bewegungen*; or Vittorio Lanternari, *The Religions of the Oppressed*.

5. See especially Lanternari, ibid., passim; and Cohn, *Pursuit*, pp. xiii–xiv, 24–32, 316–19.

6. For the most detailed statement of this position see Gil Carl Alroy, *The Involvement of Peasants in Internal Wars*.

7. For similar conclusions regarding elite involvement in this type of revitalization movement in a very different historical setting, see Donald Weinstein, "The Savonarola Movement in Florence."

8. Cohn, *Pursuit*, especially pp. 28–29, 314–15.

9. For stimulating and pioneering comparative studies of peasant rebellions in which class identification played a major role see Eric Wolf, *Peasant Wars of the Twentieth Century*; and Barrington Moore, Jr., *Social Origins of Dictatorship and Democracy*.

10. On the limitations of social banditry as a form of protest see Eric Hobsbawm, *Primitive Rebels*, pp. 23–28.

11. For a more detailed discussion of these dimensions of millenarianism see Neil J. Smelser, *Theory of Collective Behavior*, chaps. 9, 10 passim.

12. On these aspects of violent prophetic protest see especially Henri Ellenberger, "Les mouvements de libération mythique," pp. 263, 266.

13. Frantz Fanon, *The Wretched of the Earth*, pp. 92–95.

14. For a critique of these views based upon an examination of the Algerian conflict from which Fanon drew his conclusions on the effects of violence see Irene Gendzier, *Frantz Fanon: A Critical Study*, pp. 201–202. For striking counterevidence in Fanon's own writings see the moving case studies in the section "Colonial War and Mental Disorders," in *The Wretched of the Earth*.

15. For a discussion of the contrast between the outcome of this sort of movement and those not involving direct confrontation with the colonial overlords see James W. Fernandez's typological analysis of African revitalization expression in "African Religious Movements—Types and Dynamics," pp. 535–37, 548.

Bibliography

PRIMARY SOURCES

Manuscript Sources

Cary, B. S. "Hints for the Guidance of Civil Officers in the Event of the Outbreak of Disturbances in Burma." In *Political and Judicial Correspondence*, File 7347 (1930).

Government of Burma. "(Confidential) Report on the Rebellion in Burma, April 1931–March 1932." In *Political and Judicial Correspondence*, File 7347 (1930).

———. "Secret Tribunal Judgements." In Government of India, *Political and Judicial Correspondence*, Files 7347–7351 (1930). India Office Records.

Government of Tanganyika. *Kilwa District Book*, Tanzania National Archives, Dar es Salaam (on microfilm, University of Wisconsin, Madison).

———. *Mtwara Provincial Book*, Tanzania National Archives, Dar es Salaam (on microfilm, University of Wisconsin, Madison).

———. *Rufiji District Book*, Tanzania National Archives, Dar es Salaam (on microfilm, University of Wisconsin, Madison).

Morris, R. C. "Causes of the Tharrawaddy Rebellion (1931)." In *Political and Judicial Correspondence*, File 7347 (1930), no. 2208.

Printed Official Reports

Couper, Thomas. *Report of Inquiry into the Condition of Agricultural Tenants and Labourers*. Rangoon, 1924.

Elout, Cornelis T. "Staatkundig-ekonomische Beschouwingen omtrent de Landverhuringen in Soerakarta en Djokjokarta tot op den Javaschen Oorlog van 1825–1830," *Tijdschrift voor Nederlandsch-Indië* 1 (1870): 1–36.

Government of Burma. *The Origin and Causes of the Burma Rebellion (1930–1932)*. Rangoon, 1934.

———. *Report of the Committee to Examine the Land Revenue System of Burma*. 2 vols. Rangoon, 1922.

———. *Report of the Land and Agriculture Committee*. Rangoon, 1938.

———. *Report of the Provincial Banking Enquiry Committee 1929–1930*. Rangoon, 1930.

———. *Report(s) on the Administration of the Province of Burma*.

———. *Report on the Land Revenue Administration for Burma for 1929–30*. Rangoon, 1930.

———. *Report(s) on the Police Administration of Burma*.

———. "Report on the Rebellion in Burma up to the 3rd May 1931," *Parliamentary Papers*, vol. 12, 1930–31, Cmd. 3900.

Lowry, W. E. *Report on the Revision Settlement Operations in the Myaungmya District, 1903–4*. Rangoon, 1905.

MacKenna, James. *Report on the Settlement Operations in the Myaungmya and Bassein Districts, 1901–2*. Rangoon, 1903.

Nahuys van Burgst, Huibert G. *Verzameling van officiële Rapporten betreffende den Oorlog op Java in de Jaren 1825–1830*. 4 vols. Deventer, 1835–1836.

Reid, John. *Report on the Survey and Settlement Operations in the Ranchi District, 1902–1910*. Calcutta, 1912.

Taylor, F. E. A. *Final Report on the Revisional Survey and Settlement Operations in the District of Ranchi, 1927–1935*. Patna, 1940.

Tin Gyi, U. *Report on the Second Revision Settlement of the Ma-ubin District, 1925–8*. Rangoon, 1929.

Accounts by Participants or Eyewitnesses

Babad Dipanagara. Dutch translation from the Javanese contained in Pieter F. J. Louw and Eduard S. de Klerck, *De Java-Oorlog van 1825–1830*. Batavia–The Hague, 1894–1909.

Fox, William, *The War in New Zealand*. London, 1866.

Götzen, Gustav A. von. *Deutsch-Ostafrika im Aufstand 1905–1906*. Berlin, 1909.

Gwassa, Gilbert C. K., and Iliffe, John. *Records of the Maji Maji Rising*. Nairobi, 1967.

Hogendorp, Hendrik G. van. *Willem van Hogendorp in Nederlandsch-Indië, 1825–1830*. The Hague, 1913.

Karim bin Jamaliddini, Abdul. *Utenzi wa vita vya Maji Maji*. English translation: Kampala. 1957.

Mapunda, O. B., and Mpangara, G. P. *The Maji Maji War in Ungoni*. Dar es Salaam, 1969.

Martin, William. *The Taranaki Question*. London, 1861.

Meade, Herbert. *A Ride Through the Disturbed Districts of New Zealand*. London, 1870.

Merker, Moritz. "Ueber die Aufstandsbewegung in Deutsch-Ostafrika." *Militär Wochenblatt* 9 (1906), nos. 45, 46, 47, 65.

Methner, Wilhelm. *Unter Drei Gouverneuren, 16 Jahre Dienst in Deutschen Tropen*. Breslau, 1938.

Penfold, Merimeri, trans. *Ua Rongopai* (Gospel of Te Ua). In Paul Clark, *'Hauhau': The Pai Maire Search for Maori Identity*. Auckland, 1975.

Prüsse, Albert. *Zwanzig Jahre Ansiedler in Deutsch-Ostafrika*. Stuttgart, 1929.

Saw, U. *The Burmese Situation, 1930–1931*. Rangoon, 1931.

Saya San. "Diary." Published in *Rangoon Gazette*. 5 October 1931, p. 18.

Stuers, François de. *Mémoires sur la guerre de l'île de Java de 1825 à 1830*. The Hague, 1833.

Surakarta Kraton Babad. Peter Carey's English translation from the Javanese, part 2 of his "Dipanagara and the Making of the Java War, Yogyakarta History 1785–1825." D. Phil. thesis, Oxford University, 1975.

Weitzel, August W. P. *De Oorlog op Java van 1825 tot 1830* (compiled from the posthumous papers of Merkus de Kock). 2 vols. Breda, 1852–1853.

SECONDARY SOURCES

Case Studies by Area

THE JAVA WAR (1825–1830)

Anderson, Benedict R. O'G. "The Idea of Power in Javanese Culture." In *Culture and Politics in Indonesia*, edited by Claire Holt, pp. 1–70. Ithaca, New York, 1972.

Benda, Harry. *The Cresent and the Rising Sun*. The Hague, 1958.

Carey, Peter B. R. *The Cultural Ecology of Early Nineteenth Century Java: Pangeran Dipanagara, A Case Study*. Singapore, 1974.

———. "The Origins of the Java War (1825–1830)." *English Historical Review* 91 (1976): 52–78.

———. "Javanese Histories of Dipanagara: The Buku Kedhun Kebo." *Bijdragen tot de Taal-, Land- en Volkenkunde* 130 (1974): 259–88.

Cohen Stuart, Abraham B. "Eroe Tjakra." *Bijdragen tot de Taal-, Land- en Volkenkunde* 3d ser. 7 (1872): 285–88.

Colenbrander, Hermann T. *Koloniale Geschiedenis*. 3 vols. The Hague, 1925–1926.

Day, Clive. *The Dutch in Java*. New York, 1904.

Deventer, Marinus L. Van. *Geschiedenis der Nederlanders op Java*. 2 vols. Haarlem, 1886–1887.

Drewes, Gerardus W. J. *Drie Javaansche Goeroe's: Hun Leven, Onderricht en Messiaspediking*. Leiden, 1925.

Geertz, Clifford. *Agricultural Involution*. Berkeley, 1966.

———. "The Javanese Kijaji: The Changing Role of a Cultural Broker." *Comparative Studies in Society and History* 2 (1960): 228–49.

Graaf, Hermanus J. de. *Geschiedenis van Indonesië*. The Hague, 1949.

Haan, Fonger de. *Priangan: De Preanger Regentschappen onder het Nederlandsch Bestuur tot 1811*. 4 vols. Batavia, 1910–1912.

Hageman, J. *Geschiedenis van den Oorlog op Java van 1825 tot 1830*. Batavia, 1856.

Holt, Claire, ed. *Culture and Politics in Indonesia*. Ithaca, New York, 1972.

Kartodirdjo, Sartono. "Agrarian Radicalism in Java." In *Culture and Politics in Indonesia*, edited by Claire Holt, pp. 71–125. Ithaca, New York, 1972.

———. *Peasant Protest in Rural Java*. Singapore–Kuala Lumpur, 1973.

———. *The Peasants' Revolt of Banten in 1888*. The Hague, 1966.

Kielstra, Egbert B. "Eenige Personen uit den Java oorlog." *De Tijdspiegel* 1 (1896): 290–301.

Kemp, P. H. van der. "Dipanegara, eene geschiedkundige Hamlettype." *Bijdragen tot de Taal-, Land- en Volkenkunde* 46 (1896): 281–430.

_____. "De economische Oorzaken van den Java-oorlog van 1825–30." *Bijdragen tot de Taal-, Land- en Volkenkunde* 47 (1897): 1–48.

Klerck, Eduard S. de. *History of the Netherlands East Indies.* 2 vols. Rotterdam, 1938.

Knebel, J. "Amulettes Javanaises." *Tijdschrift voor Indische Taal-, Land- en Volkenkunde* 40 (1898): 497–507.

Kroef, Justus M. van der. "Javanese Messianic Expectations, Their Origins and Cultural Context." *Comparative Studies in Society and History* 1 (1959): 299–323.

_____. "Prince Diponogoro: Progenitor of Indonesian Nationalism." *The Far Eastern Quarterly* 8 (1949): 424–50.

Kumar, Ann. "Dipanagara (1787?–1855)." *Indonesia* 13 (1972): 69–118.

Louw, Pieter F. J., and Klerck, Eduard S. de. *De Java-Oorlog van 1825–1830.* 6 vols. Batavia–The Hague, 1894–1909.

Meilink-Roelofsz, Marie A. P. *Asian Trade and European Influence in the Indonesian Archipelago between 1500 and about 1630.* The Hague, 1962.

Moertono, Soemarsaid. *State and Statecraft in Old Java.* Ithaca, New York, 1968.

Nes, J. F. Walraven van. "Verhandeling over de waarschijnlijke Oorzaken, die Aanleiding tot de Onlusten van 1825 en de volgende Jaren in de Vorstenlanden gegeven hebben." *Tijdschrift voor Nederlandsch Indië* 6 (1844): 112–71.

Onghokham. "The Residency of Madiun Pryayi and Peasant in the Nineteenth Century." Ph.D. dissertation, Yale University, 1975.

Palmier, Leslie. "The Javanese Nobility under the Dutch." *Comparative Studies in Society and History* 2 (1960): 197–227.

Parvé, J. Steijn. "Landverhuur in de Vorstenlanden en Javasche oorlog." *Tijdschrift voor Nederlandsch Indië* 2 (1850): 23–57.

Peper, A. Bram. "Population Growth in Java in the 19th Century: A New Interpretation." *Population Studies* 24 (1971): 71–84.

Pigeaud, Th. G. Th. "Erucakra-Vairocana." In *India Antiqua: A Volume of Oriental Studies, Presented by His Friends and Pupils to Jean Philippe Vogel on the Occasion of the 50th Anniversary of His Doctorate,* pp. 270–73. Leiden, 1947.

Praag, S. van. *Onrust op Java. De Jeugd van Dipanĕgara. Een Historisch-Literaire Studie.* Amsterdam, 1947.

Ricklefs, Merle C. "Dipanagara's Early Inspirational Experience." *Bijdragen tot de Taal-, Land- en Volkenkunde* 130 (1974): 227–58.

_____. *Jogjakarta under Sultan Mangkubumi, 1749–1792: A History of the Division of Java.* Oxford, 1974.

Roorda, T. "Verhaal van de Oorsprong en het Begin van de Opstand van Dipâ-nĕgârâ, volgens een Javaansch Handschrift." *Bijdragen tot de Taal-, Land- en Volkenkunde* 3 (1859): 137–97.

Rouffaer, G. P. "Vorstenlanden." *Encyclopaedia van Nederlandsch-Indië*, vol. 4, pp. 587–653. The Hague, 1905.

Schrieke, Bertram J. O. "The Native Rulers." In *Indonesian Sociological Studies*, vol. 2, pp. 167–201. The Hague, 1955–1957.

———. "The Position of the Regents from the Days of the Dutch East India Company to the Constitutional Regulation of 1854." In *Sociological Studies*, vol. 2, pp. 202–21.

Sevenhoven, Jan I. van. "De oorzaken van de Oorlog op Java van 1825 tot 1830." *Tijdschrift voor Nederlandsch Indië* 1 (1838): 102–30.

Stapel, Friedrich W., ed. *Geschiedenis van Nederlansch Indië*, vol. 5. Amsterdam, 1938.

Stuers, François de. *Mémoires sur la guerre de l'île de Java de 1825 à 1830.* The Hague, 1833.

Wiselius, Jakob A. B. "Djåjå Båjå, zijn Leven en Profetieën." *Bijdragen tot de Taal-, Land- en Volkenkunde* 7 (1872): 172–215.

Wulfften-Palte, P. M. van. *Psychological Aspects of the Indonesian Problem.* Leiden, 1949.

NEW ZEALAND: THE PAI MAIRE MOVEMENT (1864–C. 1867)

Anderson, J. "The Missionaries and the Maoris." In *The Cambridge History of the British Empire*, edited by James Hight, vol. 7, pp. 47–59. Cambridge, 1933.

Babbage, Stuart B. *Hauhauism: An Episode in the Maori Wars, 1863–66.* Dunedin, 1937.

Beaglehole, Ernest. "The Polynesian Maori." In *The Maori People Today*, edited by Ivan Sutherland, pp. 49–74.

Best, Elsdon. *The Maori as He Was.* Wellington, 1924.

———. *Maori Religion and Mythology.* Wellington, 1924.

———. *Some Aspects of Maori Myth and Religion.* Wellington, 1922.

———. *Tuhoe: Children of the Mist.* New Plymouth, New Zealand, 1925.

Binney, Judith. "Christianity and the Maoris." *New Zealand Journal of History* 3 (1969): 143–65.

Buck, Peter H. (Te Rangi Hiroa). *The Coming of the Maori.* Wellington, 1952.

Clark, Paul. *'Hauhau': The Pai Maire Search for Maori Identity.* Auckland, 1975.

Condliffe, John O., and Airey, Willis T. *A Short History of New Zealand.* Christchurch, 1953.

Cowan, James. *The Maoris of New Zealand.* Christchurch, 1910.

———. *The New Zealand Wars.* 2 vols. Wellington, 1922.

Dalton, Brian J. *War and Politics in New Zealand, 1855–1870.* Sydney, 1967.

Firth, Raymond. *Economics of the New Zealand Maori.* Wellington, 1959.

Gibson, Ann J. "Religious Organization among the Maoris of New Zealand after 1860." Ph.D. dissertation, University of California at Berkeley, 1964.

Gorst, John. *The Maori King.* London, 1864.

Greenwood, William. "The Upraised Hand, or the Spiritual Significance of the Rise of the *Ringtau* Faith." *Journal of the Polynesian Society* 51 (1942): 1–18.

Gudgeon, T. W. "Maori Superstition." *Journal of the Polynesian Society* 14 (1905): 167–92.

Harrop, Angus J. *England and the Maori Wars*. London, 1937.

Hight, James, ed. *The Cambridge History of the British Empire*, vol. 7, pt. 2. Cambridge, 1933.

_____. "The Maori Wars, 1843–1872." In *The Cambridge History of the British Empire*, edited by James Hight, vol. 7, pt. 2, pp. 121–42.

Houston, John. *Maori Life in Old Taranaki*. Wellington, 1965.

Metge, Joan. *The Maoris of New Zealand*. New York, 1967.

Miller, Harold. "Maori and Paheka, 1814–1865." In *The Maori People Today*, edited by Ivan Sutherland, pp. 75–95. New York, 1940.

_____. *New Zealand*. London, 1950.

Miller, John. *Early Victorian New Zealand*. London, 1958.

Ngata, Apirana. "Maori Land Settlement." In *The Maori People Today*, edited by Ivan Sutherland, pp. 96–154. New York, 1940.

_____. "Religious Influences." In *The Maori People Today*, edited by Ivan Sutherland, pp. 336–73. New York, 1940.

Owens, J. M. R. "Christianity and the Maoris." *New Zealand Journal of History* 2 (1968): 18–40.

Sinclair, Keith. *A History of New Zealand*. London, 1961.

_____. *The Origins of the Maori Wars*. Wellington, 1957.

Stafford, D. M. *Te Arawa: A History of the Arawa People*. Auckland, 1967.

Sutherland, Ivan L. G., ed. *The Maori People Today*. New York, 1940.

Tapp, E. J. *Early New Zealand*. Melbourne, 1958.

Vayda, Andrew P. *Maori Warfare*. Wellington, 1960.

Ward, Alan D. *A Show of Justice*. Canberra, 1974.

_____. "The Origins of the Anglo-Maori Wars: A Reconsideration." *New Zealand Journal of History* 1 (1967): 148–70.

Williams, John A. *Politics of The New Zealand Maori: Protest and Cooperation 1891–1909*. Seattle, 1969.

Wilson, O. "Papahurihia, First Maori Prophet." *Journal of the Polynesian Society* 74 (1965): 473–83.

Winiata, Maharaia. *The Changing Role of the Leader in Maori Society*. Auckland, 1967.

Winks, Robin W. "The Doctrine of Hauhauism." *Journal of the Polynesian Society* 62 (1953): 199–236.

Wi Repa, T. "Depopulation in New Zealand." *Oceania* 3 (1932): 227–34.

Wright, Harrison M. *New Zealand 1769–1840: Early Years of Western Contact*. Cambridge, Mass., 1959.

CHOTA NAGPUR (INDIA): THE BIRSA RISING (1899–1900)

Bradley-Birt, Francis B. *Chota Nagpur, A Little-Known Province of the Empire*. London, 1903.

Fuchs, Stephen. *Rebellious Prophets: A Study of Messianic Movements in Indian Religions*. London, 1965.

Hallett, M. G. *Ranchi District Gazetteer*. Patna, 1917.

Hoffman, John, et al. *Encyclopedia Mundarica*. Patna, 1930.

O'Malley, Lewis S. S. *Bengal District Gazetteer: Singbhum, Saraikela, and Kharsawan*. Calcutta, 1910.

Roy, Sarat Chundra. *The Mundas and Their Country*. London, 1970.

Sachchidananda. "Birsa—An Adivasi Fighter for Freedom." In *Profiles of Tribal Culture in Bihar*, edited by Sachchidananda, pp. 103–108. Calcutta, 1964.

———. *Culture Change in Tribal Bihar, Munda and Oraon*. Calcutta, 1964.

Singh, Suresh. *The Dust-Storm and the Hanging Mist*. Calcutta, 1966.

Sinha, Surendra P. *The Life and Times of Birsa Bhagwan*. Ranchi, 1964.

GERMAN EAST AFRICA (TANZANIA): THE MAJI MAJI REBELLION (1905–1906)

Austen, Ralph A. *Northwest Tanzania under German and British Rule*. New Haven, 1968.

Bates, Margaret. Introduction to *Utenzi wa vita vya Maji Maji*, by Abdul Karim bin Jamaliddini. Kampala, 1957.

Bell, R. M. "The Maji Maji Rebellion in the Liwale District." *Tanganyika Notes and Records* 28(1950):38–57.

Brunschwig, Henri. *L'expansion allemande outre-mer du XVe siècle à nos jours*. Paris, 1957.

Cross-Upcott, A. R. W. "The Origin of the Maji Maji Revolt." *Man* 60 (1960), no. 98: 71–73.

Davidson, Basil. *The Growth of African Civilization in East and Central Africa to the Late Nineteenth Century*. London, 1967.

Driberg, J. H. "Yakan." *Journal of the Royal Anthropological Institute of Great Britain and Ireland* 61 (1931): 413–20.

Gwassa, Gilbert C. K. "African Methods of Warfare during the Maji Maji War, 1905–1907." In *War and Society in Africa*, edited by Bethwell A. Ogot, pp. 123–48. London, 1972.

———. "The German Intervention and African Resistance in Tanzania." In *A History of Tanzania*, edited by Isaria Kimambo and Arnold J. Temu, pp. 85–123. Nairobi, 1969.

———. "Kinjikitile and the Ideology of Maji Maji." In *The Historical Study of African Religion*, edited by Terence Ranger and Isaria Kimambo, pp. 202–17. London, 1970.

Harlow, Vincent, and Chilver, E. M., eds. *History of East Africa*, vol. 2. Oxford, 1965.

Hassing, Per. "German Missionaries and the Maji Maji." *African Historical Studies* 3 (1970): 373–89.

Henderson, William O. "German East Africa, 1884–1918." In *History of East Africa*, edited by Vincent Harlow and E. M. Chilver, vol. 2, pp. 123–62. Oxford, 1965.

Hussein, Ebrahim N. *Kinjeketile*. Dar es Salaam, 1970.

Iliffe, John. "The Effects of the Maji Maji Rebellion on German Policy in East Africa." In *Britain and Germany in Africa*, edited by Prosser Gifford and William Lewis, pp. 557–75. New Haven, 1967.

_____. "The Organization of the Maji Maji Rebellion." *Journal of African History* 8 (1967): 495–512.

_____. *Tanganyika under German Rule, 1905–1912*. Cambridge, 1969.

Kimambo, Isaria N., and Temu, Arnold J., eds. *A History of Tanzania*. Nairobi, 1969.

Klamroth, Martin. "Beitrage zum Verständnis der religiösen Vorstellungen der Saramo im Bezirk Daressalam." *Zeitschrift für Kolonialsprachen* 1 (1910–11): 139–53.

Moffett, John P. *Handbook of Tanganyika*. Dar es Salaam, 1958.

Nigmann, Ernst. *Die Wahehe: Ihre Geschichte, Kult-, Rechts-, Kriegs-, und Jagd-Gebraüche*. Berlin, 1908.

Nyerere, Julius K. *Freedom and Unity*. Dar es Salaam, 1966.

Ogot, Bethwell A., ed. *War and Society in Africa*. London, 1972.

Ogot, Bethwell A., and Kiernan, J. A., eds. *Zamani*. New York, 1968.

Oliver, Roland, and Mathew, Gervase, eds. *History of East Africa*, vol. 1. Oxford, 1963.

Paasche, Hermann. *Deutsch-Ostafrika: Wirtschaftlich Dargestellt*. Berlin, 1906.

Ranger, Terence O. "Connexions between 'Primary Resistance' Movements and Modern Mass Nationalism in East and Central Africa." *Journal of African History* 9 (1968): 437–53, 631–41.

_____. "The Movement of Ideas, 1850–1939." In *A History of Tanzania*, edited by Isaria Kimambo and Arnold J. Temu, pp. 161–88. Nairobi, 1969.

Raum, O. F. "German East Africa: Changes in African Tribal Life under German Administration, 1892–1914." In *History of East Africa*, edited by Vincent Harlow and E. M. Chilver, vol. 2, pp. 163–208. Oxford, 1965.

Redmond, Patrick M. "Maji Maji in Ngoni: A Reappraisal of Existing Historiography." *International Journal of African Studies* 8 (1975): 407–24.

Roberts, Andrew. "Political Change in the Nineteenth Century." In *A History of Tanzania*, edited by Isaria Kimambo and Arnold J. Temu, pp. 57–84. Nairobi, 1969.

Sayers, Gerald F. *The Handbook of Tanganyika*. London, 1930.

Schnee, Heinrich, ed. *Deutsches Koloniale-Lexicon*. Vol. 1, "Deutsch-Ostafrika," pp. 357–407. Leipzig, 1920.

Sicard, Sigvard van. *Christian Missions on the Coast of Tanzania*. Uppsala, 1970.

Smith, Allison. "The Southern Section of the Interior, 1840–1884." In *History of East Africa*, edited by Roland Oliver and Gervase Mathew, vol. 1, pp. 253–96. Oxford, 1963.

Wehler, Hans-Ulrich. *Bismarck und der Imperialismus*. Cologne, 1969.

Wright, Marcia. *German Missions in Tanganyika*. Oxford, 1971.

BRITISH BURMA: THE SAYA SAN REVOLT (1930–1932)

Adas, Michael. *The Burma Delta: Economic Development and Social Change on an Asian Rice Frontier, 1852–1941*. Madison, Wis., 1974.

Alexander, H. R., ed. "The Pacification of Upper Burma: A Vernacular History (by Maung Tha Aung and Maung Mya Din)." *Journal of the Burma Research Society* 31 (1941): 80–136.

Anonymous. "Curiosities of the Burmese Rebellion." *Illustrated London News* 3 (1932): 350–51.

Aung Than, "Relation between the Samgha and State and Laity." *Journal of the Burma Research Society* 48 (1965): 1–8.

Ba U. *My Burma: The Autobiography of a President*. London, 1959.

Brohm, John F. "Burmese Religion and the Burmese Religious Revival." Ph.D. dissertation, Cornell University, 1957.

Cady, John. *A History of Modern Burma*. Ithaca, New York, 1962.

Cheng Siok-Hwa. *The Rice Industry of Burma, 1852–1940*. Kuala Lumpur–Singapore, 1967.

Collis, Maurice. *Into Hidden Burma*. London, 1953.

_____. *Trials in Burma*. London, 1938.

Crosthwaite, Charles. *The Pacification of Burma*. London, 1912.

Dunn, Charles W. *Studies in the History of Tharrawaddy*. Cambridge, 1920.

Furnivall, John S. *Colonial Policy and Practice*. New York, 1956.

_____. *An Introduction to the Political Economy of Burma*. Rangoon, 1957.

Furnivall, John S., and Morrison, W. S. *Insein District Gazetteer*. Rangoon, 1914.

Grantham, S. G.; McDowall, R. G.; and Swithinbank, B. W. *Tharrawaddy District Gazetteer*. Rangoon, 1920.

Harvey, Godfrey E. *British Rule in Burma, 1824–1942*. London, 1946.

Hla Baw. "Superstitions of Burmese Criminals." *Journal of the Burma Research Society* 30 (1940): 376–83.

Hewett, H. P. and Clague, J. *Bassein District Gazetteer*. Rangoon, 1916.

Htin Aung, U. *The Stricken Peacock: Anglo-Burmese Relations 1752–1948*. The Hague, 1965.

Langham-Carter, R. R. "The Burmese Army." *Journal of the Burma Research Society* 27 (1937): 254–76.

Mai Lei, Ma. "The Real Origins and Causes of the Burma Rebellion, 1930–32." In *Thu Lou Lu*. Rangoon, 1953.

Mendelson, E. Michael. "The King of the Weaving Mountain." *Royal Central Asian Society Journal* 48 (1961): 229–37.

_____. "A Messianic Buddhist Association in Upper Burma." *Bulletin of the School of Oriental and African Studies* 24 (1961): 560–80.

_____. *Sangha and State in Burma*. Ithaca, New York, 1975.

Mi Mi Khaing. *The Burmese Family*. Calcutta, 1956.

Morrison, W. S. *Henzada District Gazetteer*. Rangoon, 1915.

Moscotti, Albert. "British Policy in Burma, 1917–1937." Ph.D. dissertation, Yale University, 1951.

Mya Sein, Daw. *Administration of Burma: Sir Charles Crosthwaite and the Consolidation of Burma*. Rangoon, 1938.

Pfanner, David. "Rice and Religion in a Burmese Village." Ph.D. dissertation, Cornell University, 1962.

Phayre, Arthur. *History of Burma*. London, 1883.

Rangoon Gazette (*Weekly Budget*).

Sarkisyanz, Emanuel. *Buddhist Backgrounds of the Burmese Revolution*. The Hague, 1965.

Scott, James G., and Hardiman, John P. *Gazetteer of Upper Burma and the Shan States*. Rangoon, 1900.

Smith, Donald E. *Religion and Politics in Burma*. Princeton, 1965.

Spiro, Melford. *Burmese Supernaturalism*. Englewood Cliffs, New Jersey. 1967.

_____. *Buddhism and Society: A Great Tradition and Its Vicissitudes*. New York, 1970.

Taylor, Robert. "The Relationship between Burmese Social Classes and British-Indian Policy on the Behavior of the Burmese Political Elite, 1937–1942." Ph.D. dissertation, Cornell University, 1974.

Warren, C. V. *Burmese Interlude*. London, 1937.

White, Herbert T. *A Civil Servant in Burma*. London, 1913.

Yi Yi. "Life at the Burmese Court under the Konbaung Kings." *Journal of the Burma Research Society* 44 (1961): 85–129.

GENERAL REFERENCES

Abegg, Emil. *Der Messiasglauben in Indien und Iran*. Berlin, 1928.

Abel, Armand, et al. *Religions du salut*. Brussels, 1962.

Aberle, David. "A Note on Relative Deprivation Theory." In *Millennial Dreams in Action*, edited by Sylvia L. Thrupp, pp. 209–14. New York, 1970.

_____. *The Peyote Religion among the Navahos*. Chicago, 1966.

_____. "The Prophet Dance and Reactions to White Contact." *Southwest Journal of Anthropology* 15 (1959): 77–83.

Ake, Claude. "Charismatic Legitimation and Political Integration." *Comparative Studies in Society and History* 9 (1966): 1–13.

Alroy, Gil Carl. *The Involvement of Peasants in Internal Wars*. Princeton, 1966.

Baechler, Jean. *Revolution*. Oxford, 1975.

Balandier, Georges. "Messianismes et nationalismes en Afrique noire." *Cahiers internationaux de sociologie* 14 (1953):41–64.

_____. *Sociologie actuelle de l'Afrique noire*. Paris, 1963.

Barkun, Michael. *Disaster and the Millennium*. New Haven, 1974.

Bastide, Roger. "Messianisme et développement économique et social." *Cahiers internationaux de sociologie* 30 (1961): 3–14.

Bendix, Reinhard. "Tradition and Modernity Reconsidered." *Comparative Studies in Society and History* 9 (1967): 292–346.

Beqiraj, Mehmet. *Peasantry in Revolution*. Ithaca, New York, 1966.

Brinton, Crane. *The Anatomy of Revolution*. New York, 1938.

Brown, Karl. "The Sudanese Mahdiya." In *Protest and Power in Black Africa*, edited by Robert I. Rotberg and Ali A. Mazrui, pp. 145–68. Oxford, 1970.

Brunschwig, Henri. *Mythes et réalities de l'impérialisme colonial française*. Paris, 1960.

Burridge, Kenelm. *Mambu: A Melanesian Millennium*. London, 1960.

_____. *New Heaven New Earth*. New York, 1969.

Cairns, H. Alan C. *Prelude to Imperialism*. London, 1965.

Campbell, Arthur. *Guerillas*. New York, 1968.

Chance, Norman. "Acculturation, Self-Identification, and Personality Adjustment." *American Anthropologist* 67 (1965): 372–93.

Chesneaux, Jean, et al. *Tradition et révolution au Vietnam*. Paris, 1971.

Cipolla, Carl. *Guns, Sails and Empires*. New York, 1965.

Cohn, Norman. "Medieval Millenarianism." In *Millennial Dreams in Action*, edited by Sylvia L. Thrupp, pp. 31–43. New York, 1970.

_____. *The Pursuit of the Millennium*. New York, 1961.

Curtin, Philip. "Nationalism in Africa, 1945–1965." *Review of Politics* 28 (1966): 143–53.

Da Cunha, Euclides. *Rebellion in the Backlands*. Chicago, 1964.

Dahm, Bernhard. *Sukarno and the Indonesian Struggle for Independence*. Ithaca, New York, 1969.

Davies, James C. "Toward a Theory of Revolution." *American Sociological Review* 27 (1962): 1–19.

Dekmejian, Richard H., and Wyszomirski, Margaret J. "Charismatic Leadership in Islam: The Mahdi of the Sudan." *Comparative Studies in Society and History*. 14 (1972): 193–214.

Desroche, Henri. "Les messianismes et la catégorie de l'échec." *Cahiers internationaux de Sociologie* 35 (1963):61–84.

Douglas, Mary. *The Lele of Kasai*. London, 1963.

_____. "Techniques of Sorcery Control in Central Africa." In *Witchcraft and Sorcery in East Africa*, edited by John F. Middleton and Edward H. Winter, pp. 123–41. London, 1963.

_____, ed. *Witchcraft Confessions and Accusations*. London, 1970.

Durkheim, Emile. *The Division of Labor in Society*. New York, 1964.

Eckstein, Harry. "On the Etiology of Internal Wars." In *Studies in the Philosophy of History*, edited by Geroge H. Nadel, pp. 117–47. New York, 1965.

Eliade, Mircea. "'Cargo Cults' and Cosmic Regeneration." In *Millennial Dreams in Action*, edited by Sylvia L. Thrupp, pp. 139–44. New York, 1970.

Ellenberger, Henri. "Les mouvements de libération mythique." *Critique* 15 (1963): 248–67.

Errington, Frederick. "Indigenous Ideas of Order: Time and Transition in a New Guinea Cargo Movement." *American Ethnologist* (1974): 255–68.

Fabian, Johannes. "Führer und Führung in den prophetisch-messianischen Bewegungen der (ehemaligen) Kolonialvölker." *Anthropos* 58 (1963):773–809.

Fairbairn, Geoffrey. *Revolutionary Guerilla Warfare: The Countryside Version*. Harmondsworth, England, 1974.

Fanon, Frantz. *The Wretched of the Earth*. New York, 1971.

Fernandez, James W. "African Religious Movements: Types and Dynamics." *The Journal of Modern African Studies* 2 (1964): 531–49.

Finch, Peter. *The Idea of a Social Science and Its Relation to Philosophy*. London, 1958.

————. "Understanding a Primitive Society." *American Philosophical Quarterly* 1 (1964): 307–24.

Firth, Raymond. "Rumor in Primitive Society." *Journal of Abnormal and Social Pscyhology* 53 (1956): 122–32.

Foster, George M. "Peasant Society and the Image of Limited Good." *American Anthropologist* 67 (1965):293–315.

————. "What is a Peasant?" In *Peasant Society: A Reader*, by Jack M. Potter et al., pp. 2–14. Boston, 1967.

Friedrich Carl J. "Political Leadership and the Problem of Charismatic Power." *Journal of Politics* 23 (1961): 3–24.

Fuller, John F. C. *The Conduct of War, 1789–1961*. New Brunswick, New Jersey, 1961.

Galbraith, John. "Myths of the 'Little England' Era." *American Historical Review* 67 (1961): 34–48.

Gallagher, John, and Robinson, Ronald. "The Imperialism of Free Trade." *Economic History Review* 4 (1953): 1–15.

Gendzier, Irene. *Frantz Fanon: A Critical Study*. New York, 1973.

Girault, Arthur. *Principes de colonisation et de législation coloniale*. Paris, 1895.

Gluckman, Max. *Order and Rebellion in Tribal Africa*. London, 1963.

Goody, Jack. *Literacy in Traditional Societies*. Cambridge, 1968.

Grünenbaum, Gustav E. von. *Essays in the Nature and Growth of a Cultural Tradition*. London, 1955.

Guariglia, Guglielmo. *Prophetismus und Heilserwartungs-Bewegungen als völkerkundliches und religionsgeschichtliches Problem*. Horn-Vienna, 1959.

Gurr, Ted. *Why Men Rebel*. Princeton, 1970.

Hardgreaves, Robert. *The Nadars of Tamilnad*. Berkeley, 1969.

Heine-Geldern, Robert. "Conceptions of State and Kingship in Southeast Asia." *The Far Eastern Quarterly* 2 (1942): 15–30.

Hick, John, ed. *Faith and the Philosophers*. London, 1964.

Hill, Christopher. *The World Turned Upside Down*. New York, 1972.

Hill, Francis. "Millenarian Machines in South Vietnam." *Comparative Studies in Society and History* 13 (1971): 325–50.

Hobsbawm, Eric. *Primitive Rebels: Studies in Archaic Forms of Social Movements*. New York, 1959.

Hollis, Martin. "The Limits of Irrationality." *Archives européenne de Sociologie* 8 (1967): 265–71.

Holt, Peter M. *The Mahdist State in the Sudan 1881–1898*. Oxford, 1970.

Horton, Robin. "African Traditional Thought and Western Science." *Africa* 37 (1967): 50–71, 155–87.

Inglis, Judy. "Cargo Cults: The Problem of Explanation." *Oceania* 27 (1957): 249–63.

Jahoda, Gustav. *White Man: A Study of the Attitudes of Africans to Europeans in Ghana before Independence*. Oxford, 1961.

Jarvie, Ian C. *The Revolution in Anthropology*. London, 1964.

———. "Theories of Cargo Cults: A Critical Analysis." *Oceania* 34 (1963): pt. 1, 1–31, pt. 2, 108–36.

Jarvie, Ian C., and Agassi, Joseph. "The Problem of Rationality in Magic." *British Journal of Anthropology* 18 (1967): 55–74.

Kaminsky, Howard. *A History of the Hussite Revolution*. Berkeley, 1967.

Kaufman, Robert. *Millénarisme et acculturation*. Brussels, 1964.

Kaye, John, and Malleson, George B. *History of the Indian Mutiny*. 6 vols. London, 1864.

Kroef, Justus M. van der. "Messianic Movements in the Celebes, Sumatra, and Borneo." In *Millennial Dreams in Action*, edited by Sylvia L. Thrupp, pp. 80–121. New York, 1970.

La Barre, Weston. "Materials for the Study of Crisis Cults: A Bibliographic Essay." *Current Anthropology* 12 (1971): 3–44.

Lanternari, Vittorio. "Nativistic and Socio-Religious Movements: A Reconsideration." *Comparative Studies in Society and History* 16 (1974): 483–503.

———. *Religions of the Oppressed*. New York, 1965.

Lewy, Guenther. *Religion and Revolution*. New York, 1974.

Lindig, Wolfgang H. von, and Dauer, Alfons M. "Prophetismus und Geistertanz-Bewegungen bei nordamerikanischen Eingeborenen." In *Chiliasmus und Nativismus*, edited by Wilhelm Mühlmann, pp. 41–74. Berlin, 1964.

Linton, Ralph. "Nativistic Movements." *American Anthropologist* 45 (1943): 230–40.

Lukes, Stephen. "Some Problems about Rationality." *Archives européennes de Sociologie* 8 (1967): 247–64.

Lupsha, Peter. "Explanation of Political Violence: Some Psychological Theories vs. Indignation." *Politics and Society* (1971): 89–104.

Macintyre, Alastair. "Is Understanding Religion Compatible with Believing?" In *Faith and the Philsophers*, edited by John Hick, pp. 115–33. London, 1964.

Mair, Lucy. "Independent Religious Movements on Three Continents." *Comparative Studies in Society and History* 1 (1958–59): 113–36.

———. "The Pursuit of the Millennium in Melanesia." *British Journal of Sociology* 9 (1958): 175–82.

Malagoda, Kitsiri. "Millennialism in Relation to Buddhism." *Comparative Studies in Society and History* 12 (1970): 424–41.

Malinowski, Bronislaw. *Magic, Science, and Religion and Other Essays*. Garden City, New York, 1954.

Mannoni, Octave. *Prospero and Caliban: The Psychology of Colonization*. New York, 1964.

Mauro, Frederic. *L'expansion européenne, 1600–1870*. Paris, 1967.

Michael, Franz. *The Taiping Rebellion*. Seattle, 1966.

Middleton, John F., and Winter, Edward H., eds. *Witchcraft and Sorcery in East Africa*. London, 1963.

Mooney, James. *The Ghost Dance Religion*. Chicago, 1965.

Moore, Barrington. *Social Origins of Dictatorship and Democracy*. Boston, 1966.

Mousnier, Roland. *Peasant Uprisings in Seventeenth-Century France, Russia and China*. New York, 1970.

Mühlmann, Wilhelm, ed. *Chiliasmus und Nativismus: Studien zur Psychologie, Soziologie und historischen Kasuistik der Umsturzbewegungen*. Berlin, 1964.

———. "Zwischen Erweckung und Terror: Der Mau-mau-Aufstand in Kenya." In *Chiliasmus und Nativismus*, edited by Wilhelm Mühlmann, pp. 105–40. Berlin, 1964.

Naquin, Susan. *Millennial Rebellion in China*. New Haven, 1976.

Nguyen Tran Huan. "Histoire d'une secte religieuse au Vietnam: Le Caodaïsme." In *Tradition et révolution au Vietnam*, edited by Jean Chesneaux, pp. 189–214. Paris, 1971.

Nieburg, Harold L. *Political Violence*. New York, 1969.

Oberen, Udo. "Die Aufstandsbewegung der Pende bei Quijo Ost-Ekuadors im Jahre 1578." In *Chiliasmus und Nativismus*, edited by Wilhelm Mühlmann, pp. 75–80. Berlin, 1964.

Olson, Mancur, "Rapid Growth, A Destabilizing Force." *Journal of Economic History* 23 (1963): 529–52.

Oommen, T. K. "Charisma, Social Structure and Social Change." *Comparative Studies in Society and History* 10 (1967): 85–99.

Perira de Queiroz, Maria I. "Messiahs in Brazil." *Past and Present* 31 (1965): 62–86.

Purcell, Victor. *The Boxer Uprising*. Cambridge, 1963.

Race, Jeffry. *The War Comes to Long An*. Berkeley, 1971.

Ratnam, K. T. "Charisma and Political Leadership." *Political Studies* 12 (1964): 341–54.

Redfield, Robert. *The Primitive World and Its Transformation*. Ithaca, New York, 1953.

Reed, Nelson. *The Caste War of Yucatan*. New York, 1962.

Reussner, Andre, and Nicolas, Louis. *La puissance navale dans l'histoire*. 3 vols. Paris, 1963.

Rotberg, Robert I., and Mazrui, Ali A., eds. *Protest and Power in Black Africa*. Oxford, 1970.

Rudolph, Lloyd, and Rudolph, Susanne H. *The Modernity of Tradition*. Chicago, 1969.

Sarkisyanz, Emanuel. *Russland und Messianimus des Orients*. Tübingen, 1955.

Scheiner, Irwin. "The Mindful Peasant: Sketches for a Study of Rebellion." *Journal of Asian Studies* 32 (1973): 579–92.

Schlosser, Katesa. *Propheten in Afrika*. Braunschweig, 1949.

———. "Der Prophetismus in niederen Kulturen." *Zeitschrift für Ethnologie* 75 (1950): 60–72.

Schwartz, Benjamin. *In Search of Wealth and Power: Yen Fu and the West*. New York, 1964.

Schweitzer, Arthur. "Theory and Political Charisma." *Comparative Studies in Society and History* 16 (1974):150–81.

Scott, James C. "The Erosion of Patron-Client Bonds and Social Change in Southeast Asia." *Journal of Asian Studies* 22 (1972): 5–38.

———. *The Moral Economy of the Peasant*. New Haven, 1976.

———. "Patron-Client Politics and Political Change in Southeast Asia." *American Political Science Quarterly* 66 (1972): 91–113.

Seal, Anil. *The Emergence of Indian Nationalism*. Cambridge, 1969.

Shepperson, George, and Price, Thomas. *Independent African: John Chilembwe and the Origins, Setting and Significance of the Nyasaland Native Rising*. Edinburgh, 1958.

Sierksma, Fokke. *Een nieuwe Hemel en een nieuwe Aarde*. The Hague, 1961.

Silvert, Henning. "Book Review: The Religions of the Oppressed." *Current Anthropology* 6 (1965): 447–65.

Singer, Milton. "Beyond Tradition and Modernity in Madras." *Comparative Studies in Society and History* 13 (1971):160–95.

Sitaram. *From Sepoy to Soobadar, Being the Autobiography of a Sepoy*. Lahore, 1873.

Sithole, Ndabaningi. *African Nationalism*. New York, 1969.

Smelser, Neil. *The Theory of Collective Behavior*. New York, 1963.

Stoianovich, Traian. "Les structures millenaristes sud-Slaves aux XVIIe et XVIII ss." *Actes du premier congrès international des études Balkaniques et sud-est Européennes*. Sofia, 1969.

Sturtevant, David. "Philippine Social Structure and Its Relation to Agrarian Unrest." Ph.D. dissertation, Stanford University, 1958.

Sundkler, Bernt. *Bantu Prophets in South Africa*. Oxford, 1961.

Talmon, Yonina. "Pursuit of the Millennium: The Relation between Religious and Social Change." *Archives européennes de Sociologie* 3 (1962): 125–48.

Tambiah, Stanley J. *Buddhism and the Spirit Cults in North-East Thailand*. Cambridge, 1970.

Textor, Robert. "An Inventory of Non-Buddhist Supernatural Objects in a Central Thai Village." Ph.D. dissertation, Cornell University, 1960.

Thomas, Keith. *Witchcraft and the Decline of Magic*. New York, 1971.

Thrupp, Sylvia L., ed. *Millennial Dreams in Action: Studies in Revolutionary Religious Movements*. New York, 1970.

Tipps, Dean C. "Modernization Theory and the Comparative Study of Society: A Critical Perspective." *Comparative Studies in Society and History* 15 (1973): 199–226.

Tocqueville, Alexis de. *The Old Regime and the French Revolution*. Garden City, New York, 1955.

Trung Buu Lam. *Patterns of Vietnamese Response to Foreign Intervention: 1858–1900*. New Haven, 1967.

Tucker, Glenn. *Tecumseh: Vision of Glory*. Indianapolis, 1956.

Turner, Victor. *The Ritual Process*. Harmondsworth, England, 1974.

Vansina, Jan. "Les mouvements religieux Kuba (Kasai) à l'époque coloniale." *Études d'histoire africaine* 2 (1972): 155–87.

Wakeman, Frederick, Jr. *Strangers at the Gate: Social Disorder in South China, 1839–1861*. Berkeley, 1966.

Wallace, Anthony. "Handsome Lake and the Great Revival in the West." *American Quarterly* 4 (1952): 149–65.

_____. "Revitalization Movements." *American Anthropologist* 58 (1956): 264–81.

Weber, Max. *The Sociology of Religion*. Boston, 1963.

_____. *The Theory of Social and Economic Organization*. New York, 1964.

Weinstein, Donald. "The Savonarola Movement in Florence." In *Millennial Dreams in Action*, edited by Sylvia L. Thrupp, pp. 187–203. New York, 1970.

Whipper, Audrey. "The Gusii Rebels." In *Protest and Power in Black Africa*, edited by Robert I. Rotberg and Ali A. Mazrui, pp. 377–426. Oxford, 1970.

Willis, Roy G. "Instant Millennium: The Sociology of African Witch-Cleansing Cults." In *Witchcraft Confessions and Accusations*, edited by Mary Douglas, pp. 129–39. London, 1970.

Wilson, Bryan. *Magic and the Millennium*. New York, 1973.

_____. *The Noble Savages*. Berkeley, 1974.

_____, ed. *Rationality*. Oxford, 1970.

Wingate, Francis R. *Mahdism and the Egyptian Sudan*. London, 1968.

Wolf, Eric. "Aspects of Group Relations in a Complex Society." *American Anthropologist* 58 (1956): 1065–78.

_____. *Peasant Wars of the Twentieth Century*. New York, 1969.

_____. *Peasants*. Englewood Cliffs, New Jersey, 1966.

Woodside, Alexander. *Vietnam and the Chinese Model*. Cambridge, Massachusetts, 1971.

Worsley, Peter. *The Trumpet Shall Sound: A Study of "Cargo" Cults in Melanesia*. New York, 1968.

Zimmer, Heinrich. *Myths and Symbols in Indian Art and Civilization*. New York, 1962.

Index

A

Aberle, David, 44

Acculturation: and European colonialism, xiv; and revitalization movements, xviii, 183–84; in New Zealand, 12–16, 41; and Alaskan Eskimos, 15, 193 (n. 12); and social protest, 43, 44

Adat, 83, 116

Agung, Sultan, 4, 5, 142

Akida, 30, 31, 52, 82; as overseers, 64, 78, 126. *See also* Swahili

Alaungpaya, 34, 102

Amangkurat I, 5

Amerindians, 4, 11

Amulets. *See* Talismans

Anand Panre, 107

Ancestor, 113; veneration in east Africa, 105, 144–45; and the Maji Maji cult, 105; among the Maori, 111

Anglo-Burman wars, 36, 37, 130, 172

Anomie, 42, 195 (n. 49)

Apanage. *See* Tribute systems

Arabs, 126; Dutch rivals, 3; slave traders, 25, 41; of Swahili coast, 30, 32; overseers, 65; manuscripts in Java, 132; magical inscriptions, 154

Asceticism, 97, 107, 143

Askaris, 53, 83, 174

B

Bagelen, 9–10

Banditry, 80; indiscriminate label, xx; and rebellion in Burma, 38, 40, 100, 128, 130; "social bandits," 121, 186; and rebellion, 137; and talismans, 151

Banten, 4, 49

Batavia, 3, 4, 5

Bekel, 50, 51, 65, 68

Bena, 27, 32

Benteng, 10, 173

Birsa, 87, 112, 115–16, 117, 128, 131, 140, 179, 181; as a prophet-leader, 19, 23, 118, 119, 120, 125, 135, 141, 146, 148, 153, 154, 158, 159, 165, 188; deserts his followers, 24–25, 171; biographical, 25, 106–8; hostility toward Christianity, 90

Birsa rebellion, xviii, xxii, 41, 86; course of, 23–25, 136; causes of, 51, 59–60, 68–70; ideology of, 60; precipitants of, 125–26; impact of, 178–80

Bismarck, Herbert von, 30

Bokero, 105

Bombhani, 107

Bosch, Johannes van den, 177

Boxer rebellion, 150, 204 (n. 3)

British, 172; colonizers in India, 4, 68, 100; interregnum on Java, 8, 48, 95, 96; and annexation in New Zealand, 16; rule in Chota Nagpur, 22–23, 51–52, 60, 68, 78, 84; suppression of Birsa rising, 24–25, 125–26; census in Tanganyika, 29; administration in Burma, 36–37, 45, 46–48, 55, 85–86, 101, 127, 176; empire, 37, 56–57; responses to Saya San risings, 38–39, 171, 172, 174; administration in New Zealand, 53, 71, 84–85; military in New Zealand, 91, 170

Buddha Maitreya. *See Mettaya* Buddha

Buddhism: in Lower Burma, 36, 57; in Southeast Asia, 47; in precolonial Burma, 56; in colonial Burma, 56–57, 115; in Java, 58; defense of, 88, 147, 148

Buddhist, xxii, 100, 147; restoration in Burma, xiii; kingdoms in Southeast Asia, 34; monastic schools, 57; influence in Java, 97, 98; cults in Burma, 100, 102; age of decline, 101; pagodas, 148. *See also Pongyis*

Bupatis, 131

Burma, xxii, 92, 151, 162, 171; precolonial history in, 34–36, 56, 80, 130; colonization in, 36–38, 55, 130; Western education in, 57. *See also* British; Buddhism; Saya San rebellion

Burman, 41, 103, 147, 148, 166; defined, 34, 195 (n. 41); migrants, 36, 37, 47, 115; resistance to British, 36, 47, 130, 166, 167, 180; empire, 37, 100; conditions under colonialism, 76–77

Burmese: defined, 34, 195 (n. 41). *See also* Nationalism